In the beginning, all the Lord's people, from all parts of the world, spoke one language. Nothing they proposed was impossible for them. But fearing what the spirit of man could accomplish, the Lord said, "Let us go down and confuse their language so that they may not understand one another's speech."

A FILM BY ALEJANDRO GONZÁLEZ IÑÁRRITU

Photographs by MARY ELLEN MARK,
PATRICK BARD, GRACIELA ITURBIDE and MIGUEL RIO BRANCO

Ed. MARÍA ELADIA HAGERMAN

TASCHEN

HONGKONG KÖLN LONDON LOS ANGELES MADRID PARIS TOKYO

The Memory of Wounds

Foreword by Eliseo Alberto

9

Butterfly Catchers

Introduction by Alejandro González Iñárritu

18

MOROCCO

**Photographs by
Mary Ellen Mark and Patrick Bard**

*Additional photographs by
Murray Close*

20

MEXICO

**Photographs by
Graciela Iturbide**

*Additional photographs by
Eniac Martínez and Yvonne Venegas*

110

JAPAN

**Photographs by
Miguel Rio Branco**

*Additional photographs by
Junko Kato and Tsutomu Umezawa*

186

* Photo comments by Alejandro González Iñárritu

The Foundations of *Babel*

A Conversation Between Rodrigo García and Alejandro González Iñárritu

256

The Memory of Wounds

Foreword by Eliseo Alberto

**Probably there is no memory
other than the memory of wounds.**

Czeslaw Milosz

A book of photographs can be a window too, or should be. It opens to light, it closes to darkness.

Each image is fixed in the chiaroscuro of memory, imprinted there in a theft as unpunishable as it is necessary.

One eye saw it and caught it in mid-flight: then a thousand eyes appropriate it, even recreate it without asking permission.

Or forgiveness.

Those who approach this book cannot help but yield to their desire to explore it with the spyglass of emotion, the feeling of disquiet that takes people by surprise whenever they know they are participating in a creative experience, their own or someone else's.

In *Babel*, the book, emotion vibrates halfway between the extremes of passion and reason.

Each page contains a human landscape, a portrait of the time that is our inheritance.

Look at the desert of a face in the middle of the actual desert of Morocco. Or the vast plains in eyes that wander over the eternities of Tijuana like a blind bird that cannot find a nest anywhere.

In what corner of the universe do we find the sea of rocks where a barge floats without helmsman or fish or hooks? Who abandoned it there? Is this the phantom that concerns us today?

The cosmos pauses for a moment at the grief of a father embracing his naked daughter high in a Tokyo skyscraper: it must be God Himself who shelters them.

For a moment He forgets His arrogance and breathes His silence down on them and on us.

Silence explains almost everything.

The wind batters for a reason, and we don't hear it in the photographs of the masters Patrick Bard, Graciela Iturbide, Mary Ellen Mark, and Miguel Rio Branco, and the music is silent in that Tokyo den where a forsaken adolescent searches for herself so intently that eventually she will find herself in the purity of her still intact nakedness.

If it isn't because of the silence of the image, how can we explain the frozen despair of the woman lost in the desert when she feels responsible for undeserved sadness? The children in her care dehydrate in the sun, in the midst of nothing. Here the only hope is the puddle of shade cast by a bush.

Why do we listen to the hushed trembling of Moroccan shepherds, pursued as they are by the echo of a gunshot?

The bullet is mute that punctures the glass in the bus and lodges close to the heart of a woman too beautiful to die so young, and the violent grief of her husband is mute when he understands how much they need each other now that love is bleeding away in a trickle of confessions.

If a second is all we need to die, why isn't it enough to change our lives?

The world fits into the eternity of a second.

Forever vain, death does not allow her picture to be taken.

The soul of photography, and of almost everything else in this life, is peace. Peace is not meek but heroic. Sooner or later it prevails no matter the cost.

María Eladia Hagerman knew this very well when she called on four geniuses of contemporary art to join the army that would accompany the filmmaker Alejandro González Iñárritu (and his faithful colleagues on the journey) in the adventure of filming as they moved around the waist of the planet in the illusory pursuit of a feature-length film. The picture seemed, at the time, a madness as impossible as its Biblical antecedent: inventing the watchtowers of Babel, symbol of the human race's passage on earth. González Iñárritu had never undertaken so difficult a project before. The result is simply extraordinary, a cinematic masterpiece. I lost my fear of adjectives a long time ago: the narrative perfection of *Babel*, the film, demonstrates that human weaknesses and strengths are the same for all of us. That is why, when we leave the darkened screening room, it seems inevitable that eventually we think of ourselves, of the sorrows that hound us and the illusions that could save us from the sickness we call loneliness. I would even venture to state that rarely in the history of film, and of photography, has so much talent been brought together on the same artistic journey.

Babel, the book, does and does not bear graphic witness to this adventure. The eyes of the photographers are not confined to scrutinizing dramas in the story that is being filmed with rigor, professionalism, and inspiration. Each one's particular capacity for observation explores the space that surrounds them and extends from the set to the horizon, and they do this with infinite tenderness and sagacity, an irrefutable proof that intelligence is surely an indispensable requirement for art.

Not long ago I heard this shout scrawled on a wall in Mexico City: "Enough of realities: we want promises!" And it made me afraid to live in this world of desperate illusions.

Books and films like the two *Babels* return our souls to our bodies.

No matter how hard life becomes, or how pessimism crushes us, or how black the long night that tests us, life is a great feat worth taking part in.

The sonorous silence of the film runs through the book. We can also read images. Words are superfluous.

Open the window of *Babel* wide: Perhaps you'll find yourselves on the other side.

Butterfly Catchers

Introduction by Alejandro González Iñárritu

I once dreamed that it might be possible for the eyelids to capture, or imprint, the infinite labyrinths recorded by the retina, and that those eyelids, coated like tracing paper, could be pressed to extract all the memories of one's life. However, such images have a habit of vanishing and only a few survive. Just as the present is no more than an anguished slice of time being swallowed up by the past, for me, as a film director, it is anguishing, as well, to have hundreds of images and people passing by through my windshield swiftly skimming over my retina, left to right, which will disappear from my memory despite the fact that they were capable of posing questions without end and triggering countless ideas. It was three years ago that a single image of the waters at the hot springs in Hakone, Japan, unleashed the desire and need to film a story in the city of ideograms.

The master, Akira Kurosawa, said, "the most beautiful things can never be captured on film." That seems to be the case on every movie lot in the world. The book now in your hand is no more than an attempt to forestall the fatal moment of its ephemerality.

Babel is the final film of my trilogy, which was preceded by *Amores perros* and *21 Grams*. They comprise a triptych of stories that explore locally, abroad, and, finally, on a global level the profound and complex relations between parents and children. The idea of making *Babel* came to me out of a certain need that can stem only from exile and the awareness of being an immigrant. When one comes from the Third World, it is difficult to live in a First World country. Nevertheless, one's vision is broadened and takes on a new perspective. Now, it is more usual for me to ask myself "Where am I going?" rather than "Where do I come from?"

I began shooting *Babel* under the firm conviction that I would make a picture concerning the differences between human beings and their inability to communicate, not only because of language but because of physical, political, and emotional frontiers. I was going to do it from a complex and universal standpoint until the more intimate plane of two people could be reached.

From the outset, the crew was made up of Mexicans, North Americans, French, Italians, Arabs, Berbers, Germans, and, at the end, Japanese. I had a feeling alongside the film's central theme that despite all the technology that has been developed to improve communication between human beings, the reality turns out to be very different. The problem is not with the countless new tools for communicating but that nobody listens. When there is nothing to listen to there's nothing to understand; if we leave off understanding, our language is useless and ends up dividing us. To work in five different unfamiliar languages with well-known actors and also non-actors, the majority—as, in the case of the poor Moroccan communities which had never before seen a camera—called for my unwavering task of assimilation, observation. Like Gypsies in a huge traveling circus, my quasi-family—that is to say, my friends and coworkers of long-standing, without whom realizing this task would have been unthinkable—and my actual family traveled for almost a year on three continents.

As the weeks and months, and the faces, geographies and seasons passed together with the multiple culture shocks, as well as the physical and psychological impact of the trip, all had the effect of transforming me and the rest who made the film. In the course of the journey, there were deaths, births, instances of intense joy and pain, and many demonstrations of brotherhood and solidarity; being exposed and sensing humanity in such depth not only transformed us but the picture itself as well. The cultural orgy in which we participated caused the creative process to be shaping itself to the point of taking a very different form contrary to its original objective, and confirming that, when all is said and done, a film is nothing more than the extension of oneself.

In a considerable part of the planet, borders and airports have become a carnival of distrust and degradation where freedom is exchanged for security X-rays are the weapon and otherness the crime. In spite of all this, in filming *Babel*, I confirmed that the real borderlines are within ourselves and that more than a physical space, the barriers are in the world of ideas. I realized that what makes us happy as human beings could differ greatly, but that what make us miserable and vulnerable beyond our culture, race, language, or financial standing is the same for all. I discovered that the great human tragedy boils down to the inability to love or be loved and the incapacity to touch with or be touched by this sentiment, which is what gives meaning to the life and death of every human being. Accordingly, *Babel* became transformed into a picture about what joins us, not what separates us. For me, this filming was converted not only into an external journey but an internal one, and like all works that come out of one's guts, this picture—like its two predecessors—gives testimony to my life experience, with my virtues and many limitations. During the filming of *Amores perros* and *21 Grams*, due to the concentration and exact objectives that the story being filmed demanded, to my pain I realized the impossibility of capturing not only the best of a given moment but the multiple scenes or images taking place in parallel around me. What happened to those faces and textures of the slums of Memphis where we filmed *21 Grams*, or those exhausted trees with the crows dangling like globes in the foggy mornings at the edge of the Mississippi? What happened to the rage in the eyes of the boys who held us up at gunpoint during the filming of *Amores perros*, and who later brought us coffee during the filming their faces alight with the look of appreciated children? What became of the expression on the face of the owner of the house we rented for the character played by Benicio del Toro in *21 Grams* when we told him that we had found a rotting corpse under a mattress? Such images and such moments occur in only fractions of a second then to be lost in oblivion with no possibility of registering them in collective memory.

The reality of a picture is much more than what fits into the rectangle of a movie screen, and this reality permeates inexorably those of us engaged in making that film. This book is an effort to capture and preserve those fleeting images of shared humanity, of all that which caused *Babel* to begin as one thing and end as another, and of the faces, forms, winds, and horizons that struck and transformed all of us involved together like rolling stones from the start.

Each film could give rise to another film. When filming, one's eyes and senses are so open that you bump into a character on every street corner that is potentially more interesting than the one in your film. Curiosity, however, killed the cat, and may also kill a director. Theoretically, such curiosity can be satisfied with an ordinary camera. It's that simple. "Click," and done. In practice, it's a different story.

A proud butterfly collector can delight us with the sight of the gorgeous variegated wings of hundreds of specimens pinned in wooden display cases. But those boxes are no more than glass-covered sarcophaguses and those butterflies — despite their beauty of form and coloration — are lacking the creatures' most fascinating attribute: the gift of flight. Likewise, even though a photograph has captured the body at a moment, just like the butterfly — without its power of flight — it is dead. The reason why a tiny flash from the window of an automobile or a few seconds of an image in a park is capable of triggering an entire story or a movie in an artist's mind is that those images, brief as they may be, are alive. Their life does not depend upon the amount of time that one observes them but on their verity and on the perspective of the one seeing them. All that exists between the object and the one who looks at it is the glance; and that — the glance — is what brings art into existence and makes it an individual miracle.

Just as the glance of Rodrigo Prieto was capable of capturing and rendering in *Babel* the verity and poetry of bodies and figures in movement, four masters of still photography made the parallel worlds of frozen time their own.

The reason why the pages of this book flutter like butterfly wings, their images still alive as though seeking to escape from the page, is that those who captured them did not chase butterflies but extracted their spirit and true nature without even touching them. The unmistakable glances of Mary Ellen Mark, Graciela Iturbide, Miguel Rio Branco, and Patrick Bard made it possible for these images to be stories without sound. It is the glance that makes their photographs smell like the Sahara Desert, like that of Sonora, and even that of Tokyo. Their curiosity about the human face, an animal, a wall, and the shadow of what nobody sees is precisely the curiosity of children. Humanity alone, the genius and the universality characteristic of those four photographers enables making cultures and geographies that are remote and different so intimate and close, thereby confirming that image and music are the closest to Esperanto. Their working methods, although different, achieve the same effect: that of placing poetry at the service of the dream and subordinating beauty to the truth of a moment.

The emotion and great dignity exhibited by Mary Ellen Mark's photographs have long impressed me. She has done portraits of those that are ignored by society, thereby transcending the journalistic document in her way and via her aesthetic universe. Curiously, the emotional impact of her photographs in *American Odyssey* inspired Brigitte Broch, Rodrigo Prieto, and me in our work in *Amores perros*.

Also in Morocco, Patrick Bard let his images fly free through his way of documenting them: relating himself profoundly and humanly with the natives and extracting an honesty and naturalness out of them that is only rarely obtained. This photographer-novelist makes the weight of the ordinary felt in his every image.

Furthermore, the spirit of Graciela Iturbide, whose photographs I got to know as I grew up, is so pure and delicate that it seems to be forever floating. Behind those sparkling eyes of hers lies profound wisdom and nobility. The transparency of her images makes my country into a rather idyllic place but one that is at the same time real. It is real because she sees it and reveals it in her work; it suffices for us to believe it and celebrate it with her. Her photographs in this book smell of my country. Draw your heart up closer and you will find it to be true.

Lastly, I believe that nobody handles color like Miguel Rio Branco. The books of his earliest period inspired me and many filmmakers. One's first experience of his famous picture of the dead dog, for example, is never to be forgotten. Painter, filmmaker, photographer, multimedia artist, and, most of all, conceptual poet, Rio Branco keeps reinventing himself and evolving. The triptychs in this book seems to have captured, in an abstract manner, the complex DNA of the city of Tokyo. Nobody sees what he sees. In the most unexpected corner, the objects and their shadows speak to one another.

Having the four of them on the *Babel* set was always an honor and a privilege.

This book was the idea of my wife María Eladia. Only someone with her sensitivity would have been capable of choosing among so many butterflies in order to create a range of colors, odors, textures so disparate and yet be able to simultaneously sustain in a single volume four powerful visions of three continents and two realities. Her endless hours of work for months have finally yielded the fruit of the book that she visualized and dreamed of. Also included are some photographs by Murray Close, Eniac Martínez, Yvonne Venegas, Junko Kato, and Tsutomu Umezawa, whose talent and sensitivity handsomely completed the segments of the journey of which they were all a part. From the outset, the photographs were sought that would capture not the nature of the film but its parallel reality. The experiment behind it is to verify how much fiction resembles reality and how far reality invades fiction. It was our intention to explore that frontier. These are the communities, the faces, the cities, vertical or set into the clay that surrounded us, that became integrated, and inspired us during the shooting. These are the tangible and poetic worlds behind *Babel*.

Now that I think about it again, some of the most beautiful things can, indeed, be captured on film.

المغرب

I crossed the Atlantic at the age of 18 working as a deckhand on a freighter. I was traveling with three friends and survived for a year on a thousand dollars. After crossing the border at Ceuta, we took a bus to Marrakesh. As the writer Paul Bowles observed, "The difference between a tourist and a traveler is that the latter doesn't have a return ticket." Over the course of a year I was able to vouch for the correctness of the statement.

The bus was an inferno. I was carrying a bottle half full of lukewarm water, and right in front of me, a dark-skinned boy could not tear his beautiful green eyes off me. He had a piece of fruit in his hand, which he held out to me. I made signs of "no thank you." He insisted and I continued to refuse. He said something to me in Arabic I didn't understand. His mother and several of the passengers turned around. There was nothing I could do but accept the half-eaten fruit, and at that moment he asked for my bottle. I looked at it, then at him, thought it over, and told him no. He said something to his mother in Arabic I didn't understand, and his mother then said something to me. Now, all the passengers were watching to see if I was capable of denying the boy water. Very reluctantly, I handed him the bottle. The boy began to laugh and drink. All at once, the entire bus was doing the same: the boy offering them the bottle and they drinking from it and howling with laughter at me and my friends. Then the boy began to ask for food from the others and to hand it around. The people couldn't stop laughing. My friends and I forced laughter of the kind that greets a joke when the point is not understood. It was as though all the passengers were seeing a foreigner for the first time. The boy brought out some crumbled pieces of cracker for me and introduced himself. He said his name was Abdullah—he had a spark and exceptional charm. When we left the bus in Marrakesh, thousands of children like Abdullah began surrounding and running after us. The noise was fantastic.

I was recalling a Morocco enveloped in an aura of mystery and a cloud of hashish. Its aesthetic and cultural impact on me was enormous. I wanted to film in Morocco because I felt a link that reached back into memory. Twenty-two years after that trip, when we arrived in Marrakesh, the magical children were not long in putting in an appearance once again.

When I was a boy, my mother bought me a plaster figurine of Michelangelo's *La Pietà* from New York. All during my childhood, I went to sleep and woke up with that figurine over the headboard of my bed. I wanted Richard to carry Susan as a metaphor of the piteous image. Brad carried Cate down long alleys more than 50 times; Rodrigo Prieto, the cameraman, running behind them with a 50-kilogram camera on his shoulder. Some days later, when I wanted to reshoot the scene, it was the actors and Rodrigo begging me to take pity on them.

In the original screenplay, the conflict between Richard and Susan arose from a past infidelity of his. Some weeks before the shoot, I suggested taking the drama to a more profound level, as would be the case in the crib death of an infant. When Brad reached Morocco, he found out about the script change. Actually, it was already a complicated task to have to build a character on the basis of only 30 pages of background and to have to assimilate at one fell swoop a new dramatic element in the script. Who was Richard? Why did he do what he did? Every day under extenuating physical conditions, Brad had to dig, to discover, and invent the vulnerable character he had built up for the screen.

Despite the fact that Richard's role did not seem to be obvious for an
actor as recognizable as Brad Pitt, the adventure of building it was exciting
for him and for me. It is no easy matter for actors of his caliber to agree to
do characters like that. For me, the challenge was to get Brad Pitt, the
celebrity, to disappear behind the character in order to give way not only to
the actor but to the human being behind that image. It has always seemed
to me that Brad had a magnetic presence that transcended his popularity.
It was very risky but he valiantly accepted the challenges. He accepted,
primarily, the greatest of them, which is the one always faced by actors:
that of putting themselves into the hands of the director and leaping into
the void.

Although for everybody the filmic experience was very close to the picture's plotlines, in Cate's case fiction and reality crossed radically. While in Morocco, her one-year-old son suffered a second-degree burn on both legs. Cate would have had to cope with the emergency care of a humble Moroccan hospital and so flew the child immediately to London. Two days later, assured her son would be fine, she gave us a lesson in professionalism such as I had never seen and was back acting the part of Susan, a woman bleeding from a physical and emotional wound.

Seventeen days before shooting, I didn't have a single actor. We concentrated on locating them all in the communities. We would come to the mosques and from the minarets announce over loud-speakers that our film had now arrived and that we were looking for people to appear in the picture. Alfonso, Hervé, and Marc did remarkable work.

Sfia is a Berber woman who lives in Taguenzalte next door to the house where we were filming. The depth of feeling evident in her eyes made me give her the role without hesitation. Her scenes were difficult to set. When we were at about the twentieth take and Cate Blanchett was giving with all her intensity, the old woman would forget which way to go, turn toward the camera, and smile.

Mohamed appeared at the office looking for work as a computer technician. The dignity, mixed with the pain of his expression, caught my attention. He seemed to me to be a close match with the character of Anwar: the face of a person who wants to better himself but gets no help from life.

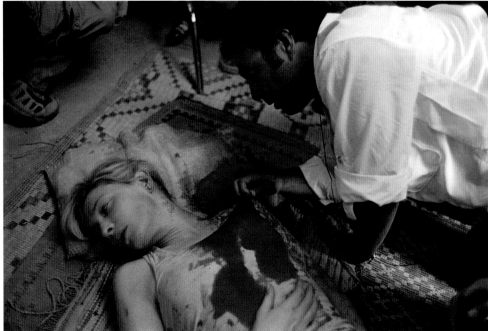

I begged Cate Blanchett to accept the part of Susan. She resisted at first, with some justification: in the script, Susan was nothing but a woman stretched out on the floor, semiconscious and bleeding. I knew, however, that only Cate could lend seriousness and reality to the role and raise the performance level for all on the set. And she did just that. Every time I saw her perform, not only was I moved but I thanked her over and over again for accepting the part. Had she known that she was going to be smeared with a sticky red syrup that smelled like shit in order to attract flies, in a dark room with no air conditioning in a temperature of over 100 degrees Fahrenheit, she would most likely not have accepted.

I cannot imagine greater generosity in the world than that which we encountered in the humble villages of southern Morocco. Whenever we passed by a house, we would inevitably be offered everything they had: tea, almonds, dates, goat's milk, smiles, and the traditional greeting of *salam alikom* accompanied by touching the heart and wafting a kiss heavenward. It was clear to me that Western consumerism is a race towards spiritual emptiness. It is true that the women work too hard while the men drink too much social tea, but all devote five or six minutes five times a day to prayer and to connecting with their spiritual part.

For the first time in its history, the little town of Taguenzalte found itself invaded by people from all over the world who interested and entertained them for over 13 weeks, as a result of which practically the entire population participated in the filming.

The first ones to believe in the project and to join forces with me were Jon Kilik and Steve Golin, my partner producers, whose friendship, experience, and support where invaluable. Together with Ann Ruark, they worked fervently and tirelessly to orchestrate this global "traveling circus" for almost one year, always providing what was necessary to make the picture.

We all had such a great time with the Taguenzalte community that the last day of shooting was very tearful for both sides. We took up a collection and raised enough to bring electricity to the town. Months after one of us returned and reported that all rooftops now had a dish antenna. I could not help reacting with sad and confused feelings.

I wanted to film in a desert that was not very romantic: a harsh, stony wasteland without dunes. To find a spot in a place as vast as the Sahara is incredibly difficult. In a space so open all the time, you ask yourself why this place is going to be any better than that one. As a dog, you have to be going in circles until you find your spot instinctively because as a hunter, once you are in dangerous fields, a film is more about your guts, your pelvis, and the amount of sunshine in your stomach than your brains and intellectual skills. No theory is worth it, because nobody but you can trigger the gun until danger arrives and you have one and only one chance. The film becomes an unpredictable animal, and your senses and spirit should be wide open even when you don't have a clue of which word to use because you are surrounded by a crew of seven different nationalities and no matter how loud you shout, nobody will understand you.

This scene portrays the moment of a Muslim family's moral collapse: It demands high physical and emotional intensity. When the language is a frontier between the director and the actors, mimicry becomes an indispensable tool. Hiam Abbass was my guardian angel: the emotional bridge between Moroccan actors and me.

One day in Tamnougalt's main square, Alfonso Gómez called me to have a look at a very special boy. He was Boubker. I explained to him that I was going to be giving him a test by saying some phrases to him and for him to answer me not with words but to tell me with his eyes what he was feeling. "Your mother died," I said. His eyes filled with tears, and all of us were stunned by his expression. It was a unique moment. I knew that I had found an actor for the part of Yussef. Afterwards, I found out that his mother had died seven years before and that his father was a man whom he rarely saw. Without realizing it, I had touched a very deep wound in the boy. There is nothing more powerful than reality and that cannot be faked.

When my friend, the writer Eliseo Alberto, saw a preliminary cut of *Babel*, he told me that it seemed that Abdullah and Hassan had come down from heaven to play their roles and gone back up afterwards. When I saw their faces among the hundreds of men lined up outside the mosques for the casting, I thought the same. The faces of those two men were biblical: likewise the humanity described in the Muslim, Jewish, and Christian bibles. Mustapha, the actor who plays Abdullah, like biblical Joseph, is a carpenter on the outskirts of Fez.

Most of the hard Moroccan faces are sweet once they smile. They do not exhibit the malice we usually attribute to them. Yet Hassan's face was difficult to break down. I needed the character to show vulnerability under police intimidation, but he had a block. Mimicry was not enough, because of which Hiam, by talking to him in his language, found a way to connect him with his emotions. Hassan told us that he had never gone to see his dead mother, and so we used the filming as a therapy session, and for over four hours nobody was able to stop his weeping. On finishing, he thanked us and I thanked Hiam.

In Morocco, we had a crew of 120: Italians, French, North Americans, Mexicans, and Moroccans, who spoke Arabic or Berber. Having six languages in one working group, gave rise to many problems because of misunderstandings. Even more than language, point of view was the problem. We were subject to debilitating heat and extreme conditions. We had to film many exteriors at high temperatures, climb hills, and suffer much dust. For many of us from the Third World, it was a bit easier to tolerate such conditions. The reality of a shepherd in Morocco is not very different from that of one in Mexico. I as well as Rodrigo Prieto and the Mexican unit of the crew were delighted with the possibility of understanding their living conditions and their limitations.

Said and Boubker became like brothers just as in the story. Said was rebellious, active, intuitive, and nonconforming while Boubker was passive, introspective, rational, and melancholy. With their earnings from the picture, Said bought a motorcycle and Boubker a computer.

On the last day of shooting in Morocco, we were filming the evening scene in which Yussef, in a close-up, weeps, imagining his brother had just died, as Said walks with his father along a sea of stony desert where I had placed an empty boat. This scene was a heavy emotional load for them to bear. Earlier in the shooting, on the spur of the moment, I had filmed a scene of the boys playing with the wind as a gift of the mountains, and all these scenes together became the epilogue of their story. Upon finishing the film, on the final day, neither Said nor Boubker were able to stop crying. We who had become their family were going to leave the next day. I promised both of them that we would be seeing one another in a year in some festival. Luckily, I was able to keep the promise. We saw each other at Cannes.

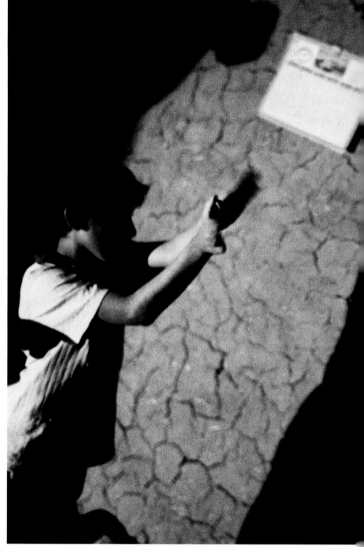

MEXICO

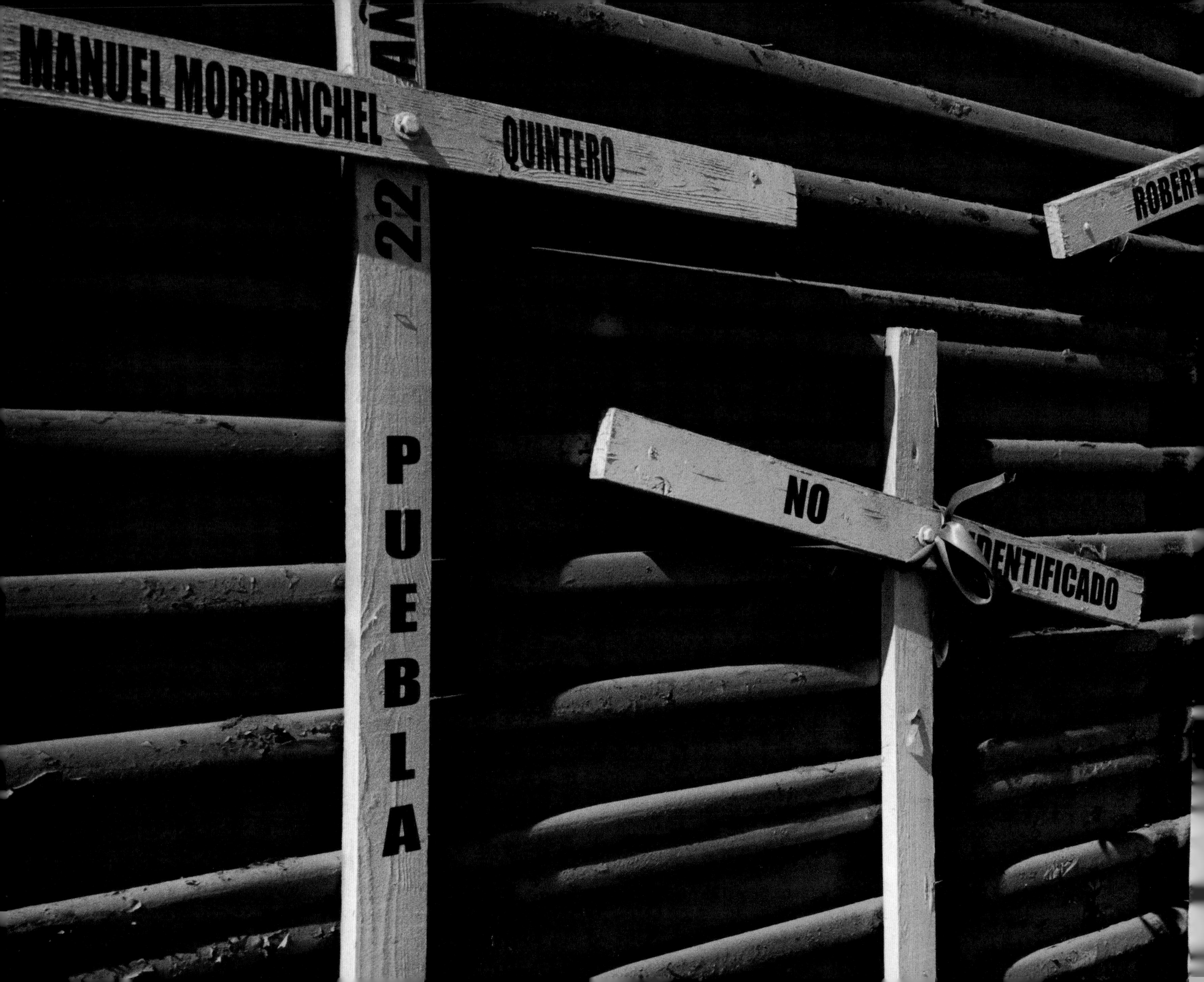
MANUEL MORRANCHEL
QUINTERO
22
PUEBLA
NO

The first thing that strikes me about this city is the fence around it [previous page]. It's called *"La Llaga"* ("The gash"): an open wound several kilometers long built out of metal barriers from the prefab airports of the Vietnam War. The stupidest and most ingenuous aspect of this fence is that it takes in part of the ocean so as to stop any terrorist in a submarine from getting in! Thousands of crosses hang from it with the names of men, women, and children who were swallowed up by the desert or disappeared at the Mexico-United States border, the busiest in the world. When completed, it will be the greatest monument to intolerance in human history.

In Tijuana, the people here aren't from here or there; they're all passing through. Only in a place like this is it possible to come upon a plaster giantess made by a man in love with his wife so she might have a bird's-eye view of the promised land she would never get to.

One day I heard that there was going to be a performance at the border [previous page]. A man was going to fly over to the other side and be arrested by the U.S. police in a circus act with a critical intent. I was five minutes away from there and decided to interrupt filming in order to take in the event. It ended up a complete fiasco.

It had to do with simply a North American "human cannonball" who had no idea or the slightest interest in the possible symbolism of his act, for which he was simply paid to carry out. Even so, the powerful and fanciful image triggered a thought of many of us there. If only we had wings…

I am a musicologist. I like the good part of all styles. However, for some reason, *norteño* music never grabbed me. I felt a kind of out-of-hand rejection of it. After living for two months in Tijuana and Sonora and exploring and trying out of necessity to connect with that music, it finally got me in another way. The hits on the radio and the song lyrics, added to my own life experience, led me to discover for the first time an emotional sense in them. The pain and frustration of their lyrics, as well as the simple and catchy melodies, are rooted deeply not in what has been had but in the yearning for what has not been or never could be had. Surrendering to that music was one of the best gifts I got out of that experience.

A Mexican woman by the name of Julia works in my house in Los Angeles. She was born in the state of Oaxaca, and it was not until after six attempts to cross the desert under extremely dangerous conditions that she managed to get in without being caught. She has a 20-year-old son who is in prison and whom she has not been able to see for over two years because she would be immediately deported. Julia lives in constant fear. Like millions of Mexicans living in the United States, she is an invisible citizen. Ironically, as Amelia, thousands of South American women have confronted the same luck crossing the Mexican border, which can be tougher and more dangerous than the one in the United States.

The work of Adriana Barraza gave for me a new meaning for the word "incarnation," since every movement of her body, her hands, and her eyes incarnate with tenderness and complexity the spirit of a character that could easily have become stereotyped. Her performance was sublime. I thought of Gael for *Babel* from the outset. Nobody better than him to play a character with so many contradictory aspects in such a short time. In *Amores perros*, Adriana was Gael's mother. Now, she is his aunt. In either instance, as her son or nephew, he has caused her much grief and driven her into various hells. The only thing that I promised Adriana and Gael is that I would not make another picture in which Gael drives an automobile. Every time he does, it ends in tragedy.

From the initial scouting of locations, I was struck by
the Carrizo community, a settlement an hour from Tijuana:
taciturn and simple but friendly and honest to a fault. There
was a subplot in *Babel,* which took place in this house involving
a pregnant bride and Amelia convincing her to attend her
own wedding. At the end, I decided to cut it but nevertheless
the atmosphere remained in the film somehow. The fatty
in the photograph is a boy who never in the three visits I
made to his house lifted himself out of his armchair. A huge
TV set and an empty plate of potato chips were in front of
him each time.

Weddings in the north of my country are very different from those in the south. The ceremonies in Tijuana are cursory, dusty, without traditional rites or customs. I went to several weddings in the course of my research for *Babel* and tried to film Amelia's wedding while remaining as faithful as possible to what I saw: plastic cups and plates, lack of a single flower or decoration, and chairs of various colors on the ever-present dust. Brigitte Broch, my friend and production designer, whose every touch breathes life into the set, did a beautiful job.

All of those who appear in the wedding scene [next page] belong to the Carrizo community. I never saw livelier and happier people. Even though I was shooting for days and until six in the morning, there was never a complaint out of them. Nothing but smiles and nonstop dancing. For me, them, and the entire crew, the wedding was indeed a fiesta. The people knew one another and that could be felt in the scene.

Just like in Morocco Gustavo Santaolalla and I settled down in a studio to record various *gnawa* music bands, in Tijuana, I shut myself in with Lynn Fainchtein for listening to and recording *norteño* groups. The *norteño* people listen to *norteño* music only. It's like a religion. There's pain and motivation in their themes, which can't be understood if not listened to from their perspective. *Los Incomparables* is a group that honors its name with their honesty, charm, and identification with the public.

153

When I met Bernie I immediately changed the idea from the one written for the character of Luis, Amelia's son. I met him in Tijuana when he went there for casting and chatted with him for about an hour. He said that he had already been everything at some time in his life: philanderer, scoundrel, foul-mouthed, musician, fireman, you name it. In other words, a conniver, as they say. But, no matter how much he insisted on appearing wicked, his innate decency betrayed him. Bernie is a typical Tijuana street character. His hip-hop Tijuana haircut plus the fierce and at the same time gentle look in his eyes interested me greatly. Like him, millions of border youngsters live with this contradiction and resent the humiliation implicit in crossing the border with the United States.

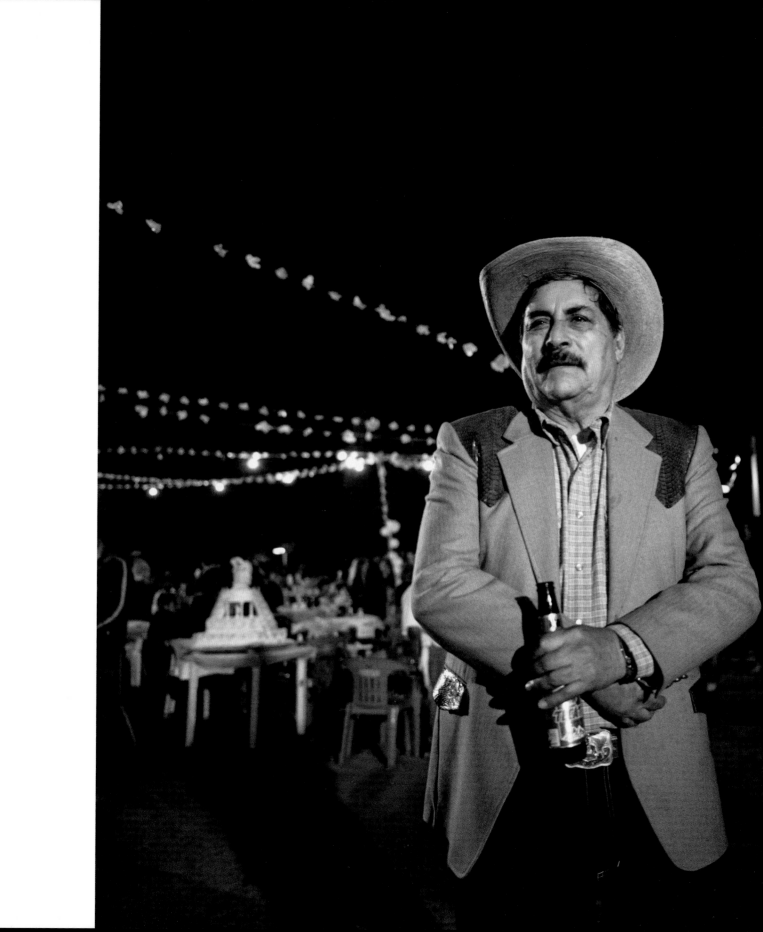

I have had to cross the border between Tijuana and the United States with my wife and children every six months for five years. No matter how many times I do this, the contrast and disparity between the two countries never ceases to impress me. Every car that comes from the United States crosses the border and enters my country without any inspection or trouble.

In contrast, all cars traveling from Mexico to the United States are carefully checked, making this crossing into a ritual of humiliation and suspicion. For me, Santiago's sudden and violent act was committed not because of an inspection but as a reaction to the accumulation of years of constant abuse of power and the manner in which it is exercised.

In three days of filming, I tried to reproduce the sensation of what I, myself, experienced, so we built a booth in the middle of the Sonora desert similar to the one in Tecate. Rodrigo Prieto, Batan Silva and I constantly checked the second unit's load that came and went for display of contents.

It is remarkable how children sometimes understand much more than seasoned actors. They have no agenda other than obedience. For Nathan Gamble and Elle Fanning, who play the children of the North American couple, there were thorny moments in the course of the filming: the Sonora desert heat was much more intense than in Morocco. By nightfall they were sleepy and cranky. In addition to the heat and drowsiness, the children had other difficult moments. We were shooting in a snake zone and, at one point, Nathan saw one coming out of a hole in the sand during a take. He was truly terrified. The take stayed in.

Adriana Barraza's heart has two slight infarcts. In order to do this scene, she had
to carry a little girl weighing over 60 pounds many times on many days while running on the
desert in a temperature of over 115 degrees Fahrenheit. On one specially hot day, five of the
crew members had to be hospitalized for dehydration. Adriana began to feel ill, nearly fainted,
and asked for an hour off to recover. I told her to go to the hotel and rest. "No," she said,
"I know what it means to lose a day and that it can cost a lot of money. Just let me have an
hour." She showered in her trailer and emerged in an hour and a half to continue with the
scene. I had never witnessed such a level of commitment and incredible physical effort.
We filmed some of the most painful moments for two hours and a bit more. Perhaps Adriana
was thinking that if the immigrant did not have the option of a rest while crossing the desert,
why should Amelia?

Rodrigo Prieto is not only a brother to me but my right arm. His almost obsessive relation to light is nearly as intense as his ability to narrate a scene and delineate a character with his paintbrush camera. Like a real butterfly chaser, even while shooting a movie with the camera on his shoulder and at times no more than inches from the actor, he never interrupts their routines. He floats and breathes with them. While filming in the Morocco desert, he had to leave the set because his parents were celebrating their 60th anniversary. He went to the fiesta with the eagerness of a child. Months later, while filming in Tijuana, Rodrigo had a call during the night that his mother had died unexpectedly. The following morning, like a soldier, he wanted to work until a replacement could be found. We held a little memorial ceremony with the crew before starting to film. Rodrigo spoke of his mother in a way I had never heard anyone speak. He brought tears to the eyes of all of us and never did a desert seem such a lonely place. When Rodrigo returned, his expression spoke of peace with himself. He told me he had had a chat with a hummingbird.

When we were filming the scene of Amelia's detention by the immigration police, all the media were focused on the story of a young man of 17 from Oaxaca who tried to cross the Arizona desert with his mother. They were with a group and the mother's legs had given out, her throat shut down, and she could go no further. The others abandoned her. Three hours later, the mother told the son to go for help or he would die too. The youth walked all by himself for two days without water, was caught, and deported to Mexico. He had told his grandfather what happened, and the 70-year-old man traveled to Arizona and started a campaign with the help of a radio station for the rescue of his daughter. Ten days later, no traces were found except her white patent leather shoes, both femurs, and a towel with a design of yellow squares that the son had put over her face before leaving.

The men in the truck had been caught in the United States several hours earlier, and we asked them if they would like to appear in a movie. Their stories were no less harrowing than the woman's.

日本

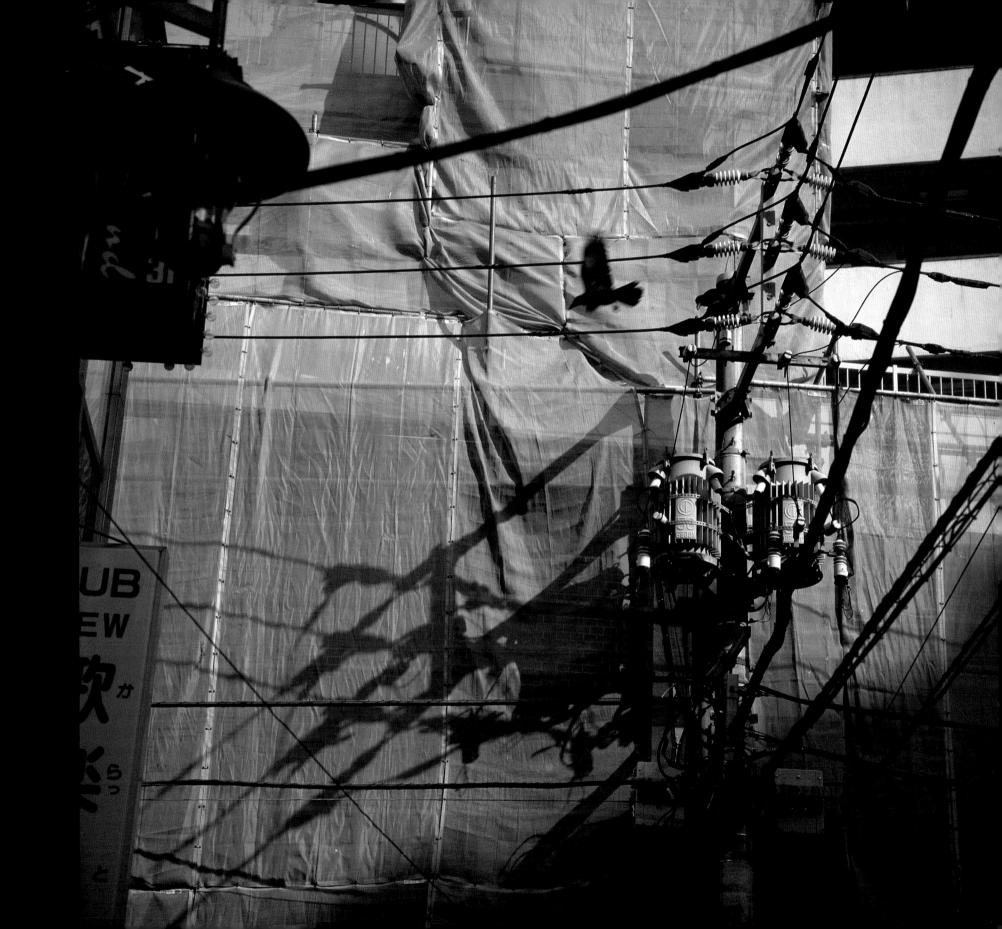

Just one single image gave me the idea for what was to be later transformed into the Japanese tale of *Babel*, an image that still echoes today with many emotions. I was walking in Hakone, a place half an hour away from Tokyo made up of bodies of sulphurous water, withered trees, constant fog, black crows like flying dogs; the ground covered with the discarded black shells of the eggs boiled by people in the waters. An atmosphere worthy of a Kurosawa film.

When I started down the mountain, I heard frightful guttural sounds. A retarded girl appeared through the fog walking slowly, helped by an elderly man. All the people going down, especially the children, were somewhat fearfully avoiding her. The old man, on the contrary, was helping her along with great tenderness, love, and dignity. I was moved by the image. On that trip and some months later, while traveling in Stockholm with my family, I saw quite a number of deaf-mutes. I was struck by their way of gesticulating and the dramatic nature of their communication. It seemed to me an unknown language ignored by practically all of us who are blessed with the power of touching and being touched by the word. "The language of silence," I was thinking. That same night I had an erotic dream about an adolescent in a dentist's office. All these images, apparently unrelated, had afforded me a justification for filming and exploring a possible story of different types of insufficiency—absence and loneliness—in one of my favorite cities for its mystery and contradictions. After two intense years of collaboration, Guillermo wrote a powerful and poignant story, which like an elegant perfume just brush the other three, leaving a delicate scent upon them.

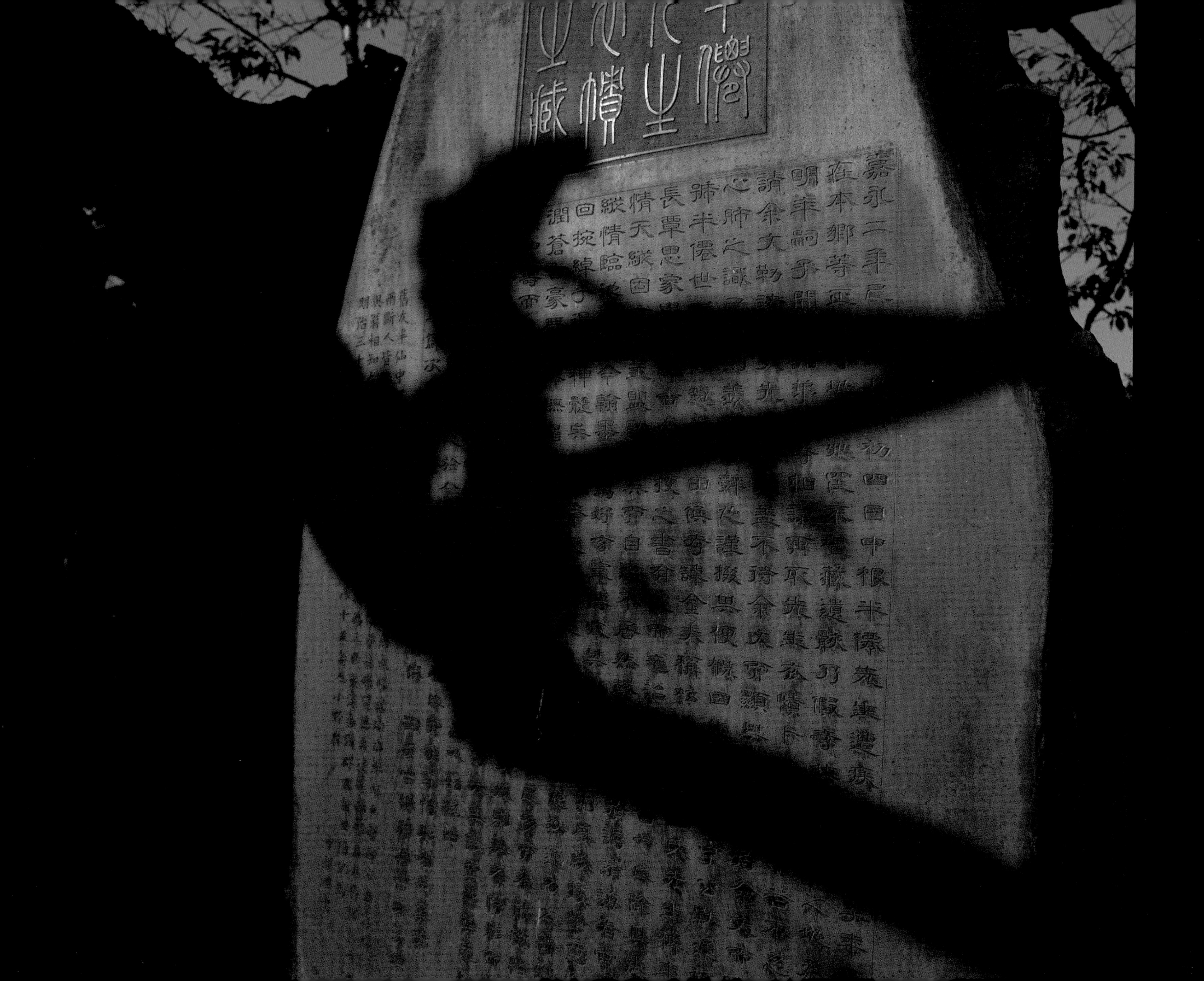

Since *Amores perros*, I have celebrated the beginning and ending day of a filming with a kind of ritual blessing. I like blessings because, as the origin in the Latin *benedicere* (to speak well) indicates, it means to say something good about something or somebody. I believe staunchly in the power and energy of words, which sometimes are nothing but what fills the heart. I use red roses on the first day and white roses on the last. On Sunday, November 6, 2005, at 5:30 a.m. in front of Tsukiji, the biggest fish market in the world, some 80 Japanamerimexicans formed a circle holding hands, prayed, observed a minute of silence, and decapitated red roses. Upon the cry of Abba Eli, we tossed their petals of blood into the pale blue sky over the city of kimonos and ideograms. It was a cold, tranquil, and romantic autumn morning, ideal for initiating the fourth and final part of *Babel*. At 7:30 a.m., the Tokyo police were chasing furiously over the city streets looking for us to shut down the filming and jail the person in charge. At 3 p.m., there was a downpour capable of washing away the island of Mishima itself. So began my first day of filming in Tokyo.

The people of Japan, like the characters in their pictures, are what they do and not what they say. No father will ever say "I love you" to his daughter. In Japan, as in good acting, feeling should be implicit in the action, not the words. For me, the words are the less important element of a scene. A well-written or well-directed scene should be understood in silence, without words, with the action delineating the character. Therein lies the greatness of the silent movies, pure cinema.

The words are only little boats that float in the great river of the emotions. A year before starting to film, I began casting in Japan, where I met Rinko Kikuchi. She introduced herself silently. We did a first reading and I was astonished. I almost took her for a deaf-mute. I couldn't take my eyes off of her. When I knew that she was not one, I hesitated. I was obsessed with finding a deaf-mute actress for the role of Chieko. I saw her again the next day. Her presence, her spirit, her intensity were perfect, but she was not a deaf-mute. I returned to Los Angeles with echoes of Rinko playing tag in my head, but unable to decide.

During the following nine months, while we were filming in Morocco and Mexico the Japanese casting director continued the search for Chieko. Rinko, on her own initiative, without notifying anybody and without the part being definitely hers, decided to take classes in sign language at her own expense. When I returned to Japan it was impossible for me to tell the difference between Rinko and a real deaf-mute. I had never before seen such determination, discipline, and need to play a part. Barely a few weeks before shooting, I told her the part was hers. Her emotion and tears were endless, profound, and silent. It has turned out to be my best decision since I started to make movies. Rinko—her presence like incense, subtle but penetrating—had incredible sensitivity and a deep inner life that made Chieko into a kinetic character.

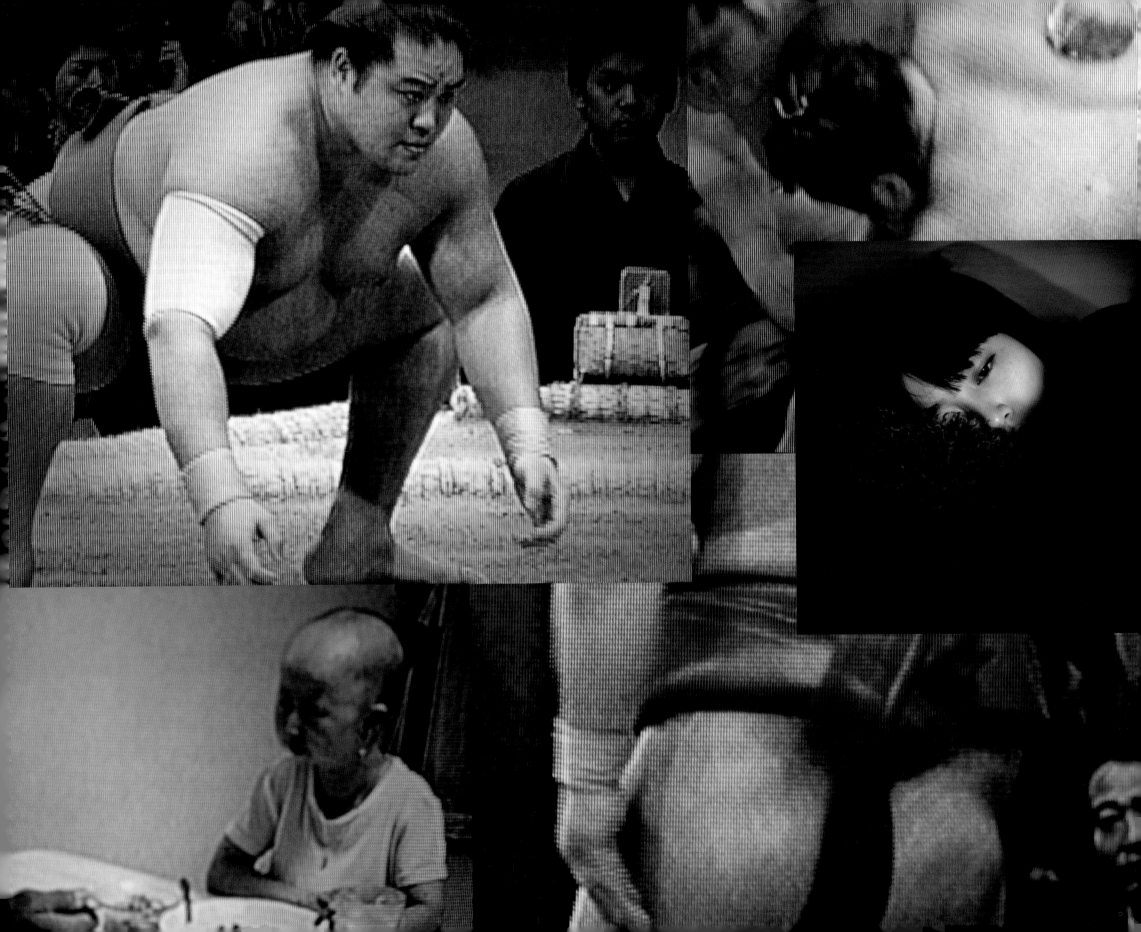

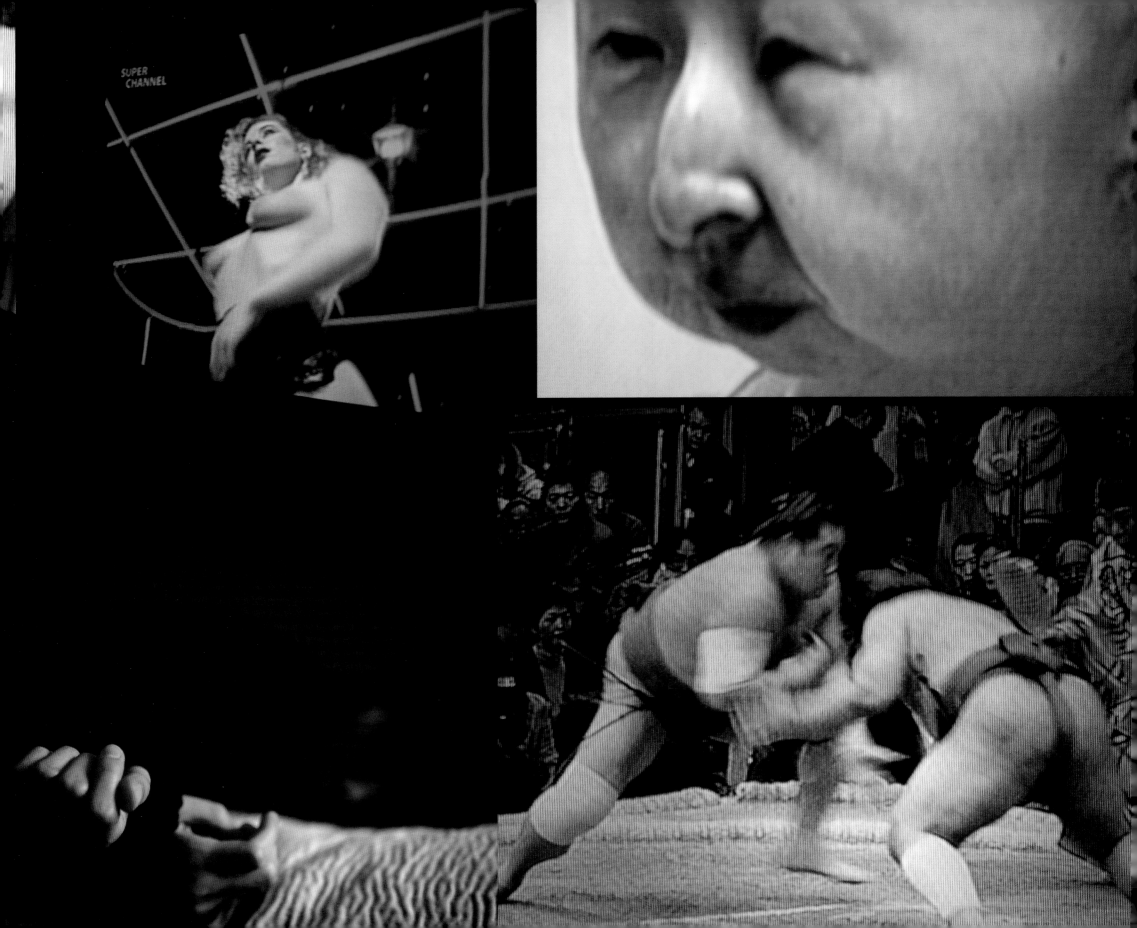

All Chieko's friends in the film, male and female, were deaf-mutes. Finding and convincing them to act was not easy, but casting the scene and rehearsing was worse. It went more or less like this: A young deaf-mute girl was sitting opposite me in a room. I had an interpreter, from English into Japanese, at my side, and next to her, an interpreter, from Japanese into sign language. When I would ask the young lady something like: "Did you ever imagine or dream the sound of anything?" the first interpreter translated to the second one in Japanese, the latter to the third one in sign language, and, finally, this one transmitted the question to the deaf-mute. The young woman thought for a few minutes and answered in sign language, which was put into Japanese by her interpreter, and finally what the English interpreter told me was: "in June". This was *Babel* at its peak.

Every day in my car on the way to the set and back to my house, I would listen to the same recording: *Chasm* by Riyuchi Sakamoto. This became my special sound track in Japan, especially the song "Only Love Can Conquer Hate." Rodrigo and Joey set up a system of rigging on the swing since I wanted to shoot that entire sequence at 30 frames and render the viewpoint and cadence of someone in ecstasy. I always felt that what in the script was a simple transition from one side to the other could be a great opportunity to get into Chieko's mind. I wanted a kind of adagio that would explode into a staccato. It wasn't until the editing room that I discovered that "Only Love Can Conquer Hate" would be the song that Chieko would be listening to if she could hear, like Sakamoto himself, the sounds of silence.

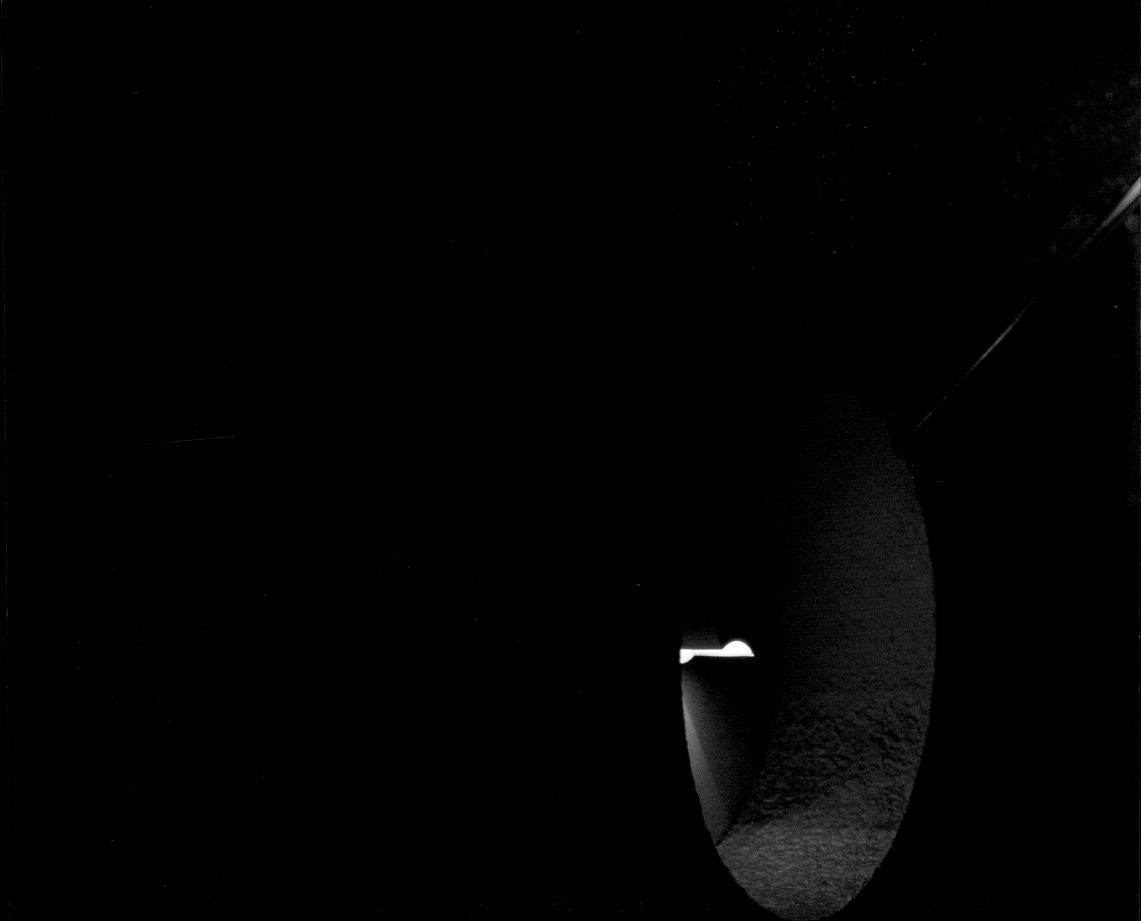

When I conceive a picture, I cannot move forward unless I have it clearly set beforehand within a musical spectrum. When I was 22 years old, I had a radio program in Mexico City in which I did, said, and played whatever I wanted to for three hours a day over a span of five years. I wrote and produced provocative stories and characters, which I combined with eclectic music. I created a space with those elements that stimulated musical and auditory ideas. That is the way I learned to entertain people for three hours nonstop. It was a question of tools that were not all that different from those of the movies.

A few weeks before beginning to film in Tokyo, we went to a club to see Shinichi Osawa, who is today one of Japan's most prestigious producers and DJs. I knew that I was going to use the "September" song of Earth, Wind & Fire for the introduction to the discotheque sequence, since I like to utilize certain songs of collective memory. At the same time, I was looking for a more current song to combine periods and atmospheres; something aggressive as opposed to something warm that would set Chieko's dramatic moment. Shinichi invited me to get behind his console. At the moment he began to play Fat Boy Slim's "The Joker," I knew that this was what I was looking for. The adolescents ceased to exist and got lost on a trip of ecstasy and sweat. Their eyes closed, they looked as though they were worshiping a guru who would lead them to a mantric and erotic land. The next day, Shinichi invited me to his studio to make a long introduction of Earth, Wind & Fire that I needed for the entrance to the discotheque and masterfully mixed Fat Boy Slim with tremendous vibes. I shot the scene against that music and, in the editing room, the magic "scissors-hands man" Stephen Mirrione and I felt throbs close to those of the adolescents' trip.

Chieko's story is not about pathological sex but about the need for affection. When words are not an alternative, and one can't touch or be touched by them, the body is transformed into our only tool of expression. To be able to suggest and support Chieko's complex past with a couple of scenes, I needed a similarly complex but profoundly human and empathetic presence. In a world in which acting styles seem to run towards shrieks of exaggeration, it was a pleasure to find myself with an actor whose spirit, reliability, and elegance are indicative of an economy of movement that very few in the world succeed in mastering. Koji Yakusho's disciplined and human warmth lent dignity to Chieko's story. The actor's micromovements, from lifting an eyelid to holding up a hand, make all the difference. In the same way, Satoshi Mikaido, who acts the part of Kenji, has a spiritual nobility necessary for him to do what he did to Chieko: dignify one considered undignified.

There is nothing sadder in a filming than the last day of shooting. Nostalgia floods the set, and a postpartum depression begins to spread for a while. However, that day in which we would be filming Chieko walking alone before the emperor's gardens, something happened that I thought at first was a joke on the part of the art department headed by Brigitte Broch. All the trees that surround the gardens were decorated with intertwined Moroccan and Japanese flags. The colors of the two flags together were green, white, and red, which are the colors of the Mexican flag. The three countries in which we had filmed were saying goodbye to us with a beautiful golden autumn day. What did a Moroccan flag have to do with that particular Japanese location on the last day of filming a picture that speaks of those two countries whose colors together make a Mexican flag? King Mohammed VI was visiting at the palace. But there is no chance or coincidence. It is all fate.

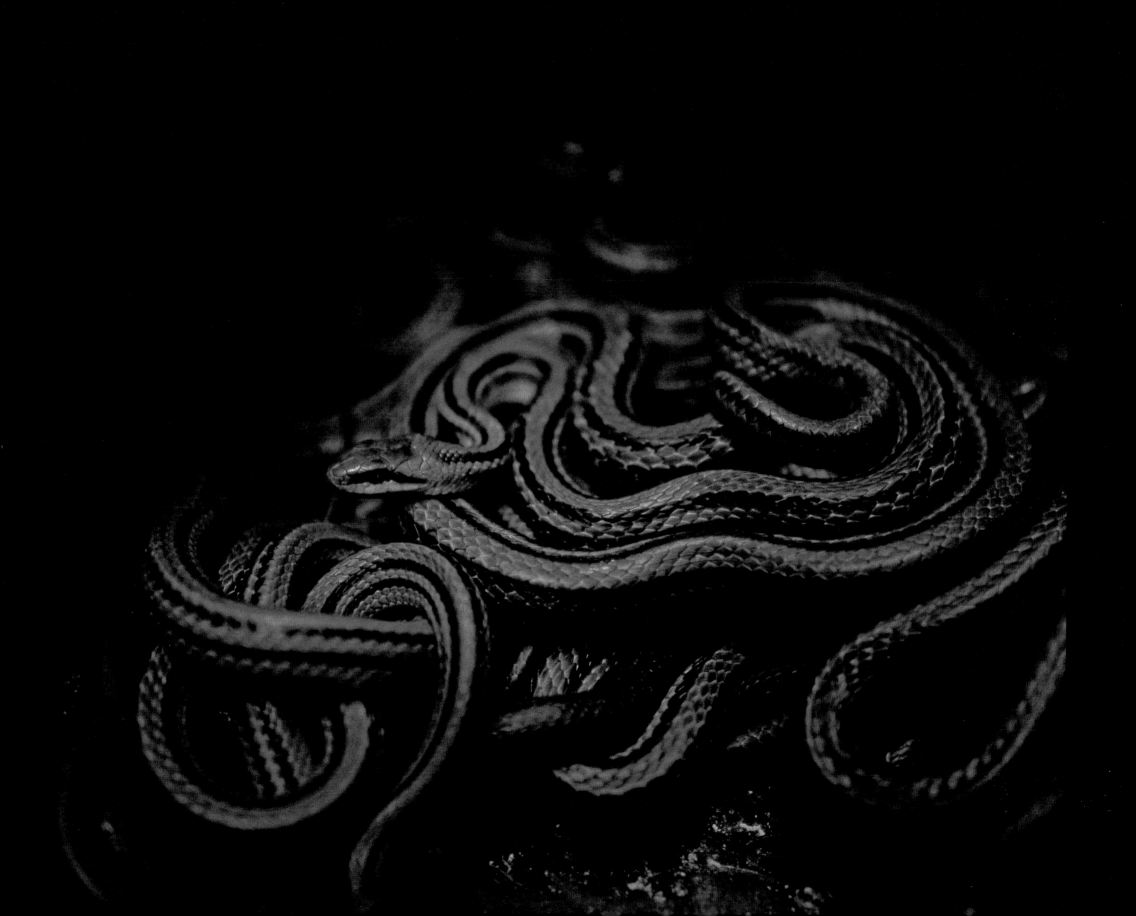

The Foundations of *Babel*

A Conversation Between Rodrigo García and Alejandro González Iñárritu

What was the image or idea that originated the project? From what seed was the script developed?

As you well know, a script is no more that the technical application of a story, which is the result of an idea, which, in turn, originates in the subconscious world, the world of intuition and irrationality.

Perhaps it was the aesthetic and cultural impact of my first trip to Morocco at the age of 18 (enveloped in a cloud of existentialism and hashish) or perhaps, the buildup of absence in exile, but at the outset, *Babel* was born of a moral need to purge myself and to speak of the things that were filling my heart and mind: the incredible and painful worldwide paradoxes that affected close and distant lands, finally pouring out as individual tragedies. First, something was cooking on the basis of something that was lodged inside me, and later on, as a concept that would close the triptych of the overlapping stories I started in *Amores perros* and *21 Grams.*

After finishing *Amores perros,* I traveled a great deal all over the world, including Japan, and went to live in Los Angeles to begin a new project. My family and I came to the United States four days before September 11, and the world was upturned around us. The experience of living in a country under a regime paranoid with aggravated nationalism was not an easy matter. It was impossible to walk a hundred yards without being faced by a United States flag and a suspicious glance.

I fell into deep depression. It was a difficult and intense phase. Nevertheless, I believe that had I not gotten out of Mexico, I would have never gotten out of my hamlet and my comfort zone, and never been obliged by need or hunger to face this challenge.

The idea of *Babel* came to me when I was on the point of starting to shoot *21 Grams* in the city of Memphis. It was the first time I would be directing a film outside my country and in a language other than my own. Again, three parallel stories concerning parents and children were set in an interesting structural context in which the central theme would be "loss."

The mere idea of trying to carry out the theory of parallel realities, now not only outside my country but on a world level, was something that cost me sleep.

I began to work on this concept with the scriptwriter and director Carlos Cuarón. Originally, five stories in five languages on five continents were involved. Carlos and I were working very briefly on a couple of tentative plots. In all of them, a decision taken in a distant land would radically alter the life of a human being who would never find out their source. We were at that point when an important Mexican newspaper published that Carlos and I were working together on a project with a worldwide theme. Not only that but, by chance, I found out that the Brazilian director Fernando Meirelles was preparing a similar project. I spoke to him and learned that it was true.

Carlos Cuarón then decided to concentrate on another story to direct that we had worked on in the past. After a while, Fernando got off on another project. It was then that I invited Guillermo Arriaga to work with me again.

Guillermo proposed five stories, of which two survived: the gorgeous, solid story of the Moroccan children, and the beginning of the story of the couple, Richard and Susan, which interwove naturally and physically with the previous one, even though, at the time, it was still quite green. I put forward the character of a Mexican nanny who was taking care of North American children, because of the need to relate something that was not just about my country but about immigrants and the tragic border situation and the character from Tokyo: an adolescent Japanese deaf-mute girl being taken care of by a man alone.

To me, the character of Amelia was always the incarnation of Julia: the Mexican woman who was working for my family in our Los Angeles home. She had told me about how she had crossed the desert six times and how she was caught by the patrol cars. Julia spent three nights and three days on the desert with seeing a trace of civilization.

The lungs of more than one of those crossing the border have collapsed from lack of water and the heat. It was not until the seventh time that Julia succeed in getting across. Her 20-year-old son is in prison, and she can't see him because the immigration authorities would deport her to Mexico. There are no sadder tales than those concerning the border. I travel to Tijuana every six months with my children in order to renew my visa. The lineup there is one in which humiliation is an institutionalized ritual. The scene that describes it in *Babel* is a faithful rendition of the form and machinery of inspection that I, myself, sometimes had to suffer.

I got the idea for the Japanese story from a single image, which, in turn, triggered many emotions. I was walking in Hakone, a place an hour and a half from Tokyo, that consisted of sulphurous waters, withered trees, constant fog, black crows like flying dogs, the ground covered with the black eggshells thrown away by the people after boiling the eggs in the waters. It seemed to me an image worthy of a Kurosawa film.

On going down the mountain, I heard horrible guttural sounds. Through the fog, there appeared a retarded girl being helped along by a man some 60 years old. All those going down, particularly the children, avoided her somewhat fearfully. The man, however, held her by the arm with great tenderness, love, and dignity.

I was moved by the image. On that very trip some months later, while traveling in Stockholm with my family, I ran into many deaf-mutes. They were everywhere. I was struck by the way they gesticulated and by the dramatic intensity of their communication. It seemed to me to be an unknown and ignored language for almost all of us who are blessed with the gift of touching and being touched by words. That same night I had an erotic dream about an adolescent girl in a dentist's office. All those apparently unconnected images provided me the justification for filming in one of my favorite cities for its mystery and contradictions. I had the idea of telling the story of a father and daughter suffering from different types of equally dreadful loneliness.

I called Guillermo from Stockholm. He liked the idea and, on the basis of it, decided that there should be four stories instead of five. We had two years of intense and demanding collaboration.

Despite the fact that Guillermo was not familiar with either Japan or Morocco, his talent enabled him to write a script, which was the blueprint for initiating the first phase of *Babel*.

Once the script was ready, still without having even the actors, much less the financing assured, I invited Jon Kilik and Steve Golin to produce the picture with me. I was personally financing the project, and they were the first to believe in it, take the risk as partners, and go along with the adventure to the end. In December 2004, the three of us got on a plane together with Brigitte Broch, my friend and production designer, and flew to Tunis and Morocco, thereby initiating the scouting and actual journey of *Babel*.

You always wanted a global frame for the film: a canvas on which an apple falling from a tree would have an economic, political, and human impact two continents away. At what point did *Babel* turn into a story less about globalization and more about three families?

The only reason why this trilogy can be considered as such, besides its having been shaped for films that have the structure of overlapping stories, is that in the very end, they are stories of parents and children. That's what *Amores perros* and *21 Grams* were. Despite the fact that social and political questions on a global scale are implicit in *Babel*, it does not cease being a quartet of very intimate tales.

The story of the Moroccan children, which originally was going to take place in Tunis, meant to me more a tragedy about the moral breakdown of a highly spiritual Muslim family than a story about a boy being chased by the police. It is equally or more important to the father of the children that Yussef is peeping on his sister while she is undressing than the fact that they had shot at a bus. When values crumble nothing makes sense anymore; when a link is broken, it's not just the link that breaks but the whole chain.

It was on the basis of that story, which was always the most solid, that the rest was built. The story of Richard and Susan, the couple traveling in Morocco, was politically slanted much more than familiarly; it focused on the politics of the government more than human politics, which are more complex. It included scenes with ambassadors, vice ministers, and TV broadcasting. It took us a long time to discover that there was no place in this story for archetypical characters.

Although much of the Moroccan story is shot from Susan's point of view, it was harder for me to find a way of narrating from Richard's perspective. Then, all at once, I realized that if I subordinated Richard's point of view to a hyperrealistic perspective, I could describe the situation of a character who never knows what is going on in the world, nor what is in the news, nor about the pressures and paranoid accusations of his government against the Moroccan government. Only on a transistor radio that broadcasts in an unfamiliar language and through a telephone conversation with a friend does Richard find out briefly what is happening around him. I considered that if the character had so few resources I ought not give the public much more information than he possessed. When do we as civilians have the opportunity to be present during conversations of

politicians and their representatives? That occurs only in the movies and I didn't want this story to sound like a movie. I wanted the public to intuit the errors of politicians and the misinterpretations of the media.

To me, Richard and Susan's story, more than one about a North American couple that comes together to get hopelessly lost in the desert, is the story of two people lost with respect to one another who come to the desert and find each other. The key to understanding who they are lies in the fact that they lose a child and in the grief and guilt arising out of that misfortune.

In Chieko's case, the Japanese adolescent, besides lacking a mother, she suffers from the lack of words. When we cannot touch or be touched by words, the body transforms itself into a tool, a weapon, an invitation.

That is what happens in the story of Amelia who besides being an invisible citizen is an unrecognized mother as well. Once again all four stories were about parents and children.

***Babel* proceeds with remarkable facility from point to point and language to language, demonstrating great empathy with human beings, regardless of their circumstances. However, I have the impression that in the Mexican segment you go a bit overboard in your affection. Were you aware of that?**

Mexico's story was extremely difficult to film not only because of the complexity of the border aspect but the harshness of the climate. We were shooting in the hottest deserts on earth in scenes involving children. Being my native country, I could be judged more severely. To get to the heart of things and examine the border subculture, which I used to avoid and reject, was no less than an anthropological undertaking.

The first decision I made for the sake of being faithful and in accordance with the picture was to leave out of the script and, subsequently in the editing room, entire blocks of stereotypes and platitudes that added nothing dramatically and portrayed the idealized and charming Mexico that no longer exists, much less on the U.S. border zone where the people are more somber and meaner.

The second decision I made was to see Mexico at least at the outset from the viewpoint of the North American children—as could happen to much of the public around the world—who go through the experience for the first time of entering Mexico through the San Jacinto border. As I had told you, I cross the border with my children every six months. Despite their being Mexicans they are impressed with the colors, the candy stores, the donkey, the mud, the whorse, the lack of grass, and the dust-laden air of their country. What is misery and poverty to an adult in the eyes of the children is colorfulness and gaiety. All who have crossed at some time from the United States into Tijuana find out that there is a certain electricity in the air and an almost absurd contrast.

Some call Tijuana the armpit of Latin America. To me it is a place where the most noble dreams overlap with the saddest ends.

In the Carrizo community, one hour from Tijuana, I filmed the wedding of Luis, Amelia's son. We went to many weddings as part of the research and some ended up with knifings. Beyond the folkloric aspect, to me, this wedding always represented the only possibility of knowing Amelia and her world. I knew that if at the moment I was unable to establish empathy with her and the audience, the character would be dead. She would just be an ignorant maid who irresponsibly put the children at risk.

For that reason I decided to build a filmic bubble of imaginary time: a capsule that would permit me to delineate Amelia as mother, friend, lover, and, particularly, as the stand-in mother of those North American children. Chavela Vargas's background song floats on the wings of melancholy, something that I had in mind beforehand and for that purpose shot at 30 frames.

Amelia, like many Mexicans, finds herself in the paradox of having to neglect her own children in order to take care of others. Like many more Mexicans who, while living in the United States, fix cars for the North Americans without having the right of a driver's license and build houses without being able to afford the rent for their own home.

I filmed the Mexican border very lovingly but, at the same time, with great pain because those are the feelings that predominate in that region.

Your shift from Mexico to the United States just as you were filming *21 Grams* was a great personal and professional challenge. What new challenges did you face this time as a director? What did you achieve that you hadn't before.

There were great physical and logistical challenges, but particularly intellectual and emotional ones. I believe that anybody can juggle three oranges at a time. However, I bet that if you take four oranges they will fall a hundred times before you are able to master them. *Babel* had four stories instead of three, as was the case with *Amores perros* and *21 Grams*, and it is different from the plan I was accustomed to. Besides, having filmed in three different continents and cultures, I had to adjust and rewrite the script in keeping with the immediate circumstances.

In this film I allowed myself a poetic license; I felt much freer and more secure than in the previous films. I tried things that I hadn't done in the others, for example, to achieve the coexistence of realism and hyperrealism with the world of the imaginary; with the congruence and logic of the silent movies but with the anarchy of music and audio as narrators in the foreground.

I converted one line of script into a 10-minute sequence related from the viewpoint of the inner world of a character, provoking the public through images, sounds, or metaphors, to submerge itself in the character's mind and his circumstances. In the case of the Chieko sequence in the park and the discotheque, I intended for the audience to experience the sound of silence just as she does in her head and from her perspective, because, at the time, it is the silence that can be truly deafening. In the scene of Richard and Susan's rescue by helicopter, I wanted the image to suggest a flying whale arriving at a desert sea and, at the same time, the clash of cultures and profound socioeconomic differences.

To me, cinema is much more than a script or illustrated anecdote. Cinema is what takes place between one dialogue and the other; what can only be told with the silence of the images. Beyond identification with the characters, their history and circumstances, I wanted the audience to connect emotionally through the use of montage, music, dialectic, and juxtaposition of visual and sensorial ideas. That is to say, in-depth utilization of all filmic resources in a way I had not done in my two previous pictures. In all this orchestration, I and the entire team must remain invisible and never allow the audience to notice us during the experience of watching a picture. If my work gets obvious on the screen, then I have failed and everything I have told you makes no sense.

Cinema is a living beast and is made in stages that seem never to end. As you know, editing is rewriting. In that sense, and because of the nature of the film, the editing of *Babel* was particularly difficult. I cannot imagine working with an editor other than Stephen Mirrione. His talent and clarity were of great importance in juggling these four oranges, and the elegance of his cutting made the transition more organic. We removed whole chunks that made the original structure of the script rickety. And once more, I found myself sculpting the stone in order to bring out its true form.

I recall, particularly, how we hit on the epilogue for Yussef and Ahmed's story. One day, going from one place to another in the Quarzazate mountains, an unexpectedly strong wind began blowing. It became almost necessary to hold on to something. I had the cameras taken out of the station wagon and asked Yussef and Ahmed to play in the wind at the edge of the road. There was no dramatic purpose to the image but, for me, it had splendid aesthetic and poetic content. In that way, I had an old abandoned boat set up in the middle of a vast valley of stony desert to suggest the existence of a sea in that region. In scouting Tunis, we found hundreds of marine fossils, even learned that skeletons of whales had been discovered in the middle of the Sahara. I was moved by that idea and, as time went by, I began getting vertigo. To me, the boat in the desert was a metaphor for Noah's ark; man's passage in the vast deserts of time.

Also on the last day of shooting, I filmed a close-up on a dolly of Yussef weeping over his brother's death. My original idea was to cut next to the scene of Noah's boat, in which his brother and father were moving off as a foreboding of the brother's death. However, on seeing the first cut, I noticed that Yussef and Ahmed's story ended very early and, for that reason, very far from the end of the picture. It seemed as though Ahmed's death was unimportant. To make matters worse, that moment for the spectator was so far from the emotional pitch of the end that it ran the risk of being forgotten. We needed an epilogue as we had in the other three stories. Now, it seems that to find a way to cut those little unconnected moments and where to put them was something obvious and easy to do, but it called for a great deal of time and work. Now, not only is it a great epilogue for that story but one of the most emotional moments of the picture, inasmuch as, besides being the only flash-back and forward in the picture's structure, it metaphorically synthesizes and fuses the deserts of Morocco and Mexico.

The wind that blows Amelia's hair upon her embracing her son at the border is the wind that shook up the children in Morocco and also the same wind created by the helicopter that came in to rescue Susan and Richard. This section, together with that of Chieko in the park and the discotheque are my favorite editing sequences and the ones in which Mirrione, with his talent and rigorousness, played a crucial part.

One of the big editing challenges was that of passing from one country to another without the change being brusque and distracting for the spectator. Here, music is an essential factor and, once again, Gustavo Santaolalla was the key.

Before traveling to each and every one of the countries where we were filming in order to record and do research, Gustavo decided to use an oud, an ancient Arabic instrument, the mother of the guitar, to be the musical DNA of the picture. Because of the tension of its strings, the oud is difficult to play. Gustavo learned how in order to express it in the score.

Despite the fact that I wanted to give the music more weight on this occasion than in the previous pictures, the tips of Santaolalla's fingers managed, in a minimalist style, to break our hearts with a single note. Besides being profoundly Afro-Mediterranean, the sound of the oud has the additional quality of recalling to us the wail of the flamenco guitar, and hence the Mexican, together with a touch of the scent of the Japanese *koto*. Santaolalla's genius made it possible to bring the three cultures together with no need for resorting to the folkloric instruments of each country, which would have been dreadful.

These are the things that I was discovering along the way; all in all, I make movies in order to learn how to make movies. Every time I begin a picture, it seems as though I had forgotten everything I learned in the previous picture. It is like having premature Alzheimer's. All in all, I do not consider myself a movie director but a fellow who has made three pictures and a couple of shorts. A frustrated musician, to boot.

My dream is to make one great film in my life, but sometimes I feel that the things I want to do are light years beyond my ability to accomplish them.

Despite *Babel*'s global and polyglot context, it has a more personal and intimate feeling than your previous films. To what do you attribute that?

In all the countries I filmed, *Babel* sought to tie my hands to prevent me from yielding to my own aesthetic temptations and ending up by making a National Geographic pseudodrama. Or, even worse, four unconnected shorts filmed from the point of view of a tourist. I had to make conflicting and even contradictory decisions: On the one hand I needed to separate and delineate the stories and at another level to unify them.

What made *Babel* end up being a film on its own, was the possibility of finding a single note that floated along it. Beyond the formal part, which I will talk to you about further on, I regard my characters with great tenderness and empathy. That look permeated the entire film and enabled the same tone and spirit to pervade, including even the visual styles and symbols in which I filmed. I tried in every scene to concentrate on obsessively filming the aspect of the intimacy and the microdetails of the inner and external world of the characters. It may sound obvious, but I was thinking locally in order to function universally.

The inner part — the picture's soul — is the same story told four times regarding the great tragedies of the vertical mammal: the inability to love and receive love, the vulnerability of the beings we love. Every time I initiated a story it was as though beginning another picture. At the end, I love my characters, suffered and wept with them, and I realized that it was nothing but the same picture told once more.

The best part of shooting *Babel* was that I began filming a picture about the difference between human beings — that which separates us, the physical barriers and those of language — but along the way I began realizing that I was filming about the things that join us, connect us, and make us only one. Those things are love and pain: What makes a Japanese or a Moroccan happy can be very different, but that which makes us miserable is the same for everybody.

Insofar as what refers to the external aspect — the formal and aesthetic — my friend and extraordinary photographer, Rodrigo Prieto, and I decided to risk making a pastiche. Each of the countries would be filmed in different styles, textures, and formats.

Theoretically, each story would have its own personality. Each style and format would be subordinate to the dramatic exigencies of the characters and their circumstances. In turn, my talented friend and art designer Brigitte Broch suggested that we divide the countries using a gamut of reds: burgundy for Morocco, bright-red for Mexico, and violet for Japan. Morocco was shot in 16mm with faded colors, Mexico in 35mm with vivid colors, and, at Rodrigo's brilliant suggestion, Japan in Panavision with anamorphic lenses, which isolate the character spectacularly and appropriately for this story's theme.

The reason why this collage worked is because behind each of these apparently disparate decisions, there was always a very compelling justification and expert teamwork approach. Rodrigo Prieto and Brigitte Broch are my right and left hands. Their collaboration enriched the final result enormously.

I always tried to make my cinematographic language consistent with the characters and my visual vocabulary and style, even when the picture was shot with hand-held camera. I saw to it that there was a rest, an inner beat backing up the quality of emotion in the staging.

Apparently, the shooting took place in what was a Tower of Babel in itself. How was it to work with people who had never acted and did not speak your language.

Directing actors is difficult. Directing actors in a language other than your own is much more difficult. Now, directing nonactors in a language you don't understand is the greatest challenge a director can have. Seventeen days before starting to shoot in Morocco, I didn't have a single actor besides Brad Pitt and Cate Blanchett.

For the the role of the children Yussef and Ahmed and their family of shepherds, as well as for all the characters throughout the story of Richard and Susan, I started out by seeking professional actors in the Moroccan community, as well as the Muslim communities of Paris. However, none of them had the appearance that I needed. I looked for weathered skins that are to be found towards the south and way into the Sahara. Most of the professionals had fine features, smooth skin, and had acquired the bad habits of the soap opera actors. No matter how much makeup we put on them, they would look like actors in a Hallmark movie. It was then that, together with Alfonso Gómez, Hervé Jacubowicz, and Marc Robert, my casting team decided to undertake a desperate search among all the poor villages around Tamnougalt and Quarzazate and find the real characters of *Babel*.

Over the noisy loudspeakers in the minarets, the good news was announced that the movie *Babel* was looking for actors to appear in it. Hundreds of people lined up and we did a video of them. At night I checked them and picked the ones that were physically interesting. Together with Hiam Abbass—a wonderful actress and a great friend who, as more than dialogue coach, transformed into my guardian angel—on the next day we tried out the individuals we had chosen with exercises I always use to sensitize myself to their emotional range.

This was my first experience of working with nonactors and ordinary people. It was enchanting; I will do it whenever possible and always. Despite the fact that the process can be frustrating and ignorance and technical limitation can be a disadvantage, innocence is and will always be more powerful than experience. The virginity, purity, and honesty one has in playing the part of himself cannot be matched.

One example is Abdullah, father of the Moroccan children, a carpenter on the outskirts of Fez whose discipline and dramatic range left me astounded. In scenes like when he strikes his children or when his son Ahmed dies—which took me three day to shoot—he kept up the intensity in each take and at every moment. Once I indicated the physical movements of the staging, he repeated them exactly and rhythmically. Scenes like those would be difficult even for midlevel professionals. It was the same with Hassan or Yussef. From the first moment, their eyes revealed that they possessed considerable inner life. It is enough to talk to somebody for a few minutes and, looking into their eyes, to find out if they have the spark or not, or if they have the emotional equipment to draw a bit of inner feeling out of themselves and metaphorically brush what happens onto the character to be portrayed.

Now, the mixture of professional actors with nonprofessionals is more complicated. In the story of Yussef and Ahmed, all were nonprofessionals. However, that was not the case in the Richard and Susan story. Apparently simple scenes like that of Cate Blanchett and Sfia, the old woman who takes care of Susan when she comes into the room bleeding or the one of the veterinarian who sews up Susan's wound with Richard looking on, were not at all easy.

Sfia was a Berber woman of 85 who had never seen a camera before. She was a native of Taguenzalte, a town without electricity and lived in the house next to where we were filming. Sfia spoke only Berber. The veterinarian is actually the town veterinarian and speaks only Arabic. A stage direction as simple as "on hearing '*what*' you get up and go close the window" became a three-hour odyssey for Sfia. It was a real achievement that she did well, a couple of times, particularly, without her turning to the camera and smiling.

What I learned is that if a director selects somebody who physically expresses what the character should express at first sight, and if that person has only one feature with which it is possible to identify with the character, once the director finds it and communicates his dramatic objectives clearly in a simple way he can make any human being on the planet act.

And what was the experience like of working with somebody like Brad Pitt, who is world-famous, amidst this ensemble of nonactors and under adverse conditions? What prompted you to pick him and Cate Blanchett?

The experience with the professional actors of *Babel* was just as rich as that of working with the nonprofessionals.

Even when fiction and reality touch several times during the filming and the circumstance and working conditions—climate, location, different languages—were difficult, I always felt support from the actors and enjoyed the privilege of their confidence.

Despite the fact that Richard's role did not seem to be obvious for an actor as recognizable as Brad Pitt, it always seemed to me that he had a magnetic presence on a level beyond his popularity. He give the feeling of a fellow who is comfortable with himself. When I met him four years ago, what impressed me from the first was his courage. We were filming together in a publicity campaign for Japanese jeans, which consisted of a series of silly takes that I was inventing as I went along.

Brad insisted on carrying things out to the point where he was putting himself in physical danger. The producer got nervous at the sight of what we were doing and put out a statement to the effect that they would not take the responsibility if Brad hurt himself and asked him to sign it. Pale and sweating, his manager asked him to stop doing reckless things and not to sign the paper. Brad, without turning around to look at him, signed it, and went on doing as he wanted. We filmed for a couple of hours more, having a lot of fun. On the last of the takes, Brad could be seen sliding down a thin railing on a huge staircase, mounted on a surfboard.

When I offered him the part of Richard four years later, he accepted without hesitation. It isn't easy for actors and celebrities of his caliber to accept doing characters of that type. After all, there is risk implicit in any independent film of low budget, and good intentions do not always result happily.

The challenge for me was to get Brad, the celebrity, to disappear behind the character in order to give way not only to the actor but to the human being behind that image. If at the end, people forgot who it was and he could blend in and not stand out among the other characters, not only Brad Pitt but the picture itself will have triumphed. A lot of risks were involved and he courageously accepted the challenges. He accepted, especially, the biggest risk actors always face: he put himself in my hands and trusted me. It was not an easy process. He was going through a difficult time in his personal life but never mixed one thing with another.

In the original script, the conflict between Richard and Susan arose from an infidelity of his in the past. Some weeks before filming I suggested taking the drama to a deeper level, such as the crib death of a child, which Guillermo wrote later. Brad did not discover the change in the script until he arrived in Morocco. Actually, it was already troublesome to build a character on the basis of only 30 pages of story. It was not easy to adjust right off the bat to this new dramatic element. Who was Richard? Why did he do what he did? Every day, under extenuating physical conditions, it was necessary to dig, to find and invent the vulnerable character that Brad built on the screen.

Between the physical exhaustion and the constant emotional intensity the part demanded, Brad, like his character, was becoming more fragile and vulnerable until reaching that moment in which he exudes great fortitude and tenderness and which to me, personally seemed very beautiful: the final phone call that Richard makes to his son, and which finally reveals to us the human being in universal guise in the face of impotence and in which Brad gave his all.

Cate Blanchett's case was different. She had been one of my favorite actresses for a long time, and I literally begged her to take on the part of Susan. She balked and for good reason. In the script, the character of Susan was that of woman who passes three-quarters of the picture stretched out on the ground semiconscious and bleeding.

However, in my opinion, it was only from Susan's viewpoint that the events would take on power and relevance, and I explained it to her in those terms. To make it possible in 28 minutes for the public to become fond of and empathize with a character who starts out by wiping her hands with disinfectant, throwing her husband's Coca-Cola on the ground and showing that she is intensely uncomfortable with every inch of her life and body, called for an actress of Cate's caliber. Her character's every moment, standing up, sleeping, or sitting down is fraught with emotion.

From the first scene on, she establishes the rules and level of the game. It never ceases to surprise me, even after so many times of having seen that moment when she smokes the pipe. It seems like something simple but what she does, says, and makes you feel with her eyes, and her eyes alone—since she is unable to move any other part of her body, is mesmerizing.

Even though, for reasons explained to you before, I had to do 25 takes of a single angle alone for the veterinarian or Sfia to be able to find their line or rhythm, Cate, in each take, gave me the same intensity. Her generosity and command of her tools made the work of the director easier.

What impact did traveling around half the world and living side by side with people of such diverse origins and customs have on your life. How did *Babel* change your way of looking at things?

I believe that all pictures are transforming, but this is the one that has changed me by far the most. More than a professional decision, it signified a life change. I was aware that it would imply sacrifice and transformation in the ordinary course of the life of my family, which is my nucleus and my base. I knew that my children, my wife, and I were going to benefit humanly but that many sacrifices would be in order as well. One cannot be the same after connecting with and being involved with so many people. If before starting to film my attitude towards life was more cynical and pessimistic, on finishing I was more hopeful and optimistic about the human being

because certainly those prejudices and inner frontiers could crumble in the face of the simple fact of touching us. I realized that the clash of the North American and Muslim cultures did not take place because of being radically disparate but because they are amazingly similar. Fanaticism, nationalism carried to an extreme, and the objectification of women, although apparently different, are close relatives. Both cultures used God for their own purposes and under his name can justify sometimes their wars and atrocities, making God an auxiliary partner instead of the Lord.

While filming *Babel*, I realized that people are basically good and that the fewer things they possess the happier and purer they are.

I know you are a deeply religious and spiritual person. Even so, and although in your pictures you touch on such Judeo-Christian themes as the fall, redemption, or culpability, religion plays no central role in your stories—even in *Babel*, which is about people from a variety of cultures. Why did you come to that decision at a moment when religion is hailed as a banner?

For me, religion is debated in the intellectual rather than in the moral sphere. In contrast to *21 Grams*, where I explored the phenomenon of religious fanaticism through the character of Benicio del Toro, there was no place for the religious questioning in *Babel*.

This picture is concerned precisely with how vulnerable and fragile the human being is; how, in the final analysis, we can be at some point just like little animals; how we love and need one another even while pissing; how loneliness kills us, indifference destroys us like a liter less of blood. In one scene, the character of Richard watches Anwar praying towards the mosque, looking at him as though seeking to find a faith that he, unfortunately, does not possess.

In *Babel* it was God who created the confusion and man who now has to find the solution. God is missing in this equation.

In your career as feature-film director you have worked with many of the same collaborators: Rodrigo Prieto, Brigitte Broch, Guillermo Arriaga, Martín Hernández. What has it been like to develop and create with them? How much influence have their styles and talents had on your films?

I met Rodrigo Prieto as director of photography when I was still doing publicity commercials. We worked together on various campaigns. I'll never forget that after sending him the script for *Amores perros*, I invited him to lunch to exchange ideas on how we could treat the project visually. I brought a series of still-photo books as reference for what I was seeking. Rodrigo pulled the same books out of his suitcase that I had brought.

From that point on I knew that there was a connection and a shared image of things. To plan shooting with Rodrigo or to be with him on the set is a pleasure; seeing him operate the camera is an experience; but to see and discover later in the editing room, in detail, his incomparable way of narrating the most minimal emotional details through the camera and impeccable composition is impressive.

In *Babel*, there are only three scenes in which we used a dolly: the first, the last, and the close-up of Yussef weeping over the death of his brother. Rodrigo filmed the rest with the camera on his shoulder. I have seen him grow in a mesmerizing way from *Amores perros* to *Babel*. His command of light and technical knowledge are vast but his elegance as a human being is even greater. During a picture there is nobody closer to me than him. We know each other so well that on the set, with just a gesture or simple grunt in code, we are able to establish an entire shooting strategy. In the more than 12 years we have known each other and worked together, never have we had a disagreeable moment.

I met Brigitte Broch at almost the same time that I met Rodrigo and we worked together for the first time in a publicity campaign that won many international prizes (and in which, curiously enough, I also worked with Gael García Bernal for the first time). Brigitte is a celebration of life. When she designs an atmosphere, each of the subjects and details, no matter how tiny they may be, speak of and describe the characters in a profound way. We enjoy filming on location and she always has a great feel for finding a better place, not based on the look but the spirit and energy of the place. In always talking colors and textures, odors and forms, during the endless scoutings around the world, we were talking of life. My pictures and life would not be the same without her.

Martín Hernández and I studied together at the university. Our first project together was when I was 20: I was the assistant director and composed the music for a short directed by a friend of ours and Martín was the soundman. Later on, we were together at a radio station where we each had a three-hour program. We were at the number-one radio station in Mexico City for five years where I wrote transgressive and provocative stories, characters, and amusing incidents and Martín produced them for the radio. Today, 22 years later, we are still working together and our affection only has grown. Better than anybody, Martín has that strange capacity to make you see and feel the role of sound. Pelayo Gutiérrez, the director of the short at which Martín and I met, was the one who introduced me to Guillermo Arriaga.

At that time, I stated in some newspaper that the level of Mexican university professors was abysmal. Guillermo, at the time, was a university teacher. When he came to the lunch at which our friend Pelayo was going to introduce us, Guillermo, without knowing me, was already angry at me. Nevertheless, throughout lunch we were discovering things we had in common and, finally, I invited him to write a script that I was developing at that time, which was the objective of the lunch. Our friendship strengthened and that first meeting gave rise to different dreams and projects we had in common. This became a very successful relationship that began with *Amores perros*. His narrative ability and talent for synthesizing complex situations in a couple of lines and finding unexpected solutions to major problems is really good. He is a collaborator in a world of his own and, at the same time, with great flexibility that permits him to work with a team while developing his own effort and so he is able to subordinate the story and characters in the service of the picture.

On the other hand, Lynn Fainchstein was our "enemy." She had a radio program at a rival station and, although she doesn't admit it, we always tore them apart. Seriously, her musical taste was impeccable and her program the only one that I, without anybody knowing, dared listen to outside of my own station. Today, we are close friends. Her taste in music remains the same: eclectic and exquisite. Being of the same epoch, we had similar musical tastes and she is the one who makes my films dance. She was the one who introduced me to Gustavo Santaolalla, when I sat down to listen to a Ron Rocco recording while looking for music for *Amores perros*.

I remember having flown to Los Angeles with a VHS cassette containing a cut of *Amores perros* to present to Santaolalla. If he liked it he would do the soundtrack. I went out to the garden while he watched and I smoked a pack of cigarettes. Two hours later, he came out with tears in his eyes. A big hug sealed our friendship for always. There is nobody like him. He is capable of breaking your heart with a single note from whatever instrument you put in his hands. Anibal is his partner and soul brother. Those two scoundrels have been the keystone of my pictures.

There is only one guru: a guy with whom everybody wants to be. Where he is becomes transformed into a space of equilibrium and good humor. He is practically a therapist. They call him "The Shark" and his real name is José Antonio García. Besides being an extraordinary soundman, his friendship and human qualities make him unique for me. Somebody who was also of vital importance in *21 Grams* and *Babel* is Alfonso Gómez Rejón: He was my personal assistant in *21 Grams* and he helped me do very valuable research for characters, and now in *Babel* he became the second unit director and also the casting supervisor and researcher. His material was indispensable and his assistance incredible in casting in the streets.

I could go on at length telling of how important people are and have been for me, like Tita Lombardo, the producer of *Amores perros* as well as *Babel*, whom I consider my cinema godmother.

Corinne Weber who has been my assistant for five years now, and was associate producer on *Babel*. Robbie and Joey, Rodrigo's gaffer and key grip, since *21 Grams* have accomplished inexplicable technical things for obtaining what the picture needed and are now family. Batan Silva, who was my assistant director for the first time on this occasion and in putting the finishing touches until the end.

Yet, the most incredible thing was to have had the opportunity and privilege to work for the first time with Jon Kilik, Steve Golin, and Ann Ruark.

In a production of this caliber it's not easy to maintain the vision of a picture and deal at the same time with the infinite logistical and financial problems to be carried out. Incredibly, there was always great communication, solidarity, and respect at the end.

The picture reached its conclusion just as we planned. Extraordinary work in the financial, technical, and human aspect was accomplished. Without the experience of Kilik and Golin this adventure would've been extremely difficult to accomplish. Ann Ruark, as associate producer and line producer, is one of those few exceptions who handles and understands all aspects of moviemaking and, above all, always with class.

Finally, who would have told me that my great friend and agent John Lesher, who would help initially get the project going and bring it to a close, would by a stroke of good luck now be the one who would launch and distribute *Babel*?

I was lucky to meet Brad Grey at the right time when he was just going in his new dream and adventure of transforming Paramount Pictures. Since the first moment, he trusted us and believed in the project 100%, giving us all the support, the respect, and freedom that we needed to make this film.

When the work is carried out within a family like ours, a filming feels more like a rock band on tour than a crew producing a film. The intense and at the same time ephemeral relations that take place in filming a picture are not easy to cope with inasmuch as for long periods of time and, generally, in distant places, one lives more with a crew than his family. When the filming ends, you know that it is very possible that the person you were so fond of you may never see again in your life. Even when being a director can be a very lonely job, and I have felt lonely many times, I have been a lucky bastard who has known all of those who make up my creative family since long before I was a movie director, which represents a double blessing: that of working at what I like and doing it with my friends.

Snapshots

La memoria de las heridas

Prefacio de Eliseo Alberto

Es probable que no haya otra memoria aparte de la memoria de las heridas.

Czeslaw Milosz

Un libro de fotografías también puede o debe ser una ventana. Se abre a la luz, se cierra a la sombra.

Toda imagen se fija en el claroscuro de la memoria. Se imprime, en robo tan impune como necesario.

Un ojo la vio y la cazó al vuelo: luego mil pupilas se la apropian, incluso la recrean sin pedir permiso.

Tampoco perdón.

Los que se acerquen a este libro no podrán evitar ceder al deseo de explorarlo con el catalejo de la emoción, ese sentimiento de ánimos turbados que sorprende al hombre cada vez que se sabe participando en una experiencia creativa, propia o ajena.

En *Babel*, el libro, la emoción vibra a mitad de camino entre los extremos de la pasión y la razón.

Cada página guarda un paisaje humano, un retrato del tiempo que nos dejaron en herencia.

Reparen en el desierto de un rostro en medio del desierto mismo de Marruecos. O en la llanura de la mirada que vaga por las eternidades de Tijuana como un pájaro ciego que no encuentra nido en ninguna parte.

¿En qué rincón del universo queda ese mar de rocas donde flota una barcaza sin timonel ni peces ni anzuelos? ¿Quién la dejó allí abandonada? ¿Es por ese fantasma que hoy nos preocupamos?

El cosmos se detiene por un instante ante el dolor de un padre que abraza a su hija desnuda, en lo alto de un rascacielos de Tokio: de seguro es el propio Dios quien los abriga.

Él ha olvidado por un rato su soberbia y sopla sobre ellos y nosotros su silencio.

El silencio lo explica casi todo.

Por algo bate el viento y no lo oímos en las fotos de los maestros Patrick Bard, Graciela Iturbide, Mary Ellen Mark y Miguel Rio Branco, y es muda la música en aquel antro de Tokio, donde una desamparada adolescente se busca tanto a sí misma que acabará por encontrarse en la pureza de su intacta desnudez.

Si no es por el silencio de la imagen, ¿cómo se explica la congelada desesperanza de esa mujer perdida en el desierto, al sentirse culpable de una tristeza inmerecida? Los niños a su cargo se deshidratan bajo el sol, en medio de la nada. Aquí, la única esperanza es el charco de sombra de un arbusto.

¿Por qué escuchamos el callado temblor de los pastorcitos marroquíes, perseguidos como están por el eco de un disparo?

Sorda es la bala que atraviesa el cristal del autobús y se clava muy cerca del corazón de una mujer demasiado bella para morir tan joven, y sordo el arrebatado dolor de su esposo al comprender cuánto se necesitaban, ahora que el amor se desangra en un hilo de confesiones.

Si un segundo basta para morir, ¿cómo no va a alcanzar para cambiarnos la vida?

El mundo cabe en la eternidad de un segundo.

Siempre presumida, la muerte no se deja retratar.

El alma de la fotografía, como de casi todo en esta vida, es la paz. La paz no es mansa, sino heroica. Tarde o temprano se impone, no importa el costo.

Bien lo sabía María Eladia Hagerman cuando convocó a cuatro genios del arte contemporáneo para que se sumaran a la tropa que acompañaría al cineasta Alejandro González Iñárritu (y a sus fieles colaboradores de viaje) en la aventura de rodar y rodar por la cintura del planeta en la soñada persecución de un largometraje que, entonces, parecía una locura tan imposible como su antecedente bíblico: inventar los miradores de Babel, símbolo del paso del hombre sobre la tierra. Nunca antes González Iñárritu se había propuesto un trabajo tan difícil. El resultado es sencillamente extraordinario, una obra maestra del cine. Hace mucho tiempo que le perdí el miedo a los adjetivos: la perfección narrativa de *Babel*, la película, nos demuestra que las fragilidades y las fortalezas humanas son iguales para todos nosotros. Por eso, cuando abandonamos la sala a oscuras, parece inevitable que acabemos pensando en nosotros mismos, en los dolores que nos acosan y en las ilusiones que podrían salvarnos de ese mal que llamamos soledad. Me atrevo a asegurar que pocas veces en la historia del cine, también de la fotografía, se ha conseguido unir tanto talento en una misma expedición artística.

Babel, el libro, es y no es el testimonio gráfico de esa andanza. Las miradas de los fotógrafos no se limitan a escudriñar en los dramas de la historia que se pretende filmar con rigor, profesionalismo e inspiración. La particularísima capacidad de observación de cada uno de ellos explora el espacio que los rodea, el que va de la escena hasta el horizonte, y lo hace con infinita ternura y sagacidad, prueba irrebatible de que, sin lugar a dudas, la inteligencia es requisito indispensable del arte.

No hace mucho, escuché en una pared de Ciudad de México este grito pintado a mano: «¡Basta ya de realidades: queremos promesas!». Y me dio miedo habitar en este mundo de ilusiones desesperadas.

Libros y películas como las dos *Babel* nos devuelven el alma al cuerpo.

Por dura que se ponga la vida, por mucho que nos abrume el pesimismo, y negra que sea la larga noche que nos toque, la vida es una hazaña en la que vale la pena participar.

El sonoro silencio del filme recorre el libro. La imagen también se lee. Sobran palabras.

Abran de par en par esta ventana de Babel: tal vez se encuentren con ustedes mismos, al otro lado.

Cazadores de mariposas

Introducción de Alejandro González Iñárritu

Alguna vez soñé con la posibilidad de que los párpados pudieran retener o grabar los infinitos laberintos de imágenes que son capturados por las retinas; y que esos párpados, impregnados como papel carbón, se pudieran exprimir para extraer de ellos todos los recuerdos de nuestra vida. Sin embargo, todas esas imágenes suelen desvanecerse y son pocas las que sobreviven. Así como el presente no es sino una angustiosa rebanada de tiempo que está siendo devorada por el pasado, para mí, como director de cine, también es angustiante ver pasar a través de la ventanilla de mi auto cientos o miles de imágenes y de personas que velozmente se deslizan por mis retinas, de izquierda a derecha, y que desaparecerán de mi memoria a pesar de que en un solo segundo fueron capaces de plantearme infinitas preguntas e inspirarme un sinnúmero de ideas. Fue hace tres años, por ejemplo, cuando una sola imagen en las aguas termales de Hakone (Japón) detonó en mí el deseo y la necesidad de filmar toda una historia en la urbe de los ideogramas.

Decía el maestro Akira Kurosawa que «lo más bonito nunca se puede capturar en una película». Esto parece hacerse realidad en todo set cinematográfico alrededor del mundo. El libro que ahora sostienes no es sino un intento de liberar el instante de su condena: la fugacidad.

Babel es la última película de mi trilogía, iniciada con *Amores perros* y continuada por *21 gramos*. Se trata de un tríptico de historias que explora en un nivel primero local, luego foráneo y finalmente global, las profundas y complejas relaciones entre padres e hijos. La idea de hacer *Babel* me vino de una cierta necesidad que solo te da el exilio y la conciencia de ser inmigrante. Es difícil vivir en un país del Primer Mundo cuando uno proviene del Tercero; sin embargo, tu visión se hace más amplia y adquieres una nueva perspectiva. Ahora me pregunto más hacia dónde voy que de dónde vengo.

Inicié el rodaje de *Babel* con la firme convicción de que haría una película sobre las diferencias entre los seres humanos y su incapacidad de comunicarse, debida no sólo a sus distintos lenguajes, sino también a sus fronteras físicas, políticas y emocionales. Lo haría desde una perspectiva compleja y universal hasta llegar al plano más íntimo, entre dos personas.

Desde un principio, el equipo de producción estuvo formado por mexicanos, americanos, franceses, italianos, árabes, bereberes y alemanes; y, al final, japoneses. En paralelo al tema central de la película, sentía que, a pesar de todas las herramientas que se han desarrollado para mejorar la comunicación entre los seres humanos, la realidad acababa siendo muy distinta. El problema no son las nuevas e infinitas herramientas que tenemos para comunicarnos, sino que nadie escucha. Cuando no hay nada que escuchar no hay nada que entender; si dejamos de entender, nuestro lenguaje es inútil y termina por dividirnos. Trabajar en cinco idiomas distintos y desconocidos, con actores reconocidos, pero también con no-actores (la mayoría) que, como en el caso de las humildes comunidades marroquíes, jamás habían visto una cámara, me exigió la paciente tarea de observar y absorber. Como gitanos en un gran circo ambulante, mi familia postiza (es decir, mis amigos y colaboradores de siempre, sin los que hubiera sido imposible lograr esta aventura) y mi familia de sangre viajamos por tres continentes durante casi un año.

Conforme fueron pasando las semanas, los meses, los rostros, las geografías y las estaciones del año, la impresión de observar tantas culturas, así como el impacto físico y psicológico del viaje, acabaron por transformarme a mí y a todos los que hicimos la película. A lo largo del viaje hubo muertes, nacimientos, situaciones intensas de alegría y de dolor, y muchas razones de fraternidad y comunión: al ser expuestos a tanta humanidad y experimentar tan profundamente con ella, no sólo nos transformamos nosotros, sino también la propia película. La orgía cultural de la que participamos hizo que el proceso creativo fuera esculpiéndose hasta llegar a ser algo muy distinto y opuesto a su objetivo original; con lo que se confirmó que, al fin y al cabo, una película no es sino la extensión de uno mismo.

En gran parte del planeta, las fronteras y los aeropuertos se han convertido en un carnaval de desconfianza y degradación donde se intercambian la libertad por la seguridad, el arma son los rayos X y el delito es la otredad. A pesar de todo esto, al filmar *Babel* confirmé que las verdaderas líneas fronterizas existen dentro de nosotros mismos y que, más que en un espacio físico, las barreras existen en el mundo de las ideas. Me di cuenta de que lo que nos hace felices como seres humanos puede ser muy diferente, pero lo que nos hace miserables y vulnerables, más allá de nuestra cultura, raza, idioma o posición económica, es lo mismo para todos. Descubrí que la gran tragedia humana se reduce a la incapacidad de poder amar o ser amado y a la imposibilidad de tocar o ser tocado por este sentimiento, que es lo que da sentido a la vida y a la muerte de todo ser humano. Por lo tanto, *Babel* se transformó en una película acerca de lo que nos une, no de lo que nos separa.

Para mí, este rodaje se convirtió en un viaje no sólo exterior, sino también interior. Además, como toda obra que proviene de las entrañas, esta película (como las dos anteriores) es un testimonio de mi experiencia vital, con mis virtudes y mis múltiples limitaciones. Durante el rodaje de *Amores perros* y *21 gramos*, debido a la concentración y a los objetivos precisos que te demanda la historia que estás filmando, resentí con dolor la imposibilidad de capturar no sólo lo más bonito de algún momento, sino también las múltiples escenas o imágenes que ocurrían de manera paralela a mi alrededor. ¿Dónde se quedaron esos rostros y esas texturas de los barrios bajos de Memphis, donde filmamos *21 gramos*, o aquellos árboles fatigados, con cuervos colgando como esferas en las mañanas brumosas, al borde del río Mississippi? ¿Dónde se quedaron los ojos furiosos de los niños que nos asaltaron pistola en mano durante el *scouting* de *Amores perros* y que más tarde fueron quienes, con cara de niños comprendidos, nos sirvieron el café durante el rodaje? ¿Dónde se quedó el gesto del dueño de la casa que alquilamos para el personaje de Benicio del Toro en *21 gramos* cuando le dijimos que habíamos encontrado un cadáver putrefacto bajo el colchón de una habitación? Esas imágenes y esos momentos sólo existieron durante una fracción de segundo para luego perderse en el olvido, sin poder ser documentados en la memoria colectiva.

La realidad de una película es mucho más de lo que cabe en el rectángulo de la pantalla de cine; y esta realidad se incrusta de manera inexorable en todos los que ejecutamos la película.

Este libro es un intento de rescatar esas imágenes fugaces de humanidad compartida, de todo aquello que provocó que *Babel* empezara siendo una cosa y terminara siendo otra, y de los rostros, formas, vientos y horizontes que a todos los que anduvimos juntos desde el principio, como piedras rodantes, nos impactaron y transformaron.

Cada película podría generar otra película. Cuando uno se encuentra filmando, los ojos y los sentidos están tan abiertos que en cada esquina te topas con un personaje en potencia más interesante que el propio personaje de tu película. No obstante, la curiosidad mató al gato y también puede matar a un director. En teoría, esta curiosidad podría ser satisfecha con una simple cámara fotográfica. Así de simple: clic, y ya está. La práctica es otra cosa.

Un orgulloso cazador de mariposas nos puede mostrar cientos de ellas clavadas con un alfiler dentro de sus cajas de madera y nos puede embelesar con los múltiples y fascinantes colores de sus alas. Pero esas cajas de madera no son sino sarcófagos cubiertos con vidrio, y esas mariposas (a pesar de ser hermosas por su forma y su colorido) carecen de lo más fascinante que posee una mariposa: la gracia de volar. De la misma manera, aunque una fotografía haya capturado el cuerpo en un momento, igual que la mariposa, si no posee también su vuelo, está muerta. La razón por la que un ligero destello desde la ventanilla de un automóvil o unos cuantos segundos de una imagen en un parque son capaces de disparar toda una historia o toda una película en la mente de un artista es que estas imágenes, por más breves que sean, están vivas. Su vida no depende del tiempo que uno dedica a observarlas, sino de su verdad y de la perspectiva de quien las ve. Lo único que existe entre el objeto y quien lo mira es la mirada; y ella (la mirada) es lo que hace que el arte exista y sea un milagro individual.

Así como la mirada de Rodrigo Prieto fue capaz de capturar y dibujar en *Babel* la verdad y la poesía de cuerpos y figuras en movimiento, cuatro maestros de la fotografía fija hicieron lo propio con los mundos paralelos del tiempo congelado.

La razón por la que en este libro las hojas revolotean como alas de mariposa, con imágenes aún vivas, como queriendo escapar del papel, es que quienes las capturaron no cazaron mariposas, sino que, sin tocarlas siquiera, extrajeron de ellas su espíritu y su verdad. Las miradas inconfundibles de Mary Ellen Mark, Graciela Iturbide, Miguel Rio Branco y Patrick Bard hacen posible que estas imágenes sean historias sin sonido. Es su mirada lo que hace que sus fotografías huelan al desierto del Sahara, al de Sonora e incluso al de Tokio. Su curiosidad por el rostro humano, el animal, el muro y las sombras de lo que nadie ve es la misma curiosidad de los niños. Sólo la humanidad, el genio y la universalidad propios de estos cuatro fotógrafos podían hacer de culturas y geografías tan lejanas y distintas algo tan íntimo y cercano; confirmando así que la imagen y la música son lo más cercano al esperanto y que todos los mundos existen solo a través del ojo de quien los mira. Sus métodos de trabajo, aun siendo tan diferentes, logran el mismo efecto: poner la poesía al servicio del sueño y subordinar la belleza a la verdad de un momento.

La emoción y la gran dignidad que muestran los personajes de las fotografías de Mary Ellen Mark son cosas que me han impresionado desde hace muchos años. Ella ha retratado a aquellos que la sociedad ignora trascendiendo a su manera, y a través de su universo estético, el documento periodístico. Curiosamente, el impacto emocional de sus fotografías en *American Odyssey* nos inspiró a Brigitte Broch, Rodrigo Prieto y a mí para nuestro trabajo en *Amores perros*.

También en Marruecos, Patrick Bard dejó volar libres las imágenes a partir de su manera de documentarlas: relacionándose profunda y humanamente con los nativos y extrayendo de ellos una honestidad y naturalidad que pocas veces se consigue. En cada imagen, este fotógrafo-novelista nos hace sentir el peso de la ordinariedad.

El espíritu de Graciela Iturbide, de quien puedo decir que crecí viendo sus fotografías, es tan puro y fino que ella parece estar siempre flotando. Detrás de sus ojos chispeantes se esconden una gran sabiduría y nobleza. La transparencia de sus imágenes hace de mi país algo idílico y a la vez verdadero. Es verdadero porque lo ve y nos lo revela en su trabajo; eso nos basta para creerla y celebrarlo con ella. Sus fotografías en este libro huelen a mí país. Acerca el corazón y comprobarás que es cierto.

Finalmente, creo que nadie maneja el color como lo hace Miguel Rio Branco. Los libros de su primera etapa han sido fuente de inspiración para mi y muchos directores. Por ejemplo, su famosa fotografía del perro muerto no puede abandonar la mente de quien haya sido expuesta a ella. Pintor, cineasta, fotógrafo, artista multimedia y, sobre todo, poeta conceptual, Rio Branco se mantiene en constante reinvención y evolución. Los trípticos que aparecen en este libro parecen haber capturado de manera abstracta el complejo ADN de la ciudad de Tokio. Nadie ve lo que él ve. En el rincón menos pensado, los objetos y sus sombras hablan entre sí.

Tener a los cuatro en el set de *Babel* fue siempre un honor y un privilegio.

La idea de hacer este libro fue de mi esposa María Eladia. Sólo alguien con su sensibilidad podía elegir entre tantas mariposas para reunir una gama de colores, olores y texturas tan diferentes y, aun así, poder sostener en un solo libro cuatro visiones poderosas en tres continentes y dos realidades. Sus interminables horas de trabajo durante meses han dado por fin como fruto el libro que ella visualizó y soñó. También la reunión de algunas fotografías adicionales de Murray Close, Eniac Martínez, Yvonne Venegas, Junko Kato y Tsutomu, quienes con su talento y su sensibilidad completaron hermosamente las piezas de este viaje del que también formaron parte, permitió que este libro pudiera llegar a su meta. Desde un principio, se pretendió que las fotografías capturaran no la naturaleza de la película, sino su realidad paralela. El experimento detrás de ello era averiguar qué tanto se parece la ficción a la realidad y qué tanto la realidad incursiona en la ficción. Fue nuestra intención explorar esa frontera. Estas son las comunidades, los rostros y las ciudades verticales o enclavadas en el barro que nos rodearon, se integraron y nos inspiraron durante el rodaje. Estos son los mundos tangibles y poéticos detrás de *Babel*.

Ahora que lo pienso otra vez, lo más bonito sí se pueda capturar en un pequeño pedazo de película.

Marruecos

Pág. 28

A los dieciocho años crucé el Atlántico trabajando como limpiapisos en un barco carguero. Me fui con tres amigos y sobreviví durante un año con mil dólares. Después de cruzar por la frontera de Ceuta, tomamos un camión colectivo hacia Marrakech. Según el escritor Paul Bowles, la diferencia entre un turista y un viajero es que el segundo no trae boleto de regreso. A lo largo de ese año, comprobé que era cierto.

El calor en el camión era infernal. Yo llevaba una botella de agua tibia por la mitad; frente a mí, había un niño moreno con hermosos ojos verdes que no dejaba de mirarme. Tenía una fruta en la mano y me la ofreció. Con señas le dije que no, que gracias; insistió y me volví a negar. Su madre y algunos pasajeros voltearon, así que tuve que aceptar su fruta medio mordida. En el momento en que tomé la fruta, me pidió la botella de agua. Volteé para ver mi botella y después volví a mirarlo a él; lo pensé y le dije que no. Entonces le dijo algo a su madre y su madre me dijo algo a mí. De pronto, todo el camión me miraba como esperando ver si iba a ser capaz de negarle agua al niño. Con mucho pesar, le di la botella. El niño empezó a reírse y a beber. De pronto, todo el camión hizo lo mismo: el niño ofreció sorbos a todos y todos sorbían y se reían a carcajadas de mí y de mis amigos. Luego, el niño empezó a pedir comida a otros pasajeros y a repartir la comida entre todos. La gente no paraba de reír. Mis amigos y yo nos reíamos a medias, como cuando te esfuerzas por entender un chiste. Era como si todos los pasajeros estuvieran viendo a un extranjero por primera vez. El niño me trajo unos pedazos de galleta y se presentó. Se llamaba Abdullah, y tenía una gracia y una chispa inigualables. Al bajarnos en Marrakech, miles de niños como Abdullah nos empezaron a rodear y corrieron detrás de nosotros. El sonido era fantástico.

Recordaba Marruecos con un halo de misterio y entre una nube de hachís. Su impacto estético y cultural fue tremendo en mí. Veintidós años después de ese viaje, quise filmar en Marruecos porque sentía un vínculo que me venía de la memoria. Una vez más, los niños mágicos no tardaron en aparecer.

Pág. 49

Cuando era niño, mi madre me trajo de Nueva York una figurita de yeso de *La piedad* de Miguel Ángel; Durante toda mi infancia, dormí y me desperté con esa figurita detrás de la cabecera. Quise que Richard cargara a Susan como metáfora de la dolorosa imagen: Brad cargó a Cate más de cincuenta veces por largos callejones; y Rodrigo Prieto, el director de fotografía, corría detrás de ellos con una cámara de cincuenta kilos al hombro. Días después, quise repetir la escena y fueron los actores y Rodrigo quienes me pidieron piedad.

Pág. 50

En el guión original, el conflicto entre Richard y Susan surgía de una infidelidad cometida en el pasado por él. Unas semanas antes del rodaje, sugerí llevar el drama a un nivel más profundo, como lo es la muerte de cuna a un hijo. Brad no se enteró del cambio en el guión hasta que llegó a Marruecos; de hecho, ya era complicado construir un personaje a partir de sólo treinta páginas de historia. No fue fácil asimilar de golpe este nuevo elemento dramático en el libreto. ¿Quién era Richard? ¿Por qué hizo lo que hizo? Todos los días, bajo condiciones físicas extenuantes, Brad tenía que escarbar, encontrar e inventar el personaje vulnerable que construyó en la pantalla.

Pág. 53

A pesar de que el papel de Richard no era en apariencia adecuado para un actor como Brad Pitt, la aventura de construirlo fue excitante para él y para mí. No es fácil que actores de su calibre acepten interpretar este tipo de personajes. Para mí, el reto era lograr que Brad Pitt, la celebridad, desapareciera detrás del personaje para dar así pie no sólo al actor, sino al ser humano detrás de esa imagen. Siempre me ha parecido que Brad tiene una presencia magnética que va más allá de su popularidad. Había muchos riesgos y con valor aceptó los retos; aceptó, sobre todo, el riesgo más grande al que se enfrentan siempre los actores: ponerse en manos de un director y tirarse al vacío.

Pág. 56

Si bien la experiencia del rodaje estuvo para todos íntimamente ligada con los temas de la película, la ficción y la realidad se cruzaron de una forma radical en el caso de Cate. Estando en Marruecos, su hijo de un año sufrió quemaduras de segundo grado en ambas piernas: Cate tuvo que enfrentarse a la emergencia en un humilde hospital de Marruecos y, de inmediato, volar a Londres para solventarla. Un día después, regresaba para interpretar a Susan, una mujer que sangra a causa de una herida física y otra emocional.

Pág. 61

Diecisiete días antes del rodaje no tenía un solo actor, así que nos dedicamos a localizar actores en todas las comunidades. Llegábamos a las mezquitas y anunciábamos a través de megáfonos que ya había llegado la película y que buscábamos gente para aparecer en ella.

Sfia es una mujer bereber que vive en Taguenzalt, al lado de la casa donde filmamos. La profundidad de su mirada me hizo darle el papel sin dudarlo. Sus escenas fueron difíciles de lograr: cuando íbamos por la vigésima toma y Cate Blanchett me daba toda su intensidad, a la anciana se le olvidaba hacia dónde caminar, volteaba a la cámara y sonreía.

Mohamed apareció en la oficina buscando trabajo como técnico de computadoras. Me llamó la atención su rostro noble y al mismo tiempo doloroso: el rostro de alguien que quiere superarse sin que la vida le preste demasiada atención. Me pareció muy cercano a la naturaleza del personaje de Anwar.

Pág. 62

Rogué a Cate Blanchett que aceptara interpretar a Susan. Al principio se resistía, y con algo de razón: en el guión, Susan no era más que una mujer tirada en el suelo y que sangraba semiinconsciente. Yo sabía, sin embargo, que solo Cate podía darle gravedad y realidad al personaje, y que elevaría el nivel de juego en el set para todos. Y lo hizo: cada vez que la veía actuar, no sólo me emocionaba, sino que agradecía siete veces siete que hubiese aceptado el papel.

En cualquier caso, si ella hubiera sabido que iba a estar embarrada de miel roja pegajosa, impregnada de un olor fecal para atraer a las moscas y a una temperatura de cuarenta grados centígrados en un cuarto oscuro sin aire acondicionado, es muy probable que no hubiera aceptado.

Pág. 70

No puedo imaginar una mayor generosidad en el mundo que la que presenciamos en los humildes pueblos del sur de Marruecos. Invariablemente, al pasar frente a una casa nos ofrecían té, almendras, dátiles, leche de cabra, sonrisas y el tradicional saludo *salam aleikum*, tocándose el corazón y lanzando un beso al cielo con la mano. Me quedó claro que el consumismo occidental es una carrera hacia el vacío espiritual: es cierto que las mujeres trabajan de más mientras que los hombres toman demasiado té social, pero todos dedican cinco o seis minutos, cinco veces al día, a orar y conectarse con su parte espiritual.

Pág. 72

Por primera vez en su historia y durante trece semanas, el pequeño pueblo de Taguenzalte se vio invadido por personas del mundo entero que despertaron su interés y entretenimiento, ya que prácticamente el pueblo entero participó en la película.

Los primeros en creer y sumarse a este proyecto fueron mis socios productores Jon Kilik y Steve Golin, quienes incansable e intensamente junto con Ann Ruark orquestaron un «circo rodante» durante casi un año alrededor del mundo e hicieron que éste funcionara sin que faltara o sobrara nada. Su amistad, experiencia y apoyo incondicional fueron invaluables. El último día de rodaje hubo muchas lágrimas por ambas partes. Recolectamos dinero entre todos para llevar la electricidad a Taguenzalte y, meses después, uno de nosotros regresó y nos contó que todas las azoteas ya tenían antenas parabólicas. No pude más que sentir tristeza y confusión.

Pág. 85

Quería filmar en un desierto que no fuera muy romántico: un desierto duro y rocoso, no de dunas. Encontrar un punto concreto en un lugar tan enorme como el Sáhara es increíblemente difícil: en un espacio tan abierto, te preguntas constantemente por qué este lugar va a ser mejor que aquél.

Pág. 88

Esta escena muestra el momento del colapso moral de la familia musulmana, así que requería de

Pág. 62

alta intensidad física y emocional. Cuando el idioma es una frontera entre el director y los actores, la mímica se vuelve una herramienta indispensable. Hiam Abbass fue mi intérprete y mi ángel de la guarda: el puente emocional entre los actores marroquíes y yo.

Pág. 90

Un día, en la plaza principal de Tamnougalt, Alfonso Gómez me llamó para que viera a un niño muy especial: era Boubker. Le expliqué que le iba a hacer una prueba y que le iba a decir algunas frases, pero que no quería que me contestara con palabras, sino que me dijera con los ojos lo que sentía. «Tu mama murió», le dije. Se le llenaron los ojos de lágrimas y todos nos quedamos pasmados con su expresión. Fue un momento único: supe que había encontrado a mi actor para el personaje de Yussef. Después me enteré de que su madre había muerto hacía siete años y de que su padre era un enano a quien nunca veía. Sin saberlo, yo había tocado una herida muy profunda en él. No hay nada más poderoso que la realidad, y esta no se puede fingir.

Pág. 92

Cuando mi amigo el escritor Eliseo Alberto vio un primer corte de *Babel*, me dijo que parecía que Abdullah y Hassan habían descendido del cielo para interpretar sus papeles y que después habían ascendido de nuevo. Cuando vi sus rostros entre los cientos de hombres que hacían fila fuera de las mezquitas para hacer *casting*, pensé lo mismo. El rostro de estos hombres es bíblico: es el mismo rostro de la humanidad escrita en los testamentos musulmán, judío y cristiano. Abdullah, como José en la Biblia, es un carpintero de las afueras de Fez.

Pág. 93

La mayoría de los duros rostros marroquíes son dulces una vez que sonríen; no tienen la malicia que solemos atribuirles. Sin embargo, el rostro de Hassan fue difícil de quebrar. Yo necesitaba que su personaje se mostrara vulnerable frente a la intimidación policíaca, pero él estaba bloqueado. La mímica fue insuficiente, así que Hiam, platicando en su idioma con él, encontró la manera de conectarlo con sus emociones. Hassan nos dijo que nunca había ido a visitar a su madre muerta, así que usamos la filmación como sesión de terapia y, durante más de seis horas, no hubo quien detuviera su llanto. Al terminar, nos dio las gracias y yo se las di a Hiam.

Pág. 94

En Marruecos tuvimos un equipo de rodaje de ciento veinte personas: italianos, franceses, americanos, mexicanos y marroquíes que hablaban árabe o bereber. Al haber seis idiomas en un equipo de trabajo, surgieron muchos problemas por falta de entendimiento. El lenguaje no era el problema, sino el punto de vista. Nos sometimos a un calor extenuante y a condiciones extremas; tuvimos que filmar muchos exteriores padeciendo altas temperaturas, subir cuestas arriba y tolerar mucho polvo. Para los muchos de nosotros que proveníamos del Tercer Mundo era un poco más fácil soportar estas condiciones: la realidad de un pastor en Marruecos no es muy distinta de la realidad de un pastor en México. Tanto yo como Rodrigo Prieto, y los departamentos mexicanos del equipo de rodaje, estábamos encantados con la posibilidad de entender sus condiciones de vida y sus limitaciones.

Pág. 104

Said y Boubker acabaron sintiéndose casi como hermanos. Igual que en la ficción, Said era rebelde, activo, intuitivo e inconforme; mientras que Boubker era pasivo, introspectivo, racional y melancólico. Con el sueldo de la película, Said se compró una moto y Boubker una computadora.

El último día de rodaje en Marruecos filmamos la escena del atardecer en donde Yussef, en un *close up*, llora e imagina a su hermano, que acaba de morir, caminando junto a su padre sobre un mar de desierto rocoso en el que ordené colocar una barca vacía. Al igual que la escena en donde juegan con el viento, que fue un regalo de las montañas y que filmé por instinto para convertirla, junto con la escena anterior, en el epílogo de su historia, estos momentos fueron de mucha carga emotiva para ambos. El último día, al término de la filmación, ni Said ni Boubker podían parar de llorar: nosotros, que nos habíamos convertido en su familia, nos iríamos al día siguiente. Les prometí a ambos que en un año nos veríamos en algún festival, afortunadamente pude cumplir mi promesa, nos vimos en Cannes.

México

Pág. 114

En Tijuana la gente no es de aquí ni de allá: todos están de paso. Sólo en un lugar como éste se puede encontrar una giganta de yeso como la que construyó un enamorado a su mujer para que pudiera ver desde arriba la tierra prometida a la que nunca llegaría.

Lo que primero te llama la atención de esta ciudad es la barda que la rodea. Le dicen *«la Llaga»* una herida abierta de varios kilómetros de largo construida con los desechos de las bardas metálicas utilizadas en los aeropuertos prefabricados de la guerra de Vietnam. Lo más estúpido e ingenuo es que esta barda se incrusta en el océano, ¡no vaya a ser que cruce un terrorista en submarino! Tiene colgadas miles de cruces con los nombres de hombres, mujeres y niños que han sido devorados por el desierto o han desaparecido en la frontera entre México y Estados Unidos, la más transitada del mundo. Una vez terminada, se convertirá en el monumento a la intolerancia más grande de la historia de la humanidad.

Pág. 120

Un día me enteré de que habría una *performance* en la frontera (página anterior): un hombre volaría al otro lado y sería detenido por la policía norteamericana en un acto de circo y crítica. Yo estaba a cinco minutos

de ahí y decidí detener la filmación para presenciar el evento. Al final fue un fiasco total; se trataba de un simple «hombre bala» norteamericano que no tenía ni idea de lo simbólico que podía resultar su acto, ni interés en ello, y al que simplemente pagaron por hacerlo. Aun así, la poderosa y onírica imagen se antojó como el sueño de muchos de los que estábamos ahí. Si tan solo tuviéramos alas…

Pág. 121

Yo soy un musicólogo; me gusta lo bueno de todos los géneros. Sin embargo, por alguna razón, la música norteña jamás me había «entrado»: sentía por ella una especie de rechazo a priori. Después de vivir más de dos meses en Tijuana y en Sonora, y de explorar y tratar de conectarme con esa música por necesidad, al fin se me reveló de una manera diferente. Los *hits* de la radio y las letras de las canciones, sumados a mis vivencias personales, hicieron que por primera vez encontrara en esa música un sentido emocional. El dolor y la frustración de sus letras, así como sus melodías simples y pegajosas, están arraigados en las raíces no de lo que se tiene, sino de extrañar lo que nunca se ha tenido o se ha podido tener. Rendirme ante esa música fue uno de los mejores regalos que obtuve de mi experiencia.

Pág. 131

En mi casa de Los Ángeles trabaja una mujer mexicana que se llama Julia. Nació en el estado de Oaxaca y no fue hasta pasados seis intentos de cruzar el desierto en condiciones extremas de peligro que logró pasar sin que la descubrieran. Tiene un hijo de veinte años que está en la cárcel y al que no ha podido ver en más de dos años porque sería inmediatamente deportada a su pueblo natal. Julia vive en constante miedo: ella, como millones de mexicanos, es una ciudadana invisible. Irónicamente, como Amelia, miles de mujeres centroamericanas han corrido la misma suerte al cruzar la frontera de México, que puede ser más dura y peligrosa que la misma frontera de Estados Unidos.

El trabajo de Adriana Barraza caracterizándolas hizo que la palabra «encarnación» tuviera un nuevo significado para mí, ya que con cada movimiento de su cuerpo, sus manos y sus ojos encarnó con ternura y complejidad el espíritu de un personaje que fácilmente hubiera caído en el estereotipo. Su trabajo es sublime. A Gael lo tenía en mente para *Babel* desde el principio: nadie mejor que él podía representar un personaje con tantas actitudes contradictorias en tan poco tiempo. En *Amores perros*, Adriana fue la mamá de Gael; ahora, era su tía. En ambas ocasiones, como su hijo o su sobrino, le ha causado grandes penas y la ha conducido a diferentes infiernos. Lo único que les prometí a Adriana y a Gael es que no volvería a hacer una película en donde Gael manejara un automóvil, pues siempre que lo hace termina en tragedia.

Pág. 136

Desde el primer *scouting* de locaciones me llamó la atención la comunidad de El Carrizo, una ranchería a una hora de Tijuana que es parca y sobria, pero amable

y sincerota. En *Babel* había una subtrama que sucedía en esta casa sobre la novia embarazada y con Amelia convenciéndola para ir a su propia boda. Al final decidí quitarla, pero de alguna manera su atmósfera permaneció en la película. El gordito de la foto es un niño que en las tres distintas visitas que hice a su casa no se despegó de su sillón. Frente a él había una televisión enorme y un plato de papas fritas vacío.

Pág. 148

Las bodas en el norte de mi país son muy distintas a las que tienen lugar en el sur. Las ceremonias de Tijuana son duras, polvorientas y sin ritos ni tradiciones arraigados. Fui a algunas bodas para mi investigación de *Babel* y traté de filmar la boda del hijo de Amelia de la manera más fiel posible con respecto a lo que vi: con vasos y platos de plástico, ausencia de flores o adornos de cualquier clase y sillas de colores sobre el polvo perenne. Brigitte Broch, mi amiga y directora de arte, que con cada objeto y detalle llena de vida el set, hizo un bellísimo trabajo.

Todas las personas que aparecen en la escena de la boda son de la comunidad de El Carrizo. Nunca vi gente más animada y contenta. A pesar de que filmé durante muchos días y hasta las seis de la mañana, jamás hubo una queja por su parte. Puras sonrisas y baile sin parar. Para mí, para ellos y para todo el equipo de rodaje, la boda fue una fiesta de verdad. La gente ya se conocía y eso se siente en la escena.

Pág. 150

Así como en Marruecos Gustavo Santaolalla y yo nos encerramos en un estudio para grabar diferentes composiciones de música gnawa, en Tijuana me encerré con Lynn Fainchtein para escuchar y grabar muchísimas canciones del norte. La gente del norte solo escucha música norteña, es como una religión: hay un dolor y una razón en sus temas que no pueden entenderse si no se escuchan desde su misma perspectiva. Por su honestidad, su gracia y su conexión con el público, la banda de «Los incomparables» hacía honor a su nombre.

Pág. 155

Al conocer a Bernie, cambió totalmente para mí la idea que estaba escrita para el personaje de Luis, el hijo de Amelia. Lo conocí en Tijuana cuando fue a hacer *casting* y platiqué con él más o menos una hora. Decía que ya había hecho de todo en la vida: casanova, maleante, madreador, músico, bombero, de todo. Como suele decirse, un «echado para adelante». Por más que quisiera aparentar su malicia, su nobleza lo traicionaba. Bernie es un personaje típico de las calles de Tijuana; su corte de pelo de rapero tijuanense, aunado a sus ojos fieros y a la vez tiernos, me parecieron muy interesantes. Como él, millones de jóvenes fronterizos resienten la humillación que implica cruzar la frontera con Estados Unidos.

Pág. 165

A lo largo de los pasados cinco años, he tenido que cruzar, junto con mi esposa y mis hijos, la frontera entre

Tijuana y Estados Unidos cada seis meses. Por más veces que lo he hecho, no deja de impactarme el contraste y la disparidad entre ambos países: todo auto que viene de Estados Unidos cruza la frontera y entra en mi país sin ninguna revisión y sin ninguna molestia. En cambio, todo coche que pasa de México a Estados Unidos es escrupulosamente revisado haciendo que el cruce se convierta en un rito de humillación y sospecha. Para mí, el violento y repentino acto de Santiago no es a causa de una inspección, sino una reacción a la suma de años de un constante abuso de poder y de la forma de aplicarlo.

Durante tres días de filmación, intenté reproducir la sensación de lo que yo mismo en ocasiones he experimentado. Construimos una garita parecida a la de Tecate en medio del desierto de Sonora y constantemente Rodrigo Prieto, Batán Silva y yo revisábamos el material de la segunda unidad, que iba y venía para presentárnoslo.

Pág. 166

Es increíble cómo los niños, a veces, comprenden muchas más cosas que los actores con experiencia; no pretenden nada más que obedecer. Para Nathan Gamble y Elle Fanning, que interpretan a los hijos de la pareja norteamericana, hubo momentos tortuosos durante el rodaje: el calor en el desierto de Sonora era mucho más fuerte que en Marruecos. Cuando llegaba la noche, estaban irritables y adormilados. Además del calor y el sueño, los niños padecieron otros momentos difíciles: estábamos filmando en una zona de serpientes cuando, en una ocasión, Nathan vio que una salía de un hoyo en la arena durante una de las tomas. Estaba realmente aterrorizado. Esa toma permaneció en la película.

Pág. 168

Adriana Barraza tiene dos microinfartos en el corazón. Para hacer esta escena, tuvo que cargar durante muchos días y en muchas ocasiones con una niña de treinta kilos corriendo por el desierto a cuarenta grados centígrados. Un día de calor extremo, cinco personas del equipo de rodaje acabaron en el hospital por deshidratación. Adriana comenzó a sentirse mal; casi se desmayó y me pidió que le diera una hora para recuperarse. Le dije que se fuera a su hotel a descansar. «No —me dijo—. Yo sé lo que es un día de retraso y sé que se pierde mucho dinero. Dame una hora nada más.» Se bañó en su tráiler y, a la hora y media, salió lista para seguir trabajando en la escena. Nunca había visto ese nivel de profesionalidad y de esfuerzo físico tan increíble. Rodamos durante esas horas más algunos de los momentos más dolorosos de la película. Quizá Adriana pensó que, si los inmigrantes no tenían la opción de descansar al cruzar el desierto, ¿por qué la iba a tener Amelia?

Pág. 172

Rodrigo Prieto no sólo es mi hermano, sino también mi mano derecha. Su relación casi obsesiva con la luz es casi tan intensa como su capacidad de narrar una escena y dibujar un personaje con el pincel de su cámara. Como buen cazador de mariposas, incluso cuando filma la película con la cámara al hombro, y en ocasiones a centímetros de los actores, jamás interrumpe sus procesos. Flota y respira con ellos.

Filmando en el desierto marroquí, tuvo que dejar el set los últimos siete días de rodaje porque sus padres iban a celebrar su sexagésimo aniversario de boda. Iba a la fiesta con la ilusión de un niño. Meses después, mientras filmábamos en Tijuana, Rodrigo recibió una llamada por la noche: su madre había fallecido inesperadamente. A la mañana siguiente, como un soldado, quiso trabajar mientras se buscaba a un fotógrafo sustituto. Antes de iniciar la filmación, hicimos una pequeña ceremonia con el equipo de rodaje. Rodrigo habló de su madre como yo nunca había oído hablar a nadie. Nos sacó lágrimas a todos y nunca un desierto se sintió tan solo. Cuando regresó, Rodrigo tenía paz en su rostro. Me dijo que había cruzado unas palabras con un colibrí.

Pág. 174

Mientras filmábamos la escena de Amelia siendo detenida por la policía de inmigración, todos los medios estaban volcados en la historia de un joven de diecisiete años originario de Oaxaca que, junto con su madre, intentó cruzar el desierto de Arizona. Iban con un grupo de personas y a la madre se le paralizaron las piernas, se le cerró la garganta y no pudo caminar más. Los demás la abandonaron allí. La madre, tres horas más tarde, le dijo a su hijo que fuera a pedir ayuda o él también moriría. El joven partió en solitario y sin agua durante dos días y fue capturado y deportado a México. Le contó a su abuelo lo sucedido y este hombre de setenta años viajó a Arizona y emprendió una campaña con la ayuda de una estación de radio para que su hija fuera rescatada. Diez días después, lo único que encontraron fueron sus zapatos blancos de charol, sus dos fémures y una toalla de cuadritos amarillos que su hijo le había puesto en la cara antes de irse. Los hombres dentro de esta camioneta habían sido capturados unos días antes en Estados Unidos y les preguntamos si querían aparecer en una película. Sus historias no eran menos terribles que aquella otra.

Japón

Pág. 202

Fue una sola imagen la que me trajo a la mente la idea que más adelante se convertiría en la historia japonesa de *Babel*; una imagen que aún hoy resuena en mí con muchas emociones. Estaba caminando por Hakone, una montaña que se encuentra a una hora y media de Tokio y en donde hay cuerpos de aguas sulfurosas, árboles secos, niebla constante, cuervos negros como perros voladores y un suelo cubierto de cáscaras de huevo negras que la gente tira después de cocerlos en las aguas. La atmósfera era digna de una película de Kurosawa.

Al bajar el monte, escuché unos sonidos guturales terribles: de entre la niebla, surgió una niña con retraso mental caminando muy despacio, cuidada por un hombre de unos sesenta años. Todos los que bajaban, particularmente los niños, la evadían con cierto temor. El hombre, en cambio, la sostenía del brazo con gran ternura, amor y dignidad. Esa imagen me conmovió. En ese viaje y unos meses después, viajando por Estocolmo con mi familia, me topé con muchos sordomudos. Me llamaba la atención su manera de gesticular y el dramatismo de su comunicación. Me pareció un lenguaje desconocido e ignorado por casi todos los que tenemos la bendición de tocar y ser tocados por la palabra. «El lenguaje del silencio», pensé. Esa misma noche tuve un sueño erótico sobre una adolescente en el consultorio de un dentista. Todas estas imágenes, en apariencia inconexas, me habían dado la justificación para filmar y explorar una historia de diferentes ausencias y soledades en una de mis ciudades favoritas por su misterio y sus contradicciones. Después de dos años de intensa colaboración, Guillermo Arriaga escribió una historia poderosa y penetrante que, como un suave perfume, solo rozó las otras tres dejándolas poéticamente impregnadas.

Pág. 207

Desde *Amores perros*, el primer y el último día de filmación celebro una bendición colectiva a manera de ritual. Me gustan las bendiciones porque, en su origen, la palabra procede del latín *benedicere*, que significa «bien decir»: decir algo bueno de algo o de alguien. Creo firmemente en el poder y en la energía de las palabras, que en ocasiones no son sino aquello de lo que está lleno el corazón. Uso rosas rojas para el primer día y rosas blancas para el último. El domingo 6 de noviembre de 2005, a las 5:30 de la mañana frente al Tsukiji, el mercado de pescado más grande del mundo, unos ochenta japoamericanomexicanos nos tomamos de la mano, hicimos un círculo, oramos, guardamos un minuto de silencio y decapitamos unas rosas rojas. Al grito de Abba Eli, lanzamos sus pétalos de sangre al cielo azul pálido que cubría la ciudad de los kimonos y los ideogramas. Era una fría, pasiva y romántica mañana de otoño, ideal para dar inicio a la cuarta y última parte de *Babel*. A las 6:30 de la mañana, la policía de Tokio nos estaba buscando y nos perseguía furiosamente por las calles de la ciudad para clausurar la filmación y encarcelar a su responsable. A las 15:00 horas, cayó un aguacero capaz de hacer desaparecer la mismísima isla de Mishima. Así empezó mi primer día de rodaje en Tokio.

Pág. 208

Como en los personajes de sus películas, en Japón la gente es lo que hace, no lo que dice. Por ejemplo, ningún padre le dice a su hija «te amo». En Japón, como en la buena actuación, los sentimientos deben estar implícitos en las acciones, no en las palabras. Para mí, lo menos importante en una escena son las palabras. Una escena bien escrita o bien dirigida debería entenderse en silencio, sin palabras, pues la acción define

al personaje. De ahí la grandeza del cine mudo, el cine puro.

Las palabras son solo pequeñas barcas que flotan en el gran río de las emociones. Un año antes de iniciar el rodaje, puse en marcha el *casting* en Japón y conocí a Rinko Kikuchi. Se presentó en silencio, hicimos una primera lectura y me quedé pasmado: pensé que era sordomuda. Sin embargo, cuando supe que no era sordomuda, dudé, pues yo estaba obsesionado por conseguir una actriz sordomuda para el papel de Chieko. Más adelante, repetimos la lectura. Su rango, su espíritu y su intensidad eran perfectos, pero no era sordomuda. Regresé a Los Ángeles con Rinko resonando en mi cabeza, pero sin haber tomado aún una decisión.

Durante los nueve meses siguientes, mientras filmábamos en Marruecos y México, Rinko, por iniciativa propia, sin avisar a nadie y sin el papel asegurado, decidió tomar clases de lenguaje de sordomudos por su cuenta. Cuando regresé a Japón para empezar a filmar me era imposible diferenciar a Rinko de una sordomuda real: jamás había visto semejante convicción, disciplina y necesidad de hacer un personaje. Apenas unas semanas antes de empezar el rodaje le dije que el papel era suyo. Su emoción y su llanto fueron infinitos, profundos y silenciosos. Ha sido la mejor decisión que he tomado haciendo cine. Su presencia, como el incienso, es suave pero penetrante. Su enorme sensibilidad y profunda vida interior hizo que Chieko se convirtiera en un personaje cinético.

Pág. 220

Todas las amigas y todos los amigos de Chieko en la película son sordomudos. Encontrarlos y convencerlos de que actuaran no fue fácil, pero resultó menos fácil aún hacerles el *casting* o ensayar una escena. La cosa era más o menos así: en un salón, frente a mí, se sentaba una jovencita sordomuda. Yo tenía junto a mí a una traductora del inglés al japonés, mientras que ella tenía a su lado a una traductora del japonés al lenguaje de signos. Cuando yo le preguntaba a la jovencita, por ejemplo, «¿Alguna vez has imaginado o soñado el sonido de algo?», una de las traductoras pasaba mis palabras del inglés al japonés y la otra traducía las palabras japonesas al lenguaje de sordomudos para ella. La jovencita pensaba durante unos minutos y daba su respuesta en lenguaje de signos, que era traducido al japonés por su traductora y, finalmente, la traductora en inglés por fin me contestaba «¿En Junio?». Ese *casting* era *Babel* en su máxima expresión.

Pág. 222

Todos los días, durante el camino en coche hacia el set y de regreso a mi casa, escuchaba siempre el mismo disco: *Chasm*, del maestro Ryuichi Sakamoto. Esta se convirtió en mi banda sonora particular en Japón, especialmente la canción *Only Love Can Conquer Hate*. Cuando filmé la escena del parque, siempre imaginé algo onírico, flotante. Rodrigo y Joey montaron un sistema de *riggs* en el columpio, pues yo quería filmar toda esta secuencia a una velocidad de treinta fotogramas y

darle el punto de vista y la cadencia de quien está en *ecstasy*. Siempre sentí que lo que en el guión era una simple transición de un lado al otro podía ser una gran oportunidad de estar en la cabeza y en el mundo de Chieko. Necesitaba una especie de *adagio* que explotaría en un *staccato*. No fue hasta llegar a la sala de montaje que descubrí que era precisamente *Only Love Can Conquer Hate* la pieza que seguramente estaría oyendo Chieko si pudiera escuchar, como el mismísimo Sakamoto, los sonidos del silencio.

Pág. 236

Cuando concibo una película, no puedo avanzar si no la tengo antes ubicada claramente en un espectro musical. A los veinte años de edad yo tenía un programa de radio en Ciudad de México en el que hice, dije y toqué lo que quise durante tres horas diarias a lo largo de cinco años. Escribía y producía historias y personajes provocativos, que combinaba con música ecléctica. Con estos elementos creaba un espacio que estimulaba ideas musicales y auditivas. Es así como aprendí a entretener a la gente durante un lapso de tres horas. Se trataba de herramientas no muy distintas a las del cine.

Unas semanas antes de empezar a filmar en Tokio, fui a un club a ver a Shinichi Osawa, que es hoy uno de los más prestigiosos productores y DJ japoneses. Yo sabía que utilizaría la canción *September* (de Earth, Wind and Fire) para la introducción de la secuencia de la discoteca, pues me gusta utilizar ciertas canciones de la memoria colectiva. A la vez, iba en busca de una canción más actual para combinar los tiempos y las atmósferas; algo cálido contra algo agresivo, que dibujara el momento dramático de Chieko. Shinichi me invitó a ponerme detrás de su consola. En el momento en que empezó a tocar *The Joker* de Fat Boy Slim, supe que eso era lo que estaba buscando: los adolescentes dejaron de existir y se perdieron en un viaje de *ecstasy* y sudor. Con los ojos cerrados, parecía que adoraban a un gurú que los conducía hacia un país mántrico y erótico.

Al día siguiente, Shinichi me invitó a su estudio para hacer la larga introducción de EWF que yo necesitaba para la entrada a la discoteca y allí mezcló magistralmente a Fat Boy Slim con una vibra bárbara. Filmé la escena contra esa música y, en la sala de montaje, Stephen Mirrione y yo sentimos un palpitar cercano al viaje de los adolescentes.

Pág. 239

La historia de Chieko no es sobre sexo patológico, sino sobre la necesidad de afecto. Cuando las palabras no están a nuestro alcance y no podemos tocar ni ser tocadas por ellas, el cuerpo se convierte en nuestra única herramienta de expresión.

Para poder sugerir y sostener con sólo un par de escenas el complejo pasado de Chieko, necesitaba una presencia igual de compleja, pero profundamente humana y empática. En un mundo donde los estilos actorales parecen correr hacia los gritos de la exageración, fue un placer encontrarme con un actor cuyo espíritu, solidez y elegancia representan una economía de movimientos que dominan muy pocos en el mundo. La disciplina y el calor humano de Koji Yakusho le dieron peso y gravedad a la historia de Chieko; sus micromovimientos, que van desde levantar un párpado hasta sostener una mano, marcan la diferencia. De la misma manera, Satoshi Nikaido, quien interpreta el papel de Kenji, tiene esa nobleza de espíritu necesaria para hacer lo que hizo con Chieko: dar dignidad a quien cree no tenerla.

Pág. 240

No hay nada más triste en una filmación que el último día de rodaje: la nostalgia inunda el set y empieza a sentirse una depresión posparto que se extiende durante un tiempo.

Sin embargo, el día en que filmamos a Chieko caminando a solas frente a los jardines del emperador, sucedió algo que en un principio achaqué a una broma del departamento de arte, encabezado por Brigitte Broch: todos los árboles que rodeaban los jardines estaban decorados con banderas marroquíes y japonesas entrelazadas. La suma de los colores de estas dos banderas coincidía con los colores verde, blanco y rojo de la bandera mexicana. De esta forma, los tres países en los que había filmado se despedían de nosotros en un frío y hermoso día de otoño. ¿Qué tenía que hacer una bandera de Marruecos aquel día, y en aquella precisa locación japonesa, en el último día de rodaje de una película que hablaba de esos dos países, los colores de cuyas banderas suman los de la bandera mexicana? El rey Muhammad VI estaba de visita en el palacio; sin embargo, no hay azar ni coincidencias: todo es destino.

Los cimientos de *Babel*

Conversación entre Rodrigo García y Alejandro González Iñárritu

¿Cuál fue la imagen o idea que dio origen al proyecto? Y, a partir de esa semilla, ¿cómo desarrollaste el guión?

Como tú bien sabes, un guion no es más que la aplicación técnica de una historia, la cual es el resultado de una idea que a su vez tiene su origen en el mundo subconsciente, en el mundo de lo intuitivo y lo irracional.

Quizá fue el impacto estético y cultural de mi primer viaje a Marruecos a los dieciocho años (envuelto en una nube de existencialismo y hachís), o quizá la acumulación de ausencias en el exilio; pero, en principio, *Babel* nació de una necesidad moral de purgar y hablar de las cosas de las que mi corazón y mi mente estaban llenos: las increíbles y dolorosas paradojas globales que tenían efectos en territorios cercanos o lejanos y que finalmente desembocaban en tragedias individuales. Primero se fue cociendo a partir de algo que yo traía atorado en las entrañas y, más tarde, como un concepto que cerraría el tríptico de historias cruzadas que inicié con *Amores perros* y *21 gramos*.

Al terminar *Amores perros* viajé muchísimo por el mundo entero, incluyendo Japón, e incluso me fui a vivir a Los Ángeles para levantar mi nuevo proyecto. Mi familia y yo llegamos a Estados Unidos cuatro días antes del 11 de septiembre, y el mundo a nuestro alrededor cambió.

La experiencia de vivir en el imperio bajo un régimen paranoico con un nacionalismo exacerbado no fue nada fácil. No se podía caminar más de cien metros sin encontrar una bandera norteamericana y una mirada de sospecha. Fue una etapa difícil e intensa, entré en una fuerte depresión. Sin embargo, creo que si no me hubiera ido de México, si no hubiera salido de mi ranchito y mi zona de confort, jamás habría tenido la necesidad o el hambre de enfrentar este reto.

La idea de *Babel* se me ocurrió cuando estaba a punto de iniciar el rodaje de *21 gramos* en la ciudad de Memphis. Era la primera vez que me enfrentaba a dirigir una película fuera de mi país y en un idioma distinto al mío. Otra vez, se trataría de tres historias paralelas de padres e hijos, resueltas en un ejercicio estructural interesante en donde el tema central sería la pérdida. La sola idea de intentar llevar a cabo la teoría de las realidades paralelas, ya no sólo fuera de mi país, sino en una escala global, era algo que me quitaba el sueño.

Empecé a trabajar sobre este concepto con el guionista y director Carlos Cuarón. Originalmente, se trataba de cinco historias, en cinco idiomas y situadas en cinco continentes distintos. Carlos y yo trabajamos muy brevemente en un par de argumentos posibles. En todos ellos, una decisión tomada en un país lejano afectaría radicalmente la vida de seres humanos que jamás se enterarían de su origen. Estábamos en eso cuando un importante periódico mexicano publicó que Carlos y yo estábamos trabajando juntos en un proyecto con tema global. Para colmo, me enteré por casualidad de que el director brasileño Fernando Meirelles preparaba un proyecto parecido. Hablé con él y comprobé que era cierto.

Carlos Cuarón decidió entonces concentrarse en otro argumento que habíamos trabajado en el pasado para luego dirigirlo él. Después de un tiempo, Fernando se encarriló en otro proyecto y fue entonces cuando invité a Guillermo Arriaga a trabajar nuevamente conmigo.

Guillermo me propuso cinco argumentos, de los que sobrevivieron dos: la bellísima y sólida historia de los niños marroquíes y el inicio de la historia de la pareja de Richard y Susan, que se entrelazaba natural y físicamente con la anterior, aunque en aquel entonces todavía estaba muy verde. Yo puse sobre la mesa el personaje de la nana mexicana que cuida de los niños americanos debido a la necesidad de contar algo no solo sobre mi país, sino también sobre los inmigrantes y la trágica situación fronteriza y el personaje de Tokio: una adolescente sordomuda japonesa que es cuidada por un hombre solo.

Para mí, el personaje de Amelia fue siempre una encarnación de Julia: la mujer mexicana que trabaja con mi familia en nuestra casa de Los Ángeles. Ella me ha contado cómo cruzó seis veces el desierto y cómo fue atrapada en las camionetas vigilantes. Julia pasó tres noches y tres días en el desierto sin ver rastros de civilización.

A más de uno de los que cruzaban la frontera se le pararon los pulmones por la falta de agua y por el calor que atraviesa la garganta. No fue hasta la séptima ocasión que Julia logró cruzar. Su hijo de veinte años está en la cárcel y no puede verlo porque las autoridades de inmigración la regresarían a México. No hay historias más tristes que las de la frontera. Yo viajo a Tijuana cada seis meses con mis hijos a renovar mi visado. Es una línea en donde se ha institucionalizado un rito de humillación. La escena que habla de esto en *Babel* es una fiel reproducción de las formas y las mecánicas de inspección que yo mismo he padecido en ocasiones.

La idea para la historia japonesa me vino de una sola imagen que, a su vez, me disparó muchas emociones. Estaba caminando en Hakone, un lugar que se encuentra a una hora y media de Tokio formado de cuerpos de aguas sulfurosas, árboles secos, niebla constante, cuervos negros como perros voladores y un suelo cubierto de cáscaras de huevo negras que la gente tira después de cocerlos en las aguas. Me pareció una imagen digna de una película de Kurosawa.

Al bajar el monte, escuché unos sonidos guturales terribles. De entre la niebla apareció una niña con retraso mental que caminaba muy despacio y era cuidada por un hombre de unos sesenta años. Todos los que bajaban, particularmente los niños, la evadían con cierto temor. El hombre, en cambio, la sostenía del brazo con una gran ternura, amor y dignidad.

Esa imagen me conmovió. En ese mismo viaje y unos meses después, viajando por Estocolmo con mi familia, me topé con muchos sordomudos. Estaban por todas partes; me llamaba la atención su manera de gesticular y el dramatismo de su comunicación. Me pareció un lenguaje desconocido e ignorado por casi todos los que tenemos la bendición de tocar y ser tocados por la palabra. Esa misma noche, tuve un sueño erótico sobre una adolescente en el consultorio de un dentista. Todas estas imágenes, en apariencia inconexas, me dieron la justificación para filmar en una de mis ciudades favoritas por su misterio y sus contradicciones. Tuve la idea de narrar la historia de un padre y una hija con dos tipos de soledades muy diferentes, pero igual de terribles. Le hablé a Guillermo desde Estocolmo; le gustó la idea y, a partir de ahí, decidimos que serían cuatro historias en vez de cinco. Fueron dos años de colaboración difícil e intensa. A pesar de que Guillermo no conoce Japón ni Marruecos, su talento lo llevó a escribir un guión que fue el *blueprint* para iniciar la primera etapa de *Babel*.

Una vez que el guión estuvo listo, sin tener aún actores en el proyecto y mucho menos financiación asegurada, invité a Jon Kilik y a Steve Golin a producir la película conmigo. Yo estaba autofinanciando el proyecto y ellos fueron los primeros en creer en la película y arriesgar en la aventura como socios y hasta el final. En diciembre de 2004, nos subimos los tres a un avión y, junto con Brigitte Broch, mi amiga y diseñadora de producción, volamos a Túnez y a Marruecos dando así inicio al *scouting* y al verdadero viaje de *Babel*.

Siempre quisiste un marco global para tu película: un lienzo en el que una manzana que cae de un árbol tuviera un impacto económico, político y humano a dos continentes de distancia. ¿En qué momento *Babel* se volvió una historia menos sobre la globalización y más sobre tres familias?

La única razón por la que esta trilogía puede ser considerada como tal, además del hecho de estar formada por películas que tienen en común una estructura de historias cruzadas, es que, al final de todo, son historias de padres e hijos. *Amores perros* y *21 gramos* lo fueron. A pesar de que *Babel* trata de manera implícita temas sociales o políticos en una escala global, no deja de ser un cuarteto de historias muy íntimas.

La historia de los niños marroquíes, que originalmente ocurría en Túnez, significaba para mí más una tragedia sobre el colapso moral de una familia musulmana sumamente espiritual que una historia sobre unos niños perseguidos por la policía. Para el padre de los niños es igual o más importante el hecho de que Yussef espíe a su hermana, y que esta se desnude, que el hecho de que le hayan disparado a un autobús. Cuando los valores se quebrantan ya nada tiene sentido; cuando un eslabón se rompe, no se rompe el eslabón, sino toda la cadena.

A partir de esa historia, que siempre fue la más sólida, se construyeron las demás. La historia de Richard y Susan, la pareja que viaja por Marruecos, en un principio se enfocaba mucho más a lo político que a lo familiar; atendía a la política de los gobiernos y no a la política de lo humano, que es la más compleja. Incluía escenas con embajadores, viceministros y televisoras. Nos llevó mucho tiempo descubrir que en esta historia no había lugar para personajes arquetípicos.

Aunque gran parte de esta historia marroquí está filmada desde el punto de vista de Susan, lo más difícil para mí fue encontrar la manera de narrar la perspectiva de Richard. De pronto comprendí que, si subordinaba el punto de vista de Richard a una perspectiva hiperrealista, podía describir la situación de un personaje que jamás se entera de lo que está pasando en el mundo, ni de lo que se dice en las noticias, ni de las presiones y acusaciones paranoicas de su gobierno contra el gobierno marroquí. Solo a través de una radio de transistores que transmite en un idioma desconocido, y por una llamada telefónica con un amigo, Richard se entera brevemente de lo que sucede alrededor. Consideré que, si el personaje solamente contaba con tan pocos elementos, no debía a darle al público más información que la que él poseía. Nosotros, como civiles, ¿cuándo tenemos la oportunidad de estar presentes en las pláticas de los políticos y sus representantes? Eso sólo pasa en las películas, y yo no quería que esta historia se sintiera como una película. Quería que el público intuyera los errores políticos y las malinterpretaciones de los medios.

Para mí, la historia de Richard y Susan, más que una historia sobre una pareja de americanos que llegan juntos para perderse sin esperanza en el desierto, es la historia de dos seres perdidos uno con respecto al otro, que llegan al desierto a encontrarse. La clave para entender quiénes son está en el hecho de que perdieron un hijo, y en el dolor y las culpas que esa desgracia les generó.

En el caso de Chieko, la adolescente japonesa, además de la ausencia de una madre, ella sufre de la ausencia de la palabra. Cuando no podemos tocar o ser tocados por las palabras, el cuerpo se convierte en una herramienta, un arma, una invitación.

Lo mismo sucede en la historia de Amelia, que además de ser una ciudadana invisible, es también una madre no reconocida Finalmente todas las historias son de padres e hijos.

***Babel* se mueve con fluidez admirable de país en país y de idioma en idioma mostrando una gran empatía por el ser humano cualquiera que sea su circunstancia. Sin embargo, tengo la impresión de que en el segmento de México tu cariño se desborda. ¿Fuiste consciente de ello?**

Fue muy difícil filmar la historia de México, no sólo por lo complejo del tema de la frontera, sino por las duras condiciones climatológicas. Rodamos en los desiertos más calientes de la tierra con niños involucrados. Tratándose de mi país natal, se me podía ir la mano y sería juzgado más escrupulosamente. Adentrarme y escudriñar la subcultura fronteriza que anteriormente rehuía y rechazaba fue toda una aventura antropológica.

La primera decisión que tomé en aras de ser fiel y congruente con la película fue excluir del guión (y después, en la sala de montaje) bloques enteros de estereotipos y lugares comunes que dramáticamente no aportaban nada y que dibujaban ese México idealizado y gracioso que ya no existe (mucho menos en una zona como la frontera con Estados Unidos, donde la gente es más sobria y cabrona).

La segunda decisión que tomé fue la de ver México, al menos en un principio, desde el punto de vista de los niños americanos; quienes (como podría sucederle a gran parte del público alrededor del mundo) viven por primera vez la experiencia de entrar en México por la frontera de San Jacinto. Como ya te había dicho, yo cruzo la frontera con mis hijos cada seis meses. A pesar de ser mexicanos, les siguen llamando la atención los colores, las dulcerías, el burro, el barro, las putas, la falta de pasto y el aire polvoriento de su país. Lo que para un adulto es miseria y pobreza, a los ojos de un niño es colorido y alegría. Todo aquel que haya cruzado alguna vez de Estados Unidos hacia Tijuana sabrá que hay una cierta electricidad en el aire y un contraste casi absurdo. Algunos dicen que Tijuana es la axila de Latinoamérica. Para mí, es un lugar en donde se cruzan los sueños más nobles con los finales más tristes.

En la comunidad de El Carrizo, a una hora de Tijuana, filmé la boda de Luis, el hijo de Amelia. Fuimos a muchas bodas como parte de la investigación y alguna terminó a cuchillazos. Más allá del aspecto folclórico, para mí, esta boda siempre representó la única posibilidad de conocer a Amelia y su mundo. Sabía que si en ese momento no lograba establecer la empatía del público con ella, el personaje estaba muerto. No pasaría de ser una criada ignorante que arriesga a los niños de manera irresponsable.

Por eso decidí construir una burbuja cinematográfica de tiempo imaginario: una cápsula que me permitiera dibujar a Amelia como madre, como amiga, como amante y, sobre todo, como la madre postiza de los niños americanos. La canción de Chavela Vargas de fondo flota con los aires de la melancolía. Amelia, como muchos mexicanos, se encuentra en la paradoja de tener que descuidar a sus propios hijos para cuidar a los ajenos. Como muchos otros mexicanos que, viviendo en Estados Unidos, arreglan los coches pero no tienen derecho a tener permiso de conducir; les construyen sus casas pero no les alcanza para pagar el alquiler de la propia.

Filmé la frontera mexicana con mucho amor, pero también con mucho dolor, porque esos son los dos sentimientos que predominan en esa región.

Tu paso de México a Estados Unidos al filmar *21 gramos* fue un gran reto personal y profesional. ¿Qué nuevos retos enfrentaste esta vez como director? ¿Qué lograste que no hubieras logrado antes?

Hubo grandes retos físicos y de logística, pero sobre todo intelectuales y emocionales. Creo que cualquiera puede malabarear con las manos tres naranjas a la vez; sin embargo, te apuesto que, si tomas cuatro naranjas, se te van a caer un centenar de veces antes de que puedas dominarlas. *Babel* tiene cuatro historias en lugar de tres, como fue el caso de *Amores perros* y *21 gramos*, y es distinta del esquema al que yo ya estaba acostumbrado. Además, al haber sido filmada en tres continentes y tres culturas distintos, tuve que ajustar y reescribir el guión de acuerdo con las circunstancias que iba enfrentando.

En esta película me permití más licencias poéticas; me sentí mucho más libre y seguro que en las anteriores. Intenté cosas que no había hecho en las otras: por ejemplo, lograr la coexistencia del realismo y el hiperrealismo con el mundo de lo imaginario; con la congruencia y lógica del cine mudo, pero con la anarquía de la música y el audio como narradores en primer plano.

Convertí una línea de guión en una secuencia de diez minutos contada desde el punto de vista del mundo interior de un personaje; lo que provocó que el público, a través de imágenes, sonidos o metáforas, se sumergiera en el personaje y en sus circunstancias. En el caso de las secuencias de Chieko en el parque y en la discoteca, intenté que el público experimentara los sonidos del silencio tal y como lo hace ella desde su cabeza y su perspectiva; porque, en ocasiones, es el silencio lo que puede ser verdaderamente ensordecedor. En la escena del rescate en helicóptero de Richard y Susan, quería que la imagen sugiriera una ballena voladora que llega al mar del desierto y que representara un choque de culturas y diferencias socioeconómicas profundas.

Para mí, el cine es mucho más que un argumento o una anécdota ilustrada. El cine es lo que sucede entre un diálogo y otro; lo que solo puede decirse con el silencio de las imágenes. Más allá de la identificación con los personajes, su historia y sus circunstancias, quise que el público se conectara emocionalmente a través del uso del montaje, la música, la dialéctica y la yuxtaposición de ideas visuales y sensoriales. Es decir, utilizando a fondo todos los recursos del cine como no lo había hecho en mis dos películas anteriores. En toda esta orquestación, yo y todo el equipo debemos ser invisibles y nunca hacernos notar por el público durante la experiencia de ver la película. Si mi trabajo se hace obvio en la pantalla, entonces he fracasado y todo lo que te he dicho no tiene sentido.

El cine es un animal vivo y se hace por etapas que parecen no terminar nunca. Como tú sabes, montar es reescribir. En ese sentido, y por la naturaleza de la película, el montaje de *Babel* fue particularmente difícil. No concibo trabajar con otro montador que no sea Stephen Mirrione: su talento y claridad fueron de gran importancia para malabarear estas cuatro naranjas en el aire; y la elegancia de sus cortes hizo que las transiciones fueran más orgánicas. Quitamos bloques enteros que hicieron que la estructura original del guión se tambaleara y, una vez más, me encontrara esculpiendo la piedra para lograr que su verdadera forma se revelara.

Recuerdo, sobre todo, cómo encontramos el epílogo para la historia de Yussef y Ahmed. Un día, yendo de un lugar a otro por las montañas de Ouarzazate, empezó a soplar un viento insólito; casi era necesario agarrarte a algo para que no te tirara. Ordené sacar las cámaras de la camioneta y pedí a Yussef y a Ahmed que jugaran con el viento a la orilla del desfiladero. La imagen no tenía ningún sentido dramático, pero para mí tenía un contenido estético y poético magnífico. De la misma manera, mandé poner una vieja barca abandonada en el centro de un inmenso valle de desierto rocoso para que sugiriera la existencia del mar por aquella región. En el *scouting* de Túnez, encontramos cientos de fósiles marinos; incluso supe que se habían encontrado esqueletos de ballena en medio del Sáhara. Esa idea me conmovió y, con el paso del tiempo, me dio vértigo. Para mí, la barca en el desierto era una metáfora del Arca de Noe: el paso del hombre en los inmensos desiertos del tiempo.

También el último día de rodaje filmé sobre una *dolly* un *close up* de Yussef llorando la muerte de su hermano. Mi idea original era cortar junto a la escena de la barca de Noe, en la que caminaban su hermano y su padre alejándose, como una imagen premonitoria de la muerte del hermano. Sin embargo, al ver el primer corte, noté que la historia de Yussef y Ahmed terminaba muy pronto y, por lo tanto, muy lejos del final de la película. Parecía que la muerte de Ahmed no tenía importancia. Peor aún, para el espectador, ese momento quedaba tan lejos del clímax emocional del final que corría el riesgo de olvidarse.

Necesitábamos un epílogo como lo tenían las otras tres historias. Ahora parece que encontrar la manera de cortar estos pequeños momentos inconexos y en dónde meterlos era algo obvio y fácil, pero requirió de mucho tiempo y trabajo. Ahora no sólo es un gran epílogo para esa historia, sino que también es uno de los momentos más emocionales del film; ya que, además de ser el único *flashahead* en la gramática de la película, sintetiza y fusiona metafóricamente los desiertos de Marruecos y de México: el viento que sopla en el cabello de Amelia al abrazar a su hijo en la frontera es el mismo viento que sacude a los niños en Marruecos; y es también el mismo viento que genera el helicóptero que entra a rescatar a Susan y Richard. Esta sección, junto con la de Chieko en el parque y en la discoteca, son mis secuencias montadas favoritas y en donde Mirrione, con su talento y rigor, juega un papel crucial.

Otro de los grandes retos de montaje era el de pasar de un país a otro sin que el cambio fuera brusco y distrajera demasiado al espectador. Aquí la música fue un factor esencial; y Gustavo Santaolalla, otra vez, fue la clave: además de viajar a todos y cada uno de los países donde filmamos para grabar y hacer investigación, Gustavo decidió usar el *oud*, un antiquísimo instrumento árabe que es la madre de la guitarra, para que fuera el ADN musical de la película. Por la dureza de sus cuerdas, el *oud* es un instrumento difícil de tocar. Gustavo aprendió a tocarlo para poder interpretarlo en la banda sonora.

A pesar de que, en esta ocasión, yo quería hacer de la música algo más presente que en mis películas anteriores, de una forma minimalista las yemas de los dedos de Santaolalla logran destrozarnos el corazón con una sola nota. El sonido del *oud* tiene la virtud de, además de ser profundamente afromediterráneo, recordarnos los llantos de la guitarra flamenca y, por lo tanto, de la mexicana, con un perfume de *koto* japonés. En un solo instrumento, el genio de Santaolalla pudo reunir las tres culturas sin necesidad de recurrir a los instrumentos folclóricos de cada país, lo cual hubiera sido terrible.

Todas estas son cosas que fui descubriendo en el camino; a fin de cuentas, yo hago cine para aprender a hacer cine. Cada vez que empiezo una película, parece como si me hubiera olvidado de todo lo que había aprendido en la película pasada. Es como si tuviera *alzheimer* prematuro. De hecho, no me considero un director de cine, sino un tipo que ha hecho tres películas y un par de cortos. También un músico frustrado.

Sueño con hacer al menos una gran película en mi vida, pero en ocasiones siento que las cosas que quiero hacer están a años luz de la capacidad que tengo para llevarlas a cabo.

A pesar del contexto global y políglota, *Babel* se siente más íntima y personal que tus películas anteriores. ¿A qué lo atribuyes?

En todos los países en que filmé *Babel* intenté amarrarme las manos para no caer en mis propias tentaciones estéticas y acabar haciendo un docudrama tipo *National Geographic*. O, todavía peor, cuatro cortometrajes inconexos filmados desde el punto de vista de un turista. Tuve que tomar decisiones opuestas y hasta contradictorias: por un lado, debía separar y delinear las historias; por el otro, había que unificarlas. Lo que hizo que *Babel* acabara siendo una sola película fue la posibilidad de encontrar una única nota que flotara a lo largo de ella.

Más allá de la parte formal, de la que te hablaré más adelante, yo miro a mis personajes con mucha ternura y empatía. Esa mirada permeó toda la película y permitió que hubiera un mismo tono y un mismo espíritu que sobrevivieron incluso a los diferentes estilos visuales en que la filmé. En cada escena traté de concentrarme en filmar obsesivamente el aspecto de la intimidad y los microdetalles del mundo interior y exterior de los personajes. Aunque suene obvio, pensaba localmente para que funcionara universalmente.

La parte interna (el alma de la película) es la misma historia, contada cuatro veces, sobre las dos grandes tragedias del mamífero vertical: la incapacidad de amar y recibir amor, y la vulnerabilidad de los seres que amamos. Cada vez que iniciaba una historia, era como empezar otra película. Al final, amaba a mis personajes, sufría y lloraba con ellos y me daba cuenta de que no era sino la misma película contada una vez más.

Lo mejor de rodar *Babel* fue que empecé filmando una película acerca de las diferencias entre los seres humanos (lo que nos separa, las barreras físicas y del lenguaje), pero en el camino me fui dando cuenta de que estaba filmando una película de las cosas que nos unen, nos conectan y nos vuelven uno solo. Estas cosas son el amor y el dolor: lo que hace feliz a un japonés o a un marroquí podrá ser muy diferente, pero aquello que nos hace miserables es lo mismo para todos.

En lo que se refiere a la parte externa (la formal y estética), mi amigo y extraordinario fotógrafo Rodrigo Prieto y yo decidimos tomar el riesgo de hacer de *Babel* un pastiche: cada uno de los países se filmaría con diferentes estilos, texturas y formatos. En teoría, cada historia tendría su propia personalidad; cada estilo y formato se subordinaría a las necesidades dramáticas de los personajes y a sus circunstancias. A su vez, mi talentosa amiga y diseñadora de arte Brigitte Broch nos propuso dividir estos países conforme a la gama de los rojos: chedron para Marruecos, rojo vivo para México y violeta para Japón. Marruecos se filmó en 16 mm con colores deslavados; México, en 35 mm con colores vivos, y Japón, por una brillante propuesta de Rodrigo, con Panavision y lentes anamórficos, que aíslan al personaje de una forma espectacular y apropiada para el tema de esa historia.

La razón por la que este *collage* funcionó es porque detrás de cada una de estas decisiones, en apariencia diferentes, hubo siempre una razón muy profunda y un trabajo de conexión y de equipo muy grande. Rodrigo Prieto y Brigitte Broch son mis manos derecha e izquierda. Su colaboración en mi trabajo es muy importante y el nivel de entendimiento al que hemos llegado hace que se enriquezca enormemente el resultado final.

Siempre traté de que mi lenguaje cinematográfico fuera congruente con los personajes y que mi gramática visual y mi estilo, aun cuando toda la película fue filmada con cámara en mano, contuviera un respiro, un ritmo interno al servicio de la emotividad de la puesta en escena.

Al parecer, el rodaje fue en sí mismo una torre de Babel. ¿Cómo fue trabajar con personas que nunca habían actuado y que no hablaban tu idioma?

Dirigir a actores es difícil. Dirigir a actores en otro idioma que no sea el tuyo es mucho más difícil. Ahora bien, dirigir a no actores en un idioma que no entiendes es el reto más grande que he tenido como director. Faltando sólo diecisiete días para iniciar el rodaje en Marruecos, no tenía un solo actor, además de Brad Pitt y Cate Blanchett.

Para los papeles de los niños Yussef y Ahmed y de su familia de pastores, así como para todos los personajes alrededor de la historia de Richard y Susan, busqué en un principio actores profesionales de la comunidad marroquí y de las comunidades musulmanas de París. Sin embargo, ninguno de ellos tenía la apariencia que yo necesitaba. Buscaba las pieles curtidas que sólo se dan al sur del Atlas y en los adentros del Sáhara. La mayoría de los actores profesionales tenían rasgos finos, pieles tersas y habían desarrollado los malos hábitos de actuación de las telenovelas. Por más que los maquilláramos, parecerían actores de una película Hallmark.

Fue entonces cuando, junto con Alfonso Gómez, Hervé Jakubowicz y Marco Robert, mi equipo de *casting*, decidí emprender una búsqueda desesperada por todos los humildes pueblos alrededor de Tamnougalt y Ouarzazate para encontrar ahí a los verdaderos personajes de *Babel*. Desde la altura de las mezquitas y con ruidosas bocinas, se anunciaba la buena nueva de que la película *Babel* buscaba actores para aparecer en ella. Cientos de personas se formaban y nosotros les tomábamos un vídeo. Por la noche, yo revisaba esos vídeos y seleccionaba a quienes me interesaban físicamente. Junto con Hiam Abbass, una actriz y amiga maravillosa que más que *dialogue coach* se convirtió en mi ángel de la guarda, al día siguiente hacíamos ensayos con las personas elegidas y unos ejercicios que siempre hago para sensibilizarme con su rango emocional.

Para mí, esta fue la primera experiencia de trabajar con no actores, con gente común y corriente. Fue alucinante; lo haré cada vez que pueda y para siempre. A pesar de que el proceso puede ser frustrante y la ignorancia y las limitaciones técnicas pueden ser una desventaja, la inocencia es y será siempre más poderosa que la experiencia. La virginidad, la pureza y la honestidad que tiene alguien haciendo el rol de sí mismo es inigualable. Un ejemplo es Abdullah, el padre de los niños marroquíes, que es un carpintero de las afueras de Fez y, sin embargo, su disciplina y su rango dramático me dejaron con la boca abierta. En escenas como cuando pega a sus hijos o cuando muere su hijo Ahmed (que filmé en tres días), mantenía la intensidad en cada toma y en todo momento. Una vez que le indicaba los movimientos físicos de la puesta en escena, los repetía con ritmo y precisión. Escenas como esas son difíciles aun para los actores profesionales de rango mundial.

Lo mismo sucedió con Hassan o con Yussef. Desde el primer momento, sus ojos me revelaron que poseían una gran vida interior. Con sólo platicar unos minutos con alguien y mirarlo a los ojos, es fácil darse cuenta de si tiene calle o no tiene calle, o de si tiene el bagaje emocional suficiente como para extraer un poco de sentir de adentro y metafóricamente rozar lo que le pasa al personaje que va a representar.

Ahora bien, la mezcla de actores con actores no profesionales es más complicada. En la historia de Yussef y Ahmed todos eran actores no profesionales; sin embargo, no fue así en la historia de Richard y Susan. Escenas en apariencia sencillas, como la de Cate Blanchett y Sfia, la vieja que cuida de Susan cuando llega al cuarto sangrando, o la del veterinario que cose la herida de Susan con Richard presente, no fueron nada fáciles. Sfia era una mujer bereber de ochenta y cinco años que en su vida había visto una cámara. Era nativa de Taguenzalte, un pueblo en el que filmamos sin luz, y vivía en la casa de al lado de donde rodábamos. Sfia solo habla bereber. El veterinario era en verdad el veterinario del pueblo y sólo hablaba árabe. Una instrucción tan fácil como «al oír ‹what› te levantas y cierras la ventana» para Sfia se convertía en una odisea de tres horas. Era todo un logro que lo hiciera bien, un par de veces igual y, sobre todo, que no volteara a la cámara y sonriera.

Lo que aprendí es que, si un director escoge a alguien que físicamente expresa lo que el personaje debe expresar a primera vista, y que si esa persona tiene un sólo rasgo con que se pueda identificar con el personaje, una vez que el director lo encuentra y le comunica claramente sus objetivos dramáticos de una forma simple, puede hacer actuar a cualquier ser humano en el planeta.

¿Y cómo fue la experiencia de trabajar con alguien como Brad Pitt, quien es una celebridad mundial, en medio de este ensamble de no actores y circunstancias tan adversas? ¿Qué es lo que te llevó a escogerlo a él y a Cate Blanchett?

La experiencia de trabajar con los actores profesionales de *Babel* fue tan rica como la experiencia de trabajar con los no profesionales. Aun cuando la ficción y la realidad se tocaron varias veces durante el rodaje y las circunstancias y condiciones de trabajo (el clima, las localizaciones, los diferentes idiomas) fueron difíciles, siempre me sentí apoyado por los actores y tuve el privilegio de su confianza.

A pesar de que el papel de Richard no era en apariencia obvio para un actor como Brad Pitt, siempre me ha parecido que tiene una presencia magnética que va más allá de su popularidad. Da la sensación de ser un tipo que se siente a gusto consigo mismo. Cuando lo conocí hace cuatro años, lo que me llamó la atención desde un principio fue su valor: filmábamos juntos una campaña publicitaria para unos *jeans* japoneses que consistía en una serie de viñetas absurdas que yo iba inventando espontáneamente. Brad insistía en llevar las cosas hasta un punto en donde físicamente se estaba poniendo en riesgo. La casa productora se puso nerviosa al ver lo que él y yo estábamos haciendo, así que redactó un documento que decía que ellos no se responsabilizaban si Brad se lastimaba físicamente y le pidieron que lo firmara. Pálido y asustado, su representante le pidió que dejara de hacer locuras y le dijo que no se le ocurriera firmar ese papel. Brad, sin voltear a verlo, firmó el papel y siguió haciendo lo que quería hacer. Estuvimos un par de horas más filmando y nos divertimos mucho. En la última de las viñetas se veía a Brad sobre una tabla de surf bajando por el delgado barandal de unas escaleras gigantes.

Cuando, cuatro años más tarde, le ofrecí el papel de Richard en *Babel*, aceptó sin reparos. No es fácil que actores y celebridades de su calibre acepten interpretar este tipo de personajes. Después de todo, hay un riesgo implícito en toda película independiente y de bajo presupuesto, y las buenas intenciones no siempre tienen buenos resultados.

Para mí, el reto era lograr que Brad Pitt, la celebridad, desapareciera tras el personaje para así dar lugar no solo al actor, sino también al ser humano detrás de esa imagen. Si al final la gente se olvidaba de quién era y podía mezclarse y no sobresalir entre los otros personajes, no habría triunfado solo Brad Pitt, sino también la película misma. Había muchos riesgos y con valor aceptó los retos. Aceptó, sobre todo, el riesgo más grande al que se enfrentan siempre los actores: se puso en mis manos y me dio su confianza. El proceso no fue fácil: estaba pasando por momentos difíciles de su vida personal y, sin embargo, nunca mezcló una cosa con la otra.

En el guión original, el conflicto entre Richard y Susan surgía de una infidelidad cometida en el pasado por él. Unas semanas antes del rodaje, sugerí llevar el drama a un nivel más profundo, como lo es la muerte de cuna de un hijo. Cuando Brad llegó a Marruecos, se enteró del cambió en el guión. De hecho, ya era complicado construir un personaje a partir de solo treinta páginas de historia; no fue fácil asimilar de golpe este nuevo elemento dramático en el libreto: ¿quién era Richard? ¿Por qué hizo lo que hizo? Todos los días, bajo condiciones físicas extenuantes, había que escarbar, encontrar e inventar el personaje vulnerable que Brad construyó en la pantalla.

Entre el agotamiento físico y la intensidad emocional constante que demandaba el personaje, Brad, al igual que su personaje, se fue haciendo más frágil y vulnerable hasta llegar a ese momento en donde exuda un gran temple y ternura, y que en lo personal me parece muy hermoso: la llamada telefónica final que hace Richard a su hijo y que, finalmente, nos revela al ser humano ante la impotencia de una forma universal y en donde Brad entregó todo.

El caso de Cate Blanchett fue diferente: ella ha sido una de mis actrices favoritas durante mucho tiempo y literalmente le supliqué que aceptara interpretar el papel de Susan. Se resistía, y sus razones eran justas. En el guión, el personaje de Susan era el de una mujer que se pasa tres cuartas partes de la película tirada en el suelo, sangrando y semiconsciente. Sin embargo, en mi opinión, era solo desde el punto de vista de Susan que los eventos tomarían fuerza y relevancia, y así se lo expliqué. Para lograr que en veintiocho minutos el público se encariñara y sintiera empatía por un personaje que empieza limpiándose las manos con desinfectante, tirándole la Coca-Cola al suelo a su marido y mostrándose intensamente incómoda con cada centímetro de su vida y de su cuerpo, necesitaba una actriz de la talla de Cate. Cada momento de su personaje, esté parada, dormida o sentada, gira alrededor de la emoción. Desde la primera escena, ella establece las reglas y el nivel del juego.

No deja de sorprenderme, aunque lo haya visto tantas veces, ese momento en que ella fuma la pipa. Parece algo fácil, pero lo que hace, dice y te hace sentir con sus ojos (y solo con sus ojos, porque no puede mover otra parte del cuerpo) es alucinante.

Aun cuando, por las razones que expliqué antes, tenía que hacer veinticinco tomas de un solo ángulo para que el veterinario o Sfia pudieran encontrar su línea o su ritmo, Cate, en cada toma, me daba la misma intensidad. Su generosidad y el dominio de sus herramientas hacen que el trabajo de un director sea más fácil.

¿Qué impacto tuvo en tu vida viajar por medio mundo y convivir con gente de tan diversos orígenes y costumbres? ¿Cómo cambió *Babel* tu visión de las cosas?

Creo que todas las películas te transforman, pero para mí ésta ha sido, por mucho, la que más me ha cambiado. Más que una decisión profesional, significó una decisión de vida: sabía que implicaría un sacrificio y una transformación en la vida ordinaria de mi familia, que es mi núcleo y mi base. Sabía que mis hijos, mi esposa y yo nos íbamos a beneficiar humanamente, pero que también habría muchos sacrificios. Uno no puede ser el mismo después de conectarse e involucrarse con tantas personas. Si antes de iniciar el rodaje mi postura ante la vida era más cínica y pesimista, al terminar tuve más esperanza y optimismo por el ser humano, porque ciertamente esos prejuicios y fronteras internas se pueden derrumbar con el solo hecho de tocarnos. Me di cuenta de que el choque de la cultura norteamericana con la musulmana no se da porque sean radicalmente opuestas, sino porque son increíblemente parecidas. Su fanatismo, su nacionalismo llevado al extremo y la forma en que hacen de la mujer un objeto son, aunque puedan parecer distintos, parientes cercanos.

Durante el rodaje de *Babel*, me di cuenta de que la gente es esencialmente buena y de que, mientras menos cosas posee, más pura y feliz es.

Sé que eres una persona profundamente religiosa y espiritual. Aun así, y aunque en tus películas tocas temas judeocristianos como la caída, la redención o la culpa, la religión no juega un papel central en tus historias; ni siquiera en *Babel*, que es sobre gente proveniente de varias culturas. ¿Por qué lo decidiste así en un momento en que se lleva la religión como bandera?

Para mí, la religión se debate en el terreno de lo intelectual más que en el de lo moral. A diferencia de *21 gramos*, donde a través del personaje de Benicio del Toro exploré el fenómeno del fanatismo religioso, en *Babel* no había cupo para la cuestión religiosa. Esta película trata precisamente sobre lo vulnerable y frágil que es el ser humano: de los animalitos que al final somos; de que incluso cuando orinamos estamos amando y necesitando del otro; de que la soledad nos mata, el desamor nos aniquila, y un litro menos de sangre también. En una escena, el personaje de Richard observa a Anwar rezar hacia la mezquita; lo mira como queriendo encontrar una fe que él, por desgracia, no posee.

En *Babel* fue Dios quien creó la confusión y es el hombre quien ahora tiene que encontrar la solución. Dios está ausente en esta ecuación.

Has hecho toda tu carrera como director de largometrajes con muchos de los mismos colaboradores: Rodrigo Prieto, Brigitte Broch, Guillermo Arriaga, Martín Hernández. ¿Cómo ha sido desarrollarse y crecer junto con ellos? ¿Qué tanto han influido en tus películas sus estilos y talentos?

A Rodrigo Prieto lo conocí como director de fotografía cuando yo aún hacía comerciales publicitarios y trabajamos juntos en distintas campañas. Nunca se me va a olvidar que, después de mandarle el guión de *Amores perros*, lo invité a comer para intercambiar ideas sobre cómo podríamos abordar visualmente el proyecto. Yo llevaba una serie de libros de fotografía fija como referencia de lo que quería; Rodrigo sacó de su maleta los mismos libros que yo traía. Desde ahí supe que había entre nosotros una conexión y una visión compartida de las cosas. Planear las tomas con Rodrigo o estar con él en el set es un gozo; verlo operar la cámara es una experiencia; pero ver y descubrir más tarde en la sala de montaje, en detalle, su forma inigualable de narrar con la cámara los más mínimos detalles emocionales resulta impresionante.

En *Babel* sólo hubo tres escenas en las que usamos una *dolly*: la primera, la última y un *close up* de Yussef llorando por la muerte de su hermano. Lo demás fue filmado por Rodrigo con la cámara sobre los hombros. De *Amores perros* a *Babel*, lo he visto crecer de una forma alucinante. Su dominio de la luz y su conocimiento técnico son muy grandes, pero lo es aún más su elegancia como ser humano. En una película, no hay nadie más cerca de mí que él. Nos conocemos tanto que estando en el set, con un solo gesto o un simple sonido gutural en clave, podemos definir toda una estrategia de filmación. En más de doce años que llevamos de conocernos y trabajar juntos, jamás hemos tenido un momento desagradable.

A Brigitte Broch la conocí casi al mismo tiempo que a Rodrigo, y trabajamos juntos por vez primera en una campaña publicitaria que ganó muchos premios internacionales (y en donde, curiosamente, también trabajé por primera vez con Gael García Bernal). Brigitte es una celebración de la vida: cuando diseña una atmósfera, cada uno de sus objetos y detalles, por mínimos que sean, hablan y describen de una forma profunda a los personajes. Nos gusta filmar en localizaciones y siempre tiene un gran olfato para encontrar el mejor lugar, no por su aspecto, sino por su espíritu y su energía. Al hablar siempre de colores, de texturas, de olores y de formas a lo largo de interminables *scoutings* por el mundo, platicamos en realidad de la vida. Mis películas y mi vida no serían lo mismo sin ella.

Martín Hernández y yo estudiábamos juntos en la universidad. Nuestro primer proyecto conjunto fue a los veinte años: yo era el asistente de dirección y el compositor musical de un cortometraje dirigido por un amigo común y Martín era el técnico de sonido. Más tarde, empezamos juntos en una estación de radio en donde cada uno tenía un programa de tres horas. Durante cinco años fuimos la estación número uno de Ciudad de México; y, a partir de ahí, yo escribía historias, personajes y ocurrencias transgresoras y provocativas, y Martín las producía para la radio. Hoy, veintidós años más tarde, seguimos trabajando juntos y no solo nuestro cariño ha crecido. Mejor que nadie, Martín posee esa extraña capacidad para hacerte ver y sentir la piel del sonido.

Pelayo Gutiérrez, el director del corto en que Martín y yo nos conocimos, fue quien me presentó a Guillermo Arriaga. Yo, en aquella época, había declarado en algún periódico que el nivel de los profesores en las universidades mexicanas era terrible; Guillermo en ese entonces era maestro universitario. Cuando llegó a la comida en donde nuestro amigo Pelayo nos iba a presentar, Guillermo, sin conocerme, ya estaba enojado conmigo. Sin embargo, a lo largo de la reunión, fuimos encontrando cosas en común y, al final, lo invité a que escribiera un argumento que yo desarrollaba en aquel entonces y que era el objetivo de la comida. Nuestra amistad se fortaleció y aquel primer encuentro generó diferentes sueños y proyectos en común. Ahí empezó una relación muy exitosa que dio comienzo con *Amores perros*. Su capacidad narrativa y para sintetizar situaciones complejas en dos líneas y encontrar soluciones inesperadas a problemas mayúsculos es única. Es un colaborador que tiene un mundo propio y, al mismo tiempo, una gran flexibilidad que le permite trabajar en equipo mientras desarrolla su trabajo, con lo que puede subordinar la historia y los personajes al servicio de la película.

Lynn Fainchtein, por el contrario, era nuestra «enemiga». Tenía un programa de radio en una estación rival y, aunque ella no lo reconozca, siempre la hacíamos pedazos. Hablando en serio, su gusto musical era impecable y su programa era el único que yo, sin que nadie lo supiera, me atrevía a escuchar fuera de mi estación. Hoy somos grandes amigos. Su gusto por la música sigue siendo el mismo: ecléctico y exquisito. Por ser de la misma generación, compartimos un gusto musical parecido y es ella quien pone a bailar a mis películas. Fue ella misma quien me introdujo a Gustavo Santaolalla al hacerme escuchar un disco de Ron Rocco cuando estaba buscando un músico para *Amores perros*.

Recuerdo haber volado a Los Ángeles con un casete vhs que contenía un corte de *Amores perros* para enseñárselo a Santaolalla. Solo si le gustaba, haría la banda sonora. Yo salí al jardín mientras él lo veía y me fumé una cajetilla de cigarros. Dos horas después, salió con los ojos llorosos. Un fuerte abrazo selló una amistad para siempre. No hay nadie como él para, con una sola nota del instrumento que le pongas enfrente, destruirte el corazón. Aníbal es su socio y hermano del alma. Ese par de cabrones han sido claves en mis películas.

Al margen de esto, en el set hay un solo gurú, un tipo con el que todos quieren estar. El lugar en que esté se convierte en un espacio de equilibrio y buen humor; es casi un terapeuta. Le llaman *el tiburón* y su verdadero nombre es José Antonio García. Además de ser un extraordinario técnico de sonido, su amistad y sus cualidades humanas lo vuelven único para mí.

Alguien que también fue de vital importancia en *21 gramos* y en *Babel* es Alfonso Gómez Rejón. En *21 gramos* fue mi asistente personal y me ayudó a hacer una investigación muy valiosa para los personajes; ahora, en *Babel*, además de supervisor de *casting* e investigador, ha sido director de la segunda unidad. Su material fue indispensable; y su ayuda en el *casting* por las calles, increíble.

Podría seguir durante mucho tiempo diciéndote lo importantes que son y han sido para mí personas como Tita Lombardo, productora de línea de *Amores perros* y también de *Babel*. La considero como mi madrina en el cine. Corinne Weber, quien es mi asistente desde hace ya cinco años y fue en *Babel* productora asociada. Robbie y Joey, que son el *gaffer* y el *key grip* de Rodrigo y que, desde *21 gramos*, han hecho cosas técnicas inexplicables para lograr lo que la película necesitaba y son ahora de la familia. O Batán, quien fue mi asistente de dirección por primera vez en esta ocasión cerrando con broche de oro en Japón.

Sin embargo, lo más increíble fue haber tenido también el privilegio y la oportunidad de trabajar por vez primera con Jon Kilk, Steve Golin y Ann Ruark. En una producción de este calibre, no es fácil mantener a flote constantemente la visión de la película y sortear al mismo tiempo los infinitos problemas logísticos y financieros para llevarla a cabo. No obstante, increíblemente, siempre y hasta el final, hubo una gran comunicación, solidaridad y respeto. La película llegó a buen puerto tal y como la planeamos; y todos ellos hicieron un trabajo extraordinario en el aspecto financiero, técnico y humano.

Ann Ruark, como productora asociada y productora de línea, es de esas pocas excepciones que maneja y entiende todos los aspectos de hacer cine y, sobre todo, de hacerlo con clase.

En fin, ¿quién me habría dicho que la persona que me ayudó en un principio a levantar y cerrar el proyecto, mi gran amigo y agente John Lesher, sería, por azares del destino, quien ahora lanzaría y distribuiría *Babel*?

Tuve la suerte de conocer a Brad Grey justo en el momento que estaba comenzando su sueño y la aventura de transformar Paramount Pictures. Desde el primer momento, confió en nosotros y creyó en el proyecto 100%, dándonos todo el apoyo, respeto y libertad que necesitábamos para hacer ésta película.

Cuando el trabajo se lleva a cabo dentro de una familia como la que nosotros conformamos, un rodaje se siente más como una banda de rock en gira que como un equipo de rodaje produciendo una película. Las intensas y al mismo tiempo efímeras relaciones que se dan al filmar una película no son fáciles de sobrellevar, ya que por espacios largos y, por lo general, en lugares lejanos, convives más con el equipo que con tu familia. Cuando termina la filmación, sabes que es muy posible que a esa persona que tanto quisiste no la vuelvas a ver en tu vida. Mi caso es diferente, pues conozco a todos los que conforman mi familia creativa desde mucho antes de ser un cineasta, lo cual representa una doble bendición: la de trabajar en lo que me gusta y la de hacerlo con mis amigos.

Die Erinnerung der Wunden

Vorwort von Eliseo Alberto

Wahrscheinlich gibt es keine andere Erinnerung als die Erinnerung der Wunden.

Czeslaw Milosz

Ein Buch mit Fotografien kann und sollte eine Art Fenster sein. Es öffnet sich dem Licht und verschließt sich dem Schatten.

Jedes Bild wird im Helldunkel der Erinnerung festgehalten. Es hinterlässt einen Eindruck – ein ebenso ungestrafter wie notwendiger Diebstahl.

Ein Auge erfasste ein Bild und fing es im Fluge ein. Später eignen es sich tausende Pupillen an und ahmen es sogar nach, ohne um Erlaubnis zu bitten. Oder um Verzeihung.

Wer dieses Buch in die Hand nimmt, kann dem Wunsch, es zu erforschen, nicht ohne Emotion nachkommen. Dieses beunruhigende Gefühl überrascht den Menschen immer dann, wenn er sich einer eigenen oder fremden kreativen Erfahrung bewusst wird.

In *Babel*, dem Buch, vibriert die Emotion auf halbem Wege zwischen den Extremen Leidenschaft und Vernunft.

Jede Seite birgt eine menschliche Landschaft, ein Porträt der Zeit, die uns als Erbe hinterlassen wurde.

Betrachten Sie die Wüste eines Gesichtes inmitten der realen Wüste Marokkos. Oder die Weite in jenem Blick, der über die Ewigkeiten Tijuanas streift wie ein blinder Vogel, der nirgendwo sein Nest finden kann.

In welchem Winkel des Universums liegt dieses Felsenmeer, auf dem ein Boot ohne Steuermann, ohne Fische und ohne Köder treibt? Wer hat es dort zurückgelassen? Beunruhigt uns dieses Phantom heute?

Das Weltall hält einen Augenblick inne, wenn hoch oben auf einem Wolkenkratzer in Tokio ein Vater voller Schmerz seine nackte Tochter in die Arme schließt. Sicher ist es Gott, der sie beschützt.

Er hat seinen Hochmut für einen Moment vergessen und lässt seine Stille auf sie und uns herabgleiten.

Die Stille erklärt beinahe alles.

Der Wind tobt aus gutem Grund, auch wenn wir ihn in den Fotos von Patrick Bard, Graciela Iturbide, Mary Ellen Mark und Miguel Rio Branco nicht hören und die Musik in jener Spelunke in Tokio stumm ist, wo eine schutzlose junge Frauen so verzweifelt nach sich selbst sucht, dass sie sich schließlich in der Reinheit ihrer unberührten Nacktheit findet.

Wäre nicht die Stille des Bildes, wie sonst könnte man die eingefrorene Verzweiflung dieser in der Wüste verlorenen Frau erklären, die sich einer unverdienten Traurigkeit schuldig fühlt? Die Kinder, für die sie verantwortlich ist, dursten in der Sonne, mitten im Nirgendwo. Die einzige Hoffnung ist hier der pfützengroße Schatten eines Strauches. Warum vernehmen wir das stille Zittern der kleinen marokkanischen Hirten, die vom Echo eines Schusses verfolgt werden?

Taub ist die Kugel, welche die Scheibe des Busses durchschlägt und ganz nah am Herzen in den Körper einer Frau eindringt, die zum Sterben viel zu schön ist. Taub ist der ungestüme Schmerz ihres Mannes, als er jetzt, wo die Liebe in einem Rinnsal aus Geständnissen verblutet, begreift, wie sehr sie einander brauchen.

Wenn eine Sekunde zum Sterben genügt, wie könnte sie nicht ausreichen, unser Leben zu verändern? Die Welt passt in die Ewigkeit einer Sekunde. Der immer eitle Tod lässt sich nicht porträtieren.

Die Seele der Fotografie, wie fast aller Dinge im Leben, ist der Frieden. Der Frieden ist nicht still, sondern heroisch. Früher oder später setzt er sich durch, egal zu welchem Preis.

María Eladia Hagerman war sich dessen sehr wohl bewusst, als sie vier renommierte Fotografen aufrief, sich der Truppe des Regisseurs Alejandro González Iñárritu (und seinen treuen Reisegefährten) anzuschließen. Gemeinsam unternahmen sie das Abenteuer, rund um den Planeten zu filmen, im Kopf die phantastischen Pläne für einen Film, der ebenso unmöglich und undurchführbar wie sein biblischer Vorgänger zu sein schien und darin bestand, die Aussichtspunkte *Babels* – Symbol der menschlichen Präsenz auf Erden – zu erfinden. Nie zuvor hatte sich González Iñárritu ein so schwieriges Projekt vorgenommen. Das Ergebnis ist schlicht außergewöhnlich, ein filmisches Meisterwerk. Die Angst vor den Adjektiven habe ich schon vor langer Zeit verloren: Die erzählerische Perfektion von *Babel*, dem Film, zeigt uns, dass wir alle die gleichen menschlichen Schwächen und Stärken besitzen. Wenn wir also den dunklen Saal verlassen, werden unsere Gedanken unvermeidlich zu uns selbst schweifen, zu den Schmerzen, die uns bedrängen, und den Hoffnungen, die uns vor dem Übel namens Einsamkeit bewahren könnten. Ich wage zu behaupten, dass es in der Geschichte der Filmkunst wie auch der Fotografie selten gelungen ist, so viel Talent in einer einzigen künstlerischen Expedition zu vereinen.

Babel, das Buch, ist und ist doch nicht die gedruckte Dokumentation dieses Abenteuers. Die Blicke der Fotografen untersuchen nicht nur die Dramen der Geschichte, die mit Genauigkeit, Professionalität und Inspiration verfilmt werden soll. Die ganz persönliche Beobachtungsgabe jedes einzelnen Fotografen erforscht die Umgebung vom Filmset bis zum Horizont, und tun dies mit unendlicher Sensibilität und einem ebensolchen Scharfsinn. Gleichzeitig liefern sie einen unwiderlegbaren Beweis dafür, dass Intelligenz für die Kunst unerlässlich ist.

Vor kurzem las ich an einer Wand in Mexiko City den folgenden handgeschriebenen Ausruf: „Genug der Wahrheiten: Wir wollen Versprechen!" Es macht mir Angst, in dieser Welt verzweifelter Illusionen zu leben.

Bücher und Filme wie die beiden *Babel* geben unserem Körper die Seele zurück.

Wie schwer das Leben auch sein mag, wie sehr uns der Pessimismus auch bedrückt, wie schwarz unsere lange Nacht auch sein mag – das Leben ist ein Abenteuer, das zu erleben es wert ist.

Die klangvolle Stille des Films durchzieht das Buch. Ein Bild lässt sich auch lesen. Worte sind überflüssig.

Öffnen Sie das Fenster von *Babel* weit – möglicherweise finden Sie sich auf der anderen Seite wieder.

Schmetterlingsjäger

Einleitung von Alejandro González Iñárritu

Einmal habe ich geträumt, dass die Augenlider die endlosen, von der Netzhaut erfassten Bildlabyrinthe zurückhalten oder aufzeichnen können. Ich stellte mir vor, von diesen Lidern alle Erinnerungen unseres Lebens abzunehmen wie imprägniertes Kohlepapier. Meist jedoch lösen sich alle diese Bilder auf, und nur wenige bleiben erhalten. So wie die Gegenwart nichts anderes als eine beklemmende Scheibe Zeit darstellt, die von der Vergangenheit verschlungen wird, ist es für mich als Filmregisseur beängstigend zu sehen, wie hunderte oder gar tausende Bilder und Personen an meinem Autofenster vorbeiziehen, rasch – von links nach rechts – über meine Netzhaut gleiten und aus meinem Gedächtnis verschwinden werden, obwohl sie in einer einzigen Sekunde vermochten, unendlich viele Fragen in mir aufzuwerfen und mir eine Unmenge an Gedanken einzuhauchen. Vor drei Jahren beispielsweise entfachte ein einziges Bild in den Thermalquellen von Hakone (Japan) in mir den Wunsch und das Bedürfnis, eine ganze Geschichte in der Metropole der Ideogramme zu drehen.

Der Meister Akira Kurosawa pflegte zu sagen: „Die schönsten Dinge können niemals auf Film aufgenommen werden." Dies scheint für alle Filmsets auf der ganzen Welt zuzutreffen. Das Buch, das Sie gerade in den Händen halten, ist nur ein Versuch, den Augenblick von seinem Bann – der Vergänglichkeit – zu befreien.

Babel ist der letzte Film meiner mit *Amores perros* und *21 Gramm* begonnenen Trilogie. Es handelt sich um eine Trilogie mit Geschichten, die zunächst in heimischer Umgebung, später in einem fremden Ambiente und schließlich auf globaler Ebene die tiefgründigen und vielschichtigen Beziehungen zwischen Eltern und Kindern erforschen. Meine Idee zu *Babel* entsprang einem gewissen Bedürfnis, das nur das Exil und das Bewusstsein, ein Immigrant zu sein, hervorbringen kann. Es ist schwierig, in einem Erste-Welt-Land zu leben, wenn man aus der Dritten Welt stammt. Allerdings gewinnt man so eine umfassendere Sichtweise und erlangt eine neue Perspektive. Ich frage mich jetzt eher, wohin ich gehe, als woher ich komme.

Ich begann die Dreharbeiten zu *Babel* in der festen Überzeugung, einen Film über die Unterschiede zwischen den Menschen und ihre Kommunikationsunfähigkeit zu drehen, die nicht nur auf die verschiedenen Sprachen, sondern auch auf physische, politische und emotionale Barrieren zurückzuführen ist. Ich wollte die Geschichte mit einer komplexen, universellen Perspektive beginnen, um bis auf die intimste Ebene – zwischen zwei Personen – vorzudringen.

Das Filmteam bestand von Anfang an aus Mexikanern, Amerikanern, Franzosen, Italienern, Arabern, Berbern, Deutschen und gegen Ende aus Japanern. Parallel zum Hauptthema des Films fühlte ich, dass trotz aller Instrumente, die zur Verbesserung der Kommunikation zwischen den Menschen entwickelt worden waren, die Wirklichkeit am Ende ganz anders aussieht. Das Problem sind nicht die neuen, zahllosen Instrumente, die uns zur Kommunikation zur Verfügung stehen, sondern die Tatsache, dass niemand zuhört. Wenn es nichts zu hören gibt, gibt es auch nichts zu verstehen; wenn wir aufhören zu verstehen, ist unsere Sprache nutzlos und führt letztendlich zur Entzweiung. Die Arbeit mit fünf verschiedenen, unbekannten Sprachen, mit prominenten Schauspielern, aber auch (in den meisten Fällen) mit Laien, die zum Teil – wie in den einfachen marokkanischen Dörfern – nie zuvor eine Kamera gesehen hatten, stellte mich vor die Geduldsprobe, zuzuschauen und zu lernen. Wie Zigeuner in einem großen Wanderzirkus reiste ich mit meiner Ersatzfamilie (d.h. mit meinen langjährigen Freunden und Mitarbeitern, ohne die dieses Abenteuer unmöglich gewesen wäre) und mit meiner eigenen Familie fast ein Jahr lang durch drei Kontinente.

Während die Wochen, Monate, Gesichter, Landschaften und Jahreszeiten vorbeizogen, sorgten die Impressionen aus so vielen verschiedenen Kulturen sowie die physischen und psychischen Anstrengungen dieser Reise dafür, dass ich mich ebenso veränderte wie alle, die an diesem Film beteiligt waren. Im Laufe der Reise gab es Todesfälle, Geburten, Momente großer Freude oder Trauer und viele Gründe für Brüderlichkeit und Gemeinschaft. Dass wir so viel Menschlichkeit erfuhren, veränderte nicht nur uns, sondern auch den Film. Die kulturelle Vielfalt, an der wir teilnahmen, gestaltete den kreativen Prozess um und brachte ein völlig anderes, dem ursprünglichen Ziel entgegengesetztes Ergebnis hervor. Damit bestätigte sich, dass ein Film letztendlich nur ein erweitertes Selbst darstellt.

In weiten Teilen der Welt sind die Grenzen und Flughäfen zu einem Marktplatz des Misstrauens und der Erniedrigung geworden, auf dem Freiheit gegen Sicherheit eingetauscht wird; die Waffen sind die Röntgenstrahlen, das Vergehen ist die Andersartigkeit. Trotz alledem wurde mir bei den Dreharbeiten zu *Babel* bestätigt, dass die wahren Grenzen in uns selbst verlaufen und nicht greifbar sind, sondern in der Gedankenwelt existieren. Ich bemerkte, dass uns Menschen zwar unterschiedliche Dinge glücklich machen können, die Gründe für unser Unglück und unsere Verletzlichkeit jedoch – unabhängig von unserer Kultur, Rasse, Sprache oder finanziellen Lage – bei allen Menschen gleich sind. Ich entdeckte, dass sich die große menschliche Tragödie auf die Unfähigkeit, zu lieben oder geliebt zu werden, beschränkt, auf das Unvermögen, dieses Gefühl, das dem Leben und Tod jedes Einzelnen Sinn gibt, zu erfahren und von ihm durchdrungen zu werden. So verwandelte sich *Babel* in einen Film über das, was uns verbindet, und nicht über das, was uns trennt.

Für mich stellten diese Dreharbeiten nicht nur eine äußerliche, sondern auch eine innere Reise dar. Wie jedes Werk, das dem Innersten entspringt, ist dieser Film – genau wie seine beiden Vorgänger – ein Zeugnis meiner Lebenserfahrung, meiner Tugenden und meiner zahlreichen Grenzen. Während der Dreharbeiten zu *Amores perros* und *21 Gramm* schmerzte es mich angesichts der Konzentration und klaren Zielsetzung, welche die Verfilmung einer Geschichte erfordert, neben der schönsten Seite eines Augenblicks nicht auch die vielen Szenen und Bilder einfangen zu können, die sich gleichzeitig um mich herum abspielten. Was wurde aus jenen Gesichtern und Häusern der heruntergekommenen Viertel von Memphis, in denen wir *21 Gramm* filmten, oder aus jenen müden Bäumen am Ufer des Mississippi, in denen an nebligen Morgen Trauben von Krähen hingen? Was wurde aus den zornigen Augen der Kinder, die uns auf einer Erkundungstour zu *Amores perros* mit einer Pistole in der Hand überfielen und uns später, während der Filmaufnahmen, mit unschuldiger Kindermiene den Kaffee servierten? Was wurde aus der Geste des Eigentümers jenes Hauses, das wir für die von Benicio del Toro gespielte Figur in *21 Gramm* mieteten, als wir ihm mitteilten, dass wir eine verweste Leiche unter der Matratze eines Schlafzimmers gefunden hatten? Diese Bilder und Momente existierten nur für den Bruchteil einer Sekunde und gerieten später in Vergessenheit, ohne für das kollektive Gedächtnis aufgezeichnet werden zu können.

Die Realität eines Films ist sehr viel mehr als das, was auf das Rechteck einer Kinoleinwand passt, und diese Realität bleibt unvermeidlich an allen am Film beteiligten Personen haften. Dieses Buch ist der Versuch, die flüchtigen Bilder gemeinsamer Menschlichkeit aufzuzeichnen. Bilder all dessen, was *Babel* anders enden ließ, als es begonnen hatte. Bilder der Gesichter, Formen, Winde und Horizonte, die uns alle, die wir von Anfang an wie Vagabunden gemeinsame Wege gingen, beeindruckten und veränderten.

Jeder Film könnte einen anderen Film hervorbringen. Wenn man mit den Dreharbeiten beschäftigt ist, sind die Augen und Sinne derart aufnahmefähig, dass man an jeder Ecke auf eine Figur stößt, die potenziell interessanter ist als die eigentliche Figur im Film. Doch Neugier ist der Katze Tod, und das Gleiche gilt für den Regisseur. Theoretisch könnte diese Neugier mit einem einfachen Fotoapparat gestillt werden. Ganz einfach. Ein Klick, und fertig. In der Praxis sieht es jedoch ganz anders aus.

Ein stolzer Schmetterlingsjäger kann uns hunderte, mit Nadeln in Holzkästen gespießte Schmetterlinge zeigen und uns mit den vielfältigen, faszinierenden Farben ihrer Flügel begeistern. Diese Holzkästen sind jedoch nichts als mit Glas bedeckte Särge, und den Schmetterlingen fehlt (trotz ihrer wunderschönen Form und Farbenpracht) die faszinierendste Eigenschaft eines Schmetterlings: sein anmutiger Flug. Gleichermaßen ist ein Bild, das den Körper – ebenso wie den Schmetterling – in einem bestimmten Moment erfasst, ohne Bewegung tot. Der Grund, warum ein kurzer Blick aus dem Autofenster oder eine nur wenige Sekunden währende Episode in einem Park im Kopf eines Künstlers eine ganze Geschichte oder einen Film ins Rollen bringen kann, ist, dass diese Bilder, wenn auch nur von kurzer Dauer, so doch lebendig sind. Ihr Leben ist nicht abhängig von der Zeit, die man mit ihrer Beobachtung verbringt, sondern von ihrer Wahrheit und der Perspektive des Betrachters. Zwischen dem Objekt und dem Betrachter existiert nur der Blick, und dieser Blick verhilft der Kunst zu ihrer Existenz und macht sie zu einem einzigartigen Wunder.

So wie es Rodrigo Prietos Blick vermochte, die Wahrheit und Poesie der Körper und Figuren in *Babel* in Bewegung einzufangen und darzustellen, haben vier großartige Fotografen das Gleiche mit den Parallelwelten der eingefrorenen Zeit vollbracht.

Der Grund, warum die Seiten dieses Buches mit noch immer lebendigen Bildern flattern wie Schmetterlingsflügel, als wollten sie dem Papier entfliehen, ist, dass die Personen, die diese Bilder einfingen, keine Schmetterlinge jagten, sondern ihnen – ohne sie zu berühren – ihre Seele und ihre Wahrheit entlockten. Der unverwechselbare Blickwinkel von Mary Ellen Mark, Graciela Iturbide, Miguel Rio Branco und Patrick Bard hat es vermocht, diese Bilder in lautlose Geschichten zu verwandeln. Ihrer Sichtweise ist es zu verdanken, dass ihre Fotos den Geruch der Wüste Sahara, der Wüste Sonora und sogar der Wüste Tokio verströmen. Ihr Interesse für das menschliche Gesicht, das Tier, die Mauer und die Schatten dessen, was niemand sieht, gleicht der Neugier von Kindern. Nur die Menschlichkeit, das Genie und die Vielseitigkeit dieser vier Fotografen konnten so entfernte, fremde Kulturen und Gegenden in etwas derart Vertrautes und Nahes verwandeln. Damit bestätigen sie, dass Bilder und Musik dem Esperanto am ähnlichsten sind. Die Arbeitsweisen dieser Fotografen sind zwar äußerst unterschiedlich, erzielen jedoch dieselbe Wirkung. Sie stellen die Poesie in den Dienst des Traums und ordnen die Schönheit der Wahrheit eines Augenblicks unter.

Die Emotionen und die große Würde der Personen in Mary Ellen Marks Fotografien beeindrucken mich seit Jahren. Sie hat jene Menschen porträtiert, welche die Gesellschaft ignoriert, und ist dabei auf ihre eigene Art und mithilfe ihres ästhetischen Universums weit über ein journalistisches Zeugnis hinausgegangen. Interessanterweise diente die emotionale Wirkung ihrer Fotografien in *American Odyssey* Brigitte Broch, Rodrigo Prieto und mir als Inspiration für unsere Arbeit zu *Amores perros*.

Ebenfalls in Marokko ließ Patrick Bard die Bilder in dem ihm eigenen Dokumentationsstil frei fliegen. Aus den engen menschlichen Beziehungen, die er zu den Einheimischen aufbaute, schöpfte er eine Ehrlichkeit und Natürlichkeit, wie sie nur selten erzielt werden. In jedem Bild lässt uns dieser Fotograf und Geschichtenschreiber die Schwere des Gewöhnlichen spüren.

Die Seele Graciela Iturbides, mit deren Fotografien ich aufgewachsen bin, ist so rein und erlesen, dass die Künstlerin stets zu schweben scheint. Hinter ihren funkelnden Augen verbirgt sich sehr viel Weisheit und Edelmut. Die Transparenz ihrer Bilder verleiht meinem Land einen idyllischen und zugleich wahrhaftigen Charakter. Wahrhaftig deshalb, weil sie es sieht und es uns in ihrer Arbeit enthüllt. Das genügt uns, um ihr zu glauben und es mit ihr zu feiern. Ihre Fotos in diesem Buch verströmen den Duft meines Landes. Lassen Sie sich mit Ihrem Herz auf die Bilder ein, und Sie werden feststellen, dass ich Recht habe.

Zu guter Letzt glaube ich, dass niemand besser mit Farbe umzugehen weiß als Miguel Rio Branco. Seine frühen Bücher beeinflussten mich und viele andere Regisseure. Sein berühmtes Foto eines toten Hundes wird niemand, der es gesehen hat, je vergessen können. Als Maler, Filmemacher, Fotograf, Multimedia-Künstler und vor allem als Lyriker erhält sich Rio Branco einen Zustand ständiger Neuerfindung und Evolution. Die Triptychen in diesem Buch scheinen auf abstrakte Art und Weise den genetischen Code der Stadt Tokio eingefangen zu haben. Niemand sieht, was Rio Branco sieht. An einem völlig unerwarteten Ort führen die Objekte und ihre Schatten ein Zwiegespräch.

Die Anwesenheit dieser vier Fotografen am Filmset zu *Babel* war stets eine Ehre und ein Privileg.

Die Idee zu diesem Buch stammt von meiner Frau María Eladia. Nur jemand mit ihrer Sensibilität konnte aus so vielen Schmetterlingen ein solches Kaleidoskop unterschiedlicher Farben, Gerüche und Texturen auswählen und, trotz aller Vielfalt, in einem einzigen Buch vier individuelle Sichtweisen aus drei Kontinenten und zwei Realitäten vereinen. Ihre monatelange, schier endlose Arbeit ließ schließlich dieses Buch entstehen, das sie ersann und erträumte. Dass das Buch sein Ziel erreichte, ist nicht zuletzt der Aufnahme einiger weiterer Fotografien von Murray Close, Eniac Martínez, Yvonne Venegas, Junko Kato und Tsutomu zu verdanken, die mit ihrem Talent und ihrer Sensibilität die Ergebnisse dieser Reise, an der sie ebenfalls teilnahmen, wundervoll abrundeten. Von Anfang an war das Bestreben, in diesen Fotos nicht nur das Wesen des Films, sondern auch seine parallele Realität einzufangen. Das Experiment bestand darin, herauszufinden, in welchem Maße die Fiktion der Realität ähnelt und wie sehr die Realität in die Fiktion eingreift. Unsere Absicht war es, diese Grenze zu erkunden. Dies sind die Dörfer und Gesichter, die Hochhäuser oder die im Schlamm errichteten Städte, die uns während der Dreharbeiten umgaben, in den Film aufgenommen wurden und uns inspirierten. Dies sind die realen und poetischen Welten hinter *Babel*.

Wenn ich noch einmal darüber nachdenke: Einige der schönsten Dinge können tatsächlich auf Film aufgenommen werden.

Marokko

Mit achtzehn Jahren überquerte ich als Schiffsjunge auf einem Frachtschiff den Atlantik. Ich war mit drei Freunden unterwegs und hielt mich ein Jahr lang mit tausend Dollar über Wasser. Nach Überqueren der Grenze in Ceuta fuhren wir mit dem Bus nach Marokko. Dem Schriftsteller Paul Bowles zufolge besteht der Unterschied zwischen einem Touristen und einem Reisenden darin, dass Letzterer keine Rückfahrkarte hat. Im Laufe jenes Jahres stellte ich fest, dass das stimmt.

Im Bus war er es höllisch heiß. Ich hatte eine halbe Flasche mit lauwarmem Wasser dabei. Vor mir saß ein dunkelhäutiger Junge mit wunderschönen grünen Augen und schaute mich unentwegt an. In der Hand hielt er eine Frucht, die er mir anbot. Gestenreich lehnte ich es dankend ab. Er wiederholte sein Angebot, und ich lehnte erneut ab. Dann sagte er etwas auf Arabisch zu mir, das ich nicht verstand. Seine Mutter und einige Fahrgäste drehten sich um, so dass ich mich gezwungen sah, die angebissene Frucht anzunehmen. Als ich die Frucht ergriff, verlangte er nach meiner Wasserflasche. Ich drehte mich zu meiner Flasche um, schaute dann wieder den Jungen an, überlegte einen Augenblick und lehnte ab. Daraufhin sagte er etwas zu seiner Mutter, die wiederum mich ansprach. Plötzlich schauten mich alle Leute im Bus an, als wollten sie sehen, ob ich imstande war, dem Jungen das Wasser zu verweigern. Schweren Herzens gab ich ihm die Flasche. Der Junge lachte und trank. Auf einmal taten alle Businsassen das Gleiche: Der Junge bot allen einen Schluck an, und alle tranken und bedachten mich und meine Freunde mit schallendem Gelächter. Dann bat der Junge die anderen Fahrgäste um Essen und verteilte es unter ihnen. Die Leute lachten immer weiter. Meine Freunde und ich rangen uns ein gequältes Lächeln ab, als wären wir bemüht, einen Witz zu verstehen. Es war, als würden alle Fahrgäste zum ersten Mal Ausländer sehen. Der Junge gab mir ein paar Kekse und stellte sich vor. Er hieß Abdullah und besaß einen unvergleichlichen Charme und Witz. Als wir in Marokko ausstiegen, wurden wir von Tausenden von Kindern wie Abdullah umringt, die uns nachliefen. Der Lärm war großartig.

Zurückblickend erinnerte ich mich an Marokko mit einer geheimnisvollen Aura und inmitten einer Wolke von Haschisch. Das Land hinterließ einen enormen ästhetischen und künstlerischen Eindruck bei mir. Zweiundzwanzig Jahre nach dieser Reise beschloss ich, in Marokko zu drehen, weil mich die Erinnerung noch immer mit diesem Land verband. Und wieder dauerte es nicht lange, bis die magischen Kinder auftauchten.

Als ich noch ein Kind war, brachte mir meine Mutter aus New York eine Gipsnachbildung von Michelangelos *Pietà* mit. Während meiner ganzen Kindheit schlief ich mit dieser Figur am Kopfende meines Betts. Ich wollte, dass Richard Susan so in den Armen hält, als Metapher für das leidvolle Bild. Brad schleppte Cate mehr als fünfzigmal durch lange Gassen, und Rodrigo Prieto, der Kameramann, rannte mit einer fünfzig Kilogramm schweren Kamera auf der Schulter hinter ihnen her. Als ich einige Tage später die Szene wiederholen wollte, baten mich die Schauspieler und Rodrigo um *piedad* – „Erbarmen".

Die Ursache für den Konflikt zwischen Richard und Susan war laut Drehbuch ursprünglich ein von Richard in der Vergangenheit verübter Seitensprung. Einige Wochen vor Drehbeginn schlug ich ein tiefer greifendes Drama vor, nämlich den plötzlichen Tod eines Kindes. Brad erfuhr von der Änderung bei seiner Ankunft in Marokko. Es war eigentlich schon schwierig genug, eine Figur anhand einer nur dreißig Seiten langen Geschichte aufzubauen. So war es nicht leicht, plötzlich dieses neue dramatische Element im Drehbuch zu verarbeiten: Wer war Richard? Warum handelte er auf diese Art und Weise? Täglich musste die verletzliche Figur, die Brad auf der Leinwand darstellte, unter anstrengenden physischen Bedingungen neu erforscht, entdeckt und mit Leben gefüllt werden.

Obwohl die Rolle des Richard auf den ersten Blick nicht zu einem Schauspieler wie Brad Pitt passt, war die Entwicklung der Figur ein aufregendes Abenteuer für ihn und mich. Es ist nicht leicht, Schauspieler von seinem Kaliber dazu zu bringen, solche Rollen zu spielen. Für mich bestand die Herausforderung darin, den Star Brad Pitt hinter der gespielten Figur zum Verschwinden zu bringen, um nicht nur den Schauspieler, sondern auch den Menschen hinter dieser Ikone hervorzulocken. Brad schien für mich immer eine magnetische Wirkung zu haben, die über seine Popularität hinausgeht. Es gab viele Risiken, doch er nahm alle Herausforderungen mutig an. Er stellte sich vor allem der größten Gefahr, die einem Schauspieler immer droht: sich in die Hände des Regisseurs zu begeben und den Sprung ins Unbekannte zu wagen.

Wenngleich die Erfahrungen des gesamten Filmteams während der Dreharbeiten eng mit den Filmthemen verknüpft waren, erlebte Cate eine geradezu radikale Überschneidung von Fiktion und Realität. Während ihres Aufenthalts in Marokko erlitt ihr einjähriger Sohn Verbrennungen zweiten Grades an beiden Beinen. Cate musste diesen Notfall zunächst in einem einfachen marokkanischen Krankenhaus behandeln lassen und brachte ihr Kind anschließend umgehend nach London. Zwei Tage später erteilte sie uns, beruhigt von der Zusicherung, ihrem Sohn würde es bald besser gehen, eine Lektion in Sachen Professionalität wie ich sie noch nie erlebt habe. Sie spielte wieder die Rolle der Susan, einer Frau, die aus körperlichen und seelischen Wunden blutet.

Siebzehn Tag vor Drehbeginn hatte ich noch keinen einzigen Schauspieler, so dass wir überall auf die Suche gingen. Wir besuchten die Moscheen und ließen mit Megafonen verkünden, dass die Dreharbeiten beginnen würden und wir noch Leute für den Film brauchten.

Sfia (auf der gegenüberliegenden Seite) ist eine Berberin, die in Taguenzalt neben dem Haus lebt, in dem wir drehten. Ihr tiefgründiger Blick ließ mich keine Minute zweifeln, ihr die Rolle zu geben. Ihre Szenen waren schwer zu filmen. Noch bei der zwanzigsten Aufnahme, als Cate Blanchett ihre ganze intensive Ausstrahlung einsetzte, vergaß die alte Frau, in welche Richtung sie gehen musste, drehte sich zur Kamera um und lächelte.

Mohamed kam ins Büro und suchte Arbeit als EDV-Techniker. Er bezeichnete sich selbst als Hacker. Mir gefiel sein gutmütiges und gleichzeitig trauriges Gesicht, das Gesicht eines Menschen, der hoch hinaus will, aber vom Leben nicht zur Kenntnis genommen wird. Er schien mir gut geeignet für die Rolle des Anwar.

Ich bat Cate Blanchett, die Rolle der Susan zu übernehmen. Anfangs weigerte sie sich, und das nicht ganz ohne Grund. Im Drehbuch wurde Susan als eine Frau beschrieben, die die meiste Zeit des Films blutend und halb bewusstlos am Boden liegt. Ich wusste jedoch genau, dass nur Cate der Figur Intensität und Gewicht verleihen und die Leistung aller Protagonisten am Set erhöhen würde. Und so war es dann auch: Immer, wenn ich sie spielen sah, war ich nicht nur gerührt, sondern ihr auch zutiefst dankbar, dass sie die Rolle übernommen hatte.

Wenn sie jedoch gewusst hätte, dass sie – um Fliegen anzulocken – mit klebrigem, rotem Honig beschmiert und mit Fäkalgeruch durchtränkt werden würde und sich dazu in einem vierzig Grad heißen, dunklen Zimmer ohne Klimaanlage würde aufhalten müssen, hätte sie vermutlich nicht zugesagt.

Ich kann mir auf der ganzen Welt keine großzügigeren Menschen vorstellen als die, die wir in den kleinen Orten im Süden Marokkos trafen. Wo wir auch hinkamen, bot man uns Tee, Mandeln, Ziegenmilch, ein Lächeln und den traditionellen Gruß *salam aleikum* an, bei dem sich die Menschen ans Herz fassen und eine Kusshand in den Himmel werfen. Mir wurde klar, dass der westliche Konsumismus zu geistiger Leere führt. Es stimmt, dass die Frauen zu viel arbeiten, während die Männer zu viele Teekränzchen abhalten, doch alle Menschen verwenden fünfmal täglich etwa fünf bis sechs Minuten darauf, zu beten und sich ihrem spirituellen Inneren zuzuwenden.

Für den Ort Taguenzalte war *Babel* ein Zirkus, der die Einwohner drei Wochen lang unterhielt. Die ersten, die an das Projekt glaubten und mir tatkräftig beistanden waren Jon Kilik und Steve Golin, meine Produzenten-Partner, deren Freundschaft, Erfahrung und Unterstützung waren von unschätzbarem Wert. Zusammen mit Ann Ruark arbeiteten sie leidenschaftlich und unermüdlich, um diesen globalen „Wanderzirkus" fast ein Jahr lang zu orchestrieren und sorgten dabei stets für alles nötige, um den Film zu realisieren.

Wir hatten alle eine so wunderbare Zeit mit der bescheidenen Gemeinde Taguenzalte, dass am letzten Drehtag auf beiden Seiten viele Tränen flossen. Wir sammelten Geld, um eine Stromversorgung für Taguenzalt zu finanzieren, doch Monate später kehrte einer unserer Mitarbeiter von dort zurück und erzählte uns, dass jetzt auf allen Dächern Parabolantennen installiert waren. Ich fühlte nur Traurigkeit und Verwirrung.

Ich wollte in einer Wüste filmen, die nicht romantisch oder von Dünen belebt, sondern rau und felsig war. Eine solche Stelle in einem derart großen Gebiet wie der Sahara zu finden, ist unglaublich schwierig. In einem offenen Raum wie diesem fragt man sich ständig, ob jener Standort nicht vielleicht doch besser wäre als dieser.

Diese Szene zeigt den moralischen Zusammenbruch der moslemischen Familie und erforderte daher eine große körperliche und emotionale Intensität. Wenn die Sprache eine Barriere zwischen dem Regisseur und den Schauspielern darstellt, wird die Mimik zu einem unerlässlichen Instrument. Hiam Abbass war mein Dolmetscher und Schutzengel, die emotionale Brücke zwischen den marokkanischen Schauspielern und mir.

Eines Tages, auf dem Hauptplatz in Tamnougalt, bat mich Alfonso Gómez, einen Blick auf einen ganz besonderen Jungen zu werfen. Es war Boubker. Ich erklärte ihm, dass ich eine Probe mit ihm machen wolle und ihm einige Sätze sagen würde, auf die er nicht mit Worten antworten, sondern mit dem Blick seiner Augen reagieren solle. „Deine Mutter ist tot", sagte ich zu ihm. Seine Augen füllten sich mit Tränen, und wir alle waren von seiner Ausdruckskraft begeistert. Dies war ein ganz besonderer Moment, denn ich wusste, dass ich meinen Schauspieler für die Figur des Yussef gefunden hatte. Später erfuhr ich, dass Boubkers Mutter vor sieben Jahren gestorben und sein Vater ein zwergenwüchsiger Mann war, den er nie sah. Ohne es zu wissen, hatte ich eine tiefe Wunde in ihm berührt. Nichts ist mächtiger als die Realität, denn sie lässt sich nicht vortäuschen.

Mein Freund, der Schriftsteller Eliseo Alberto, sagte mir, nachdem er einen ersten Ausschnitt aus *Babel* gesehen hatte, dass Abdullah und Hassan aussähen, als seien sie für ihre Rollen vom Himmel herabgestiegen und anschließend wieder dorthin verschwunden. Als ich ihre Gesichter unter den hunderten von Männern erblickte, die vor den Moscheen für das Casting Schlange standen, dachte ich das Gleiche. Die Gesichter dieser Männer sind biblisch und entsprechen dem Antlitz der Menschlichkeit, wie es in den moslemischen, jüdischen und christlichen heiligen Schriften beschrieben wird. Wie der biblische Josef ist auch Abdullah Zimmermann und arbeitet am Stadtrand von Fes.

Seite 93

Die meisten der rauen marokkanischen Gesichter werden sanft sobald sie lächeln. Sie besitzen nicht die Verschlagenheit, die wir ihnen unterstellen. Hassans Züge waren jedoch nur schwer aus dem Gleichgewicht zu bringen. Ich benötigte eine Figur, die sich angesichts der Einschüchterung durch die Polizei verletzlich zeigt, doch Hassan war unerschütterlich. Die Mimik war unzureichend, so dass sich Hiam mit ihm in seiner Sprache unterhielt und einen Weg zu seinen Emotionen fand. Hassan erzählte uns, dass er nie das Grab seiner Mutter besucht habe. Also nutzten wir die Dreharbeiten für eine Art Therapiesitzung, und mehr als sechs Stunden lang konnte niemand Hassans Tränenfluss stoppen. Am Ende dankte er uns, und ich dankte Hiam.

Seite 94

Unser Filmteam in Marokko bestand aus einhundertzwanzig Personen, darunter Italiener, Franzosen, Amerikaner, Mexikaner und Marokkaner, die Arabisch oder Berberisch sprachen. Wenn ein Arbeitsteam sich in sechs verschiedenen Sprachen unterhält, gibt es viele Verständigungsprobleme. Noch problematischer als die Sprachen sind die verschiedenen Sichtweisen. Wir arbeiteten in glühender Hitze und unter extremen Bedingungen. Wir mussten viele Außenaufnahmen machen und dabei hohe Temperaturen ertragen, Abhänge hinaufsteigen und sehr viel Staub schlucken. Für diejenigen unter uns, die aus der Dritten Welt stammten, waren diese Umstände etwas leichter zu ertragen, denn das Leben eines Hirten in Marokko unterscheidet sich kaum vom Leben eines Hirten in Mexiko. Sowohl Rodrigo Prieto als auch die mexikanischen Mitglieder des Filmteams und ich freuten uns über die Gelegenheit, die Lebensbedingungen und Probleme der Anwohner verstehen zu lernen.

Seite 104

Said und Boubker fühlten sich am Ende fast wie Brüder. Wie im Film war auch Said rebellisch, aktiv, spontan und nonkonformistisch, während sich Boubker passiv, introvertiert, rational und melancholisch gab. Mit der Filmgage kaufte sich Said ein Motorrad, Boubker einen Computer.

Am letzten Drehtag in Marokko filmten wir die Sonnenuntergangsszene, bei der Yussef in einer Nahaufnahme den Tod seines Bruders beweint, während er sich vorstellt, wie sein Bruder zusammen mit seinem Vater über ein steiniges Wüstenmeer läuft, in das ich ein leeres Boot stellen ließ. Diese Szene war eine große emotionale Belastung für sie. Am Anfang des Drehs hatte ich ganz spontan eine Szene gefilmt, in der die Jungen mit dem Wind spielen wie mit einem Geschenk

der Berge; zusammen wurden all diese Szenen der Epilog ihrer Geschichte. Am letzten Tag, nach Drehschluss, konnten weder Said noch Boubker die Tränen zurückhalten, da wir, die wir zu ihrer Familie geworden waren, am nächsten Tag abreisen würden. Ich versprach beiden, dass wir uns ein Jahr später bei einem Festival wiedersehen. Glücklicherweise konnte ich das Versprechen halten: Wir sahen einander in Cannes.

Mexiko

Seite 114

Die Menschen in Tijuana sind weder hier noch dort zu Hause: Alle sind auf der Durchreise. Nur an einem Ort wie diesem kann man auf eine Riesenfigur aus Gips stoßen, wie die, die ein verliebter Mann für seine Frau errichtete, damit sie von oben das gelobte Land sehen könnte, das sie nie erreichen würde.

Was einem als Erstes in dieser Stadt auffällt, ist der Zaun ringsherum. Man nennt ihn *la llaga* – „die Wunde" –, denn er ist wie eine kilometerlange offene Wunde, errichtet aus den Überresten der Metallzäune, die man für die Fertigbau-Flughäfen des Vietnamkriegs verwendete. Das Dümmste und Einfältigste an dieser Einzäunung ist, dass sie bis ins Meer führt – es könnte ja sein, dass sich ein Terrorist mit einem U-Boot nähert! Am Zaun hängen Tausende von Kreuzen mit den Namen von Männern, Frauen und Kindern, die in der Wüste oder an der Grenze zwischen Mexiko und den USA – der am häufigsten passierten Grenze der Welt – verschwanden. Sobald die Umzäunung fertig ist, wird sie das größte Denkmal der Intoleranz in der Geschichte der Menschheit sein.

Seite 120

Eines Tages erfuhr ich von einer geplanten Performance an der Grenze (vorangegangene Seite). Ein Mann wollte auf die andere Seite fliegen und würde bei dieser Mischung aus Zirkusvorstellung und politischer Geste von der nordamerikanischen Polizei verhaftet werden. Ich war nur fünf Minuten vom Schauplatz entfernt und unterbrach die Dreharbeiten, um der Veranstaltung beizuwohnen. Am Ende entpuppte sie sich als völliges Fiasko. Es handelte sich um eine „menschliche Kanonenkugel", einen Nordamerikaner, der sich der Symbolik seiner Aktion weder bewusst war noch Interesse an ihr hatte – er war einfach nur dafür bezahlt worden. Dennoch verkörperte dieser mächtige, symbolhafte Anblick den Traum vieler Zuschauer: Wenn wir doch nur Flügel hätten…

Seite 121

Ich bin Musikwissenschaftler und mag das Beste aller Genres. Aus irgendeinem Grund hatte mich jedoch nie die traditionelle Musik Nordmexikos, der „Norteño", „ergriffen". Ich mochte sie von Anfang an nicht. Nachdem ich mehr als zwei Monate in Tijuana und in Sonora gewohnt und mich notgedrungen mit dieser Musik

beschäftigt hatte, betrachtete ich sie schließlich mit ganz anderen Augen. Die Hits aus dem Radio und die Liedtexte sorgten zusammen mit meinen persönlichen Erfahrungen dafür, dass ich in dieser Musik erstmals eine emotionale Seite entdeckte. Der Schmerz und die Enttäuschung, von denen die Liedtexte erzählen, und die einfachen, eingängigen Melodien entspringen nicht dem, was man besitzt, sondern dem, was man nie sein Eigen nannte bzw. nennen konnte. Mich dieser Musik hinzugeben, war eines der schönsten Geschenke, das mir diese Erfahrung bereitete.

Seite 131

In meinem Haus in Los Angeles arbeitete eine Mexikanerin namens Julia. Sie wurde im Bundesstaat Oaxaca geboren und schaffte es erst nach sechs vergeblichen Versuchen, die Wüste unter extrem gefährlichen Umständen unentdeckt zu durchqueren. Sie hat einen zwanzigjährigen Sohn, der im Gefängnis sitzt und den sie seit über zwei Jahren nicht mehr gesehen hat, weil man sie umgehend in ihre Heimat abschieben würde. Julia lebt in ständiger Furcht: Wie Millionen von Mexikanern, die in den USA leben, ist auch sie eine unsichtbare Bürgerin. Ironischerweise haben Tausende Südamerikanerinnen wie Amelia das gleiche Glück gehabt, als sie die mexikanische Grenze passierten, die schwieriger und viel gefährlicher sein kann als die in die Vereinigten Staaten.

Mit Adriana Barrazas Arbeit erhielt der Begriff „Verkörperung" für mich eine ganz neue Bedeutung, da sie mit jeder Bewegung ihres Körpers, ihrer Hände und ihrer Augen auf liebevolle und vielschichtige Weise die Seele einer Figur verkörperte, die leicht zu einem Klischee hätte werden können. Ihre Darstellung war grandios. Gael stand mir von Anfang an für *Babel* vor Augen; wer sonst könnte eine derart widersprüchliche Figur in so kurzer Zeit darstellen. In *Amores perros* spielte Adriana noch Gaels Mutter; diesmal war sie seine Tante. Beide Male – als Sohn wie auch als Neffe – bereitete er ihr großen Kummer und ließ sie oft durch die Hölle gehen. Ich versprach Adriana und Gael lediglich, keinen Film mehr zu drehen, in dem Gael Auto fahren muss. Das hat bisher immer mit einer Katastrophe geendet.

Seite 136

Schon bei der ersten Erkundungstour auf der Suche nach Drehorten fiel mir der etwa eine Stunde von Tijuana entfernt liegende kleine Ort El Carrizo auf, der einen kargen und einfachen, aber freundlichen und aufrichtigen Charakter besitzt. In *Babel* gab es eine Nebenhandlung, die sich in diesem Haus (links) abspielte und die schwangere Braut betraf, die von Amelia zur Teilnahme an ihrer eigenen Hochzeit überredet werden musste. Am Ende entschied ich, diese Szenen zu streichen, doch irgendwie ist ihre Stimmung im Film erhalten geblieben.

Das Dickerchen auf dem Foto ist ein Junge, der sich bei keinem meiner drei Besuche in diesem Haus aus seinem Sessel erhob. Vor ihm standen ein riesiger Fernseher und ein leerer Chips-Teller.

Seite 148

Die Hochzeiten im Norden meines Landes unterscheiden sich stark von denen im Süden. Die Feste in Tijuana sind nüchtern, staubig und besitzen keine festen Riten oder Traditionen. Bei meinen Erkundungen für *Babel* besuchte ich einige Hochzeiten und versuchte, die Hochzeit von Amelias Sohn so wirklichkeitsgetreu wie möglich zu drehen: Plastikbecher und -teller, keine Blumen oder sonstiger Schmuck sowie bunte Stühle im ewigen Staub. Meine Freundin und Setdesignerin Brigitte Broch leistete wunderbare Arbeit; jeder ihrer Handgriffe hauchte der Kulisse Leben ein.

Alle Personen, die in der Hochzeitsszene (auf der folgenden Seite) zu sehen sind, stammen aus dem Ort El Carrizo. Ich habe noch nie so viele fröhliche und zufriedene Menschen gesehen. Obwohl ich viele Tage lang und mitunter bis sechs Uhr morgens filmte, beklagten sie sich nie. Mit unermüdlichem Lächeln tanzten sie pausenlos. Für mich, für sie und für das ganze Filmteam war die Hochzeit ein echtes Fest. Die Menschen kannten sich bereits, was man der Szene anmerkt.

Seite 150

So wie ich mich in Marokko mit Gustavo Santaolalla im Studio einschloss, um verschiedene Stücke der Gnawa-Musik aufzunehmen, zog ich mich in Tijuana mit Lynn Fainchtein zurück, um unzählige Lieder aus dem Norden anzuhören und aufzunehmen. Die Menschen aus dem Norden hören nur Musik aus dem Norden, die wie eine Religion ist. Ihre Themen vermitteln einen Schmerz und eine Bedeutung, die man nur verstehen kann, wenn man sie aus der Perspektive der Anwohner hört. Mit ihrer Ehrlichkeit, ihrem Witz und ihrem Kontakt zum Publikum machte die Gruppe *Los incomparables* – „Die Unvergleichlichen" – ihrem Namen alle Ehre.

Seite 155

Bernie machte mir einen Vorschlag, der vollkommen von der Beschreibung der Figur des Luis, Amelias Sohn, abwich. Ich lernte ihn in Tijuana beim Casting kennen, und wir sprachen über eine Stunde miteinander. Er erzählte, dass er im Leben schon vieles probiert hatte: Casanova, Betrüger, Schläger, Musiker, Feuerwehrmann, einfach alles. Ein echter „Tausendsassa", wie man zu sagen pflegt. Auch wenn er unbedingt verschlagen wirken wollte, so machte seine Gutmütigkeit einen Strich durch die Rechnung. Bernie ist eine für die Straßen Tijuanas typische Figur. Sein Haarschnitt in der Manier der ortsansässigen Rapper erschien mir in Verbindung mit seinen wilden und gleichzeitig sanften Augen höchst interessant. Wie er leiden Millionen von Jugendlichen im Grenzgebiet unter den Demütigungen, die mit der Überquerung der Grenze zu den USA verbunden sind.

Seite 165

In den vergangenen fünf Jahren musste ich alle sechs Monate die Grenze zwischen Tijuana und den USA zusammen mit meiner Frau und meinen Kindern überqueren. Trotz dieser vielen Erfahrungen beeindrucken mich der Kontrast und die Ungleichheit zwischen beiden Ländern immer wieder: Alle aus den USA anreisenden

Autos überqueren die Grenze und fahren in mein Land, ohne sich einer Kontrolle unterziehen zu müssen, ohne Unannehmlichkeiten. Im Gegensatz dazu wird jeder Wagen, der von Mexiko in die USA fährt, peinlich genau untersucht, so dass das Passieren der Grenze zu einem Ritual der Erniedrigung und des Misstrauens wird. Für mich ist Santiagos heftige und plötzliche Reaktion nicht auf eine einzelne Kontrolle, sondern auf all die Jahre des beständigen Machtmissbrauchs und die Verhaltensweisen der Grenzbeamten zurückzuführen.

Während drei Drehtagen versuchte ich, eine Stimmung nachzuahmen, die ich selbst mitunter erfahren habe. Wir errichteten mitten in der Wüste Sonora eine Kontrollstelle, die der in Tecate glich, und Rodrigo Prieto, Batan Silva und ich überprüften wie die Polizisten an der Grenze ständig peinlich genau das Material, das die Second Unit uns brachte.

Seite 166

Es ist erstaunlich, wie Kinder manchmal mehr verstehen als erfahrene Schauspieler. Sie gehorchen einfach nur, nichts weiter. Für Nathan Gamble und Elle Fanning, die die Kinder des nordamerikanischen Paares spielen, waren die Dreharbeiten mit großen Anstrengungen verbunden. In der Wüste Sonora war es sehr viel heißer als in Marokko. Gegen Abend waren die Kinder gereizt und müde. Neben der Hitze und der Müdigkeit mussten sie noch andere Probleme meistern. Wir filmten gerade in einer schlangenreichen Gegend, als Nathan sah, wie bei einer der Aufnahmen eine Schlange aus einem Sandloch kroch. Er war vollkommen verängstigt. Diese Aufnahme ist im Film erhalten geblieben.

Seite 168

Adriana Barraza hat zwei kleinere Herzinfarkte hinter sich. Für diese Szene musste sie viele Tage hintereinander ein dreißig Kilogramm schweres Mädchen auf dem Arm tragen und durch die vierzig Grad heiße Wüste laufen. An einem besonders heißen Tag wurden fünf Mitglieder des Filmteams wegen Dehydrierung ins Krankenhaus gebracht. Adriana fühlte sich immer schlechter; sie wurde fast ohnmächtig und bat mich um eine Stunde Pause, um sich zu erholen. Ich wollte sie zum Ausruhen ins Hotel schicken, doch sie sagte: „Nein. Ich weiß, was ein eintägiger Verzug bedeutet und wie viel Geld man dabei verliert. Gib mir einfach nur eine Stunde Zeit." Sie nahm ein Bad in ihrem Wohnwagen und kehrte eineinhalb Stunden später zurück, um weiter an der Szene zu arbeiten. Ich hatte noch nie ein solches Maß an Professionalität und eine derart außergewöhnliche körperliche Energie gesehen. Wir drehten noch zwei Stunden lang einige der schmerzlichsten Szenen des Films. Vielleicht dachte Adriana, dass wenn die Immigranten beim Durchqueren der Wüste keine Rast machen können, auch Amelia keine braucht.

Seite 172

Rodrigo Prieto ist nicht nur mein Bruder, sondern auch meine rechte Hand. Sein fast schon zwanghaftes Verhältnis zum Licht wird an Intensität nur noch von seiner Fähigkeit übertroffen, eine Szene zu erzählen

und eine Figur mit dem Pinsel seiner Kamera zu entwerfen. Als guter Schmetterlingsjäger stört er die Schauspieler nie, auch wenn er mit geschulterter Kamera und manchmal nur wenige Zentimeter von ihnen entfernt filmt. Er fließt und atmet mit ihnen.

Während wir in der marokkanischen Wüste drehten, musste Rodrigo das Set für die letzten sieben Drehtage verlassen, weil seine Eltern ihren sechzigsten Hochzeitstag feierten. Er freute sich wie ein Kind auf das Fest. Monate später, als wir in Tijuana filmten, erhielt Rodrigo eines Abends einen Anruf: Seine Mutter war überraschend gestorben. Am nächsten Morgen wollte er wie ein Soldat seine Arbeit verrichten und suchte gleichzeitig einen Ersatz-Kameramann. Vor Drehbeginn hielten wir mit dem Filmteam eine kleine Zeremonie ab. Rodrigo sprach von seiner Mutter, wie ich nie zuvor jemanden von einer anderen Person reden gehört hatte. Er brachte uns alle zum Weinen und ließ uns die Wüste noch einsamer erscheinen. Als Rodrigo zurückkehrte, sah man ihm an, dass er Frieden gefunden hatte. Er erzählte mir, dass er ein paar Worte mit einem Kolibri gewechselt habe.

Seite 174

Während wir die Szene drehten, in der Amelia von der Einwanderungspolizei verhaftet wird, beschäftigten sich alle Medien mit der Geschichte eines Siebzehnjährigen aus Oaxaca, der zusammen mit seiner Mutter versucht hatte, die Wüste von Arizona zu durchqueren. Sie waren mit einer größeren Gruppe unterwegs, als die Beine der Mutter plötzlich wie gelähmt waren, ihre Kehle zugeschnürt war und sie nicht mehr weitergehen konnte. Die anderen ließen die beiden dort zurück. Drei Stunden später bat die Frau ihren Sohn, Hilfe holen zu gehen, oder er würde ebenfalls sterben. Der Junge zog ganz allein und ohne Wasser zwei Tage lange weiter, wurde schließlich festgenommen und nach Mexiko deportiert. Er erzählte seinem Großvater, was geschehen war, woraufhin der siebzigjährige Mann nach Arizona reiste und mithilfe eines Radiosenders eine Kampagne startete, um seine Tochter zu bergen. Zehn Tage später fand man nur noch ihre weißen Lacklederschuhe, ihre beiden Oberschenkelknochen und das gelb karierte Handtuch, mit dem ihr der Sohn das Gesicht abgedeckt hatte, bevor er sie zurückließ. Die Männer in diesem Lieferwagen waren einige Tage zuvor in den USA festgenommen worden, und wir fragten sie, ob sie im Film mitspielen wollten. Ihre Geschichten waren nicht weniger schrecklich als die des Jungen.

Japan

Seite 202

Die Idee, aus der später die japanische Geschichte in *Babel* hervorging, kam mir mit einem einzigen Bild, das noch heute viele Emotionen in mir weckt. Ich spazierte gerade durch Hakone, einen etwa eineinhalb Stunden von Tokio entfernt liegenden Ort mit Schwefel-

wasser-Quellen, vertrockneten Bäumen, Dauernebel, schwarzen, flughundähnlichen Raben und einem Boden voller schwarzer Eierschalen, welche die Menschen nach dem Kochen ihrer Eier in den heißen Quellen dort zurücklassen. Es schien mir wie ein Bild aus einem Kurosawa-Film.

Als ich den Berg hinabstieg, vernahm ich schreckliche gutturale Laute. Aus dem Nebel tauchte ein geistig zurückgebliebenes Mädchen auf, das sehr langsam ging und von einem etwa sechzigjährigen Mann begleitet wurde. Alle Passanten, besonders die Kinder, mieden das Mädchen furchtsam. Der Mann aber hielt sie sehr zärtlich, liebevoll und würdevoll am Arm. Dieser Anblick berührte mich. Monate später, als ich noch immer unterwegs war und mit meiner Familie nach Stockholm reiste, traf ich auf viele taubstumme Menschen. Sie fielen mir wegen ihrer Gestik und der Dramatik ihrer Kommunikation auf. Für mich war dies eine fremde Sprache, welche die meisten von uns, die wir mit der Fähigkeit zu hören und zu sprechen gesegnet sind, nicht kennen. „Die Sprache der Stille", dachte ich. In der gleichen Nacht hatte ich einen erotischen Traum über eine junge Frau in einer Zahnarztpraxis. Ich rief Guillermo Arriaga aus Stockholm an. All diese scheinbar zusammenhanglosen Bilder boten mir einen Grund, in einer meiner Lieblingsstädte zu filmen, die ich wegen ihres mysteriösen Charakters und ihrer Widersprüchlichkeiten bewundere. Guillermo schrieb später eine wunderschöne Geschichte über zwei Formen von Mangel, Abwesenheit und Einsamkeit, die zwar verschieden, aber gleichermaßen schrecklich sind. Mitunter lassen mich Städte die Einsamkeit stärker fühlen als die Wüste.

Seite 207

Seit *Amores perros* erteile ich am ersten und letzten Drehtag eine Art rituelle Gemeinschaftssegnung. Ich mag Segnungen bzw. *bendiciones*, wie sie auf Spanisch heißen, denn das Wort *bendición* stammt ursprünglich vom lateinischen *benedicere* ab, das im Sinne von *bene dicere* so viel bedeutet wie „etwas Gutes über etwas oder jemanden sagen". Ich glaube fest an die Macht und die Kraft der Worte, die oft das ausdrücken, was unser Herz erfüllt. Ich verwende rote Rosen für den ersten Tag und weiße Rosen für den letzten Tag. Am Sonntag, dem 6. November 2005, trafen wir – eine achtzigköpfige japanisch-amerikanisch-mexikanische Crew – uns morgens um 5:30 Uhr vor Tsukiji, dem größten Fischmarkt der Welt. Wir fassten uns an den Händen, bildeten einen Kreis, beteten, legten eine Schweigeminute ein und köpften einige rote Rosen. Auf einen Ruf von Abba Eli hin warfen wir die blutroten Blütenblätter in den blassblauen Himmel über der Stadt der Kimonos und Ideogramme. Es war ein kalter, ruhiger und romantischer Herbstmorgen, ideal, um mit dem vierten und letzten Teil von *Babel* zu beginnen. Um 6:30 Uhr morgens suchte uns Tokios Polizei und verfolgte uns hektisch durch die Straßen der Stadt, um die Dreharbeiten zu beenden und den Verantwortlichen ins Gefängnis zu stecken. Um 15:00 Uhr ging ein Wolkenbruch nieder, der selbst die Insel Mishima hätte verschwinden lassen können. So begann mein erster Drehtag in Tokio.

Wie die Personen in den japanischen Filmen zeichnen sich die Menschen in diesem Land durch das aus, was sie tun, und nicht durch das, was sie sagen. So sagt beispielsweise kein japanischer Vater zu seiner Tochter: „Ich liebe dich." Japan und die Schauspielerei haben gemeinsam, dass die Gefühle in den Taten, nicht in den Worten enthalten sind. Für mich haben die Worte in einer Szene nur wenig Bedeutung. Eine gut geschriebene bzw. geführte Szene sollte selbst in völliger Stille und ohne Worte verständlich sein, da die Figur über die Handlung definiert wird. Daher rührt auch die Kraft des Stummfilms, der Kino in Reinform darstellt.

Worte sind nur kleine Boote auf dem großen Fluss der Emotionen. Ein Jahr vor Drehbeginn begann ich mit dem Casting in Japan und lernte Rinko Kikuchi kennen. Sie stellte sich stumm vor und wir führten erste Proben durch, bei denen sie mir den Eindruck machte, sie sei taubstumm. Als ich erfuhr, dass dies nicht der Fall war, bekam ich jedoch Zweifel, weil ich für die Rolle der Chieko wie besessen nach einer taubstummen Schauspielerin suchte. Später wiederholten wir die Proben. Ihr Repertoire, ihr Charakter und ihre Intensität waren perfekt, doch sie war nicht taubstumm. Als ich nach Los Angeles zurückkehrte, konnte ich Rinko nicht vergessen, wenngleich ich noch keine Entscheidung getroffen hatte.

Während der folgenden neun Monate, in denen wir in Marokko und Mexiko drehten, nahm Rinko auf eigene Faust und Kosten Unterricht in der Gebärdensprache, ohne jemanden davon zu erzählen und ohne zu wissen, ob sie die Rolle bekommen würde. Als ich nach Japan zurückkam, um mit den Dreharbeiten zu beginnen, konnte ich Rinko nicht von einer echten Taubstummen unterscheiden: Ich hatte noch nie eine solche Überzeugungskraft, Disziplin und ein derartiges Verlangen nach einer Rolle erlebt. Nur wenige Wochen vor Drehbeginn sagte ich Rinko die Rolle zu. Die Antwort war eine grenzenlose, tiefe und stille Freude voller Tränen.

Seite 220

Alle Freundinnen und Freunde von Chieko werden im Film von Taubstummen gespielt. Es war nicht leicht, sie zu finden und zum Mitwirken zu bewegen, doch noch viel schwieriger waren das Casting und die Szenenproben mit ihnen. Das Ganze lief in etwa so ab: In einem Raum saß mir ein taubstummes Mädchen gegenüber. Neben mir befand sich eine Dolmetscherin, die aus dem Englischen ins Japanische übersetzte, während eine andere Dolmetscherin dem Mädchen das Gesagte aus dem Japanischen in die Gebärdensprache übertrug. Wenn ich also das Mädchen fragte „Hast du dir schon einmal den Klang von etwas vorgestellt oder davon geträumt?", wurden meine Worte von einer Dolmetscherin aus dem Englischen ins Japanische und von der anderen aus dem Japanischen in die Taubstummensprache übersetzt. Sie dachte einige Minuten nach und antwortete in der Gebärdensprache, die von ihrer

Dolmetscherin ins Japanische und von meiner Dolmetscherin ins Englische übersetzt wurde: „Im Juni." Dieses Casting war *Babel* in reinster Form.

Seite 222

Jeden Tag, wenn ich mit dem Auto zum Set bzw. zurück nach Hause fuhr, hörte ich dieselbe CD: *Chasm* von Ryuichi Sakamoto. Sie wurde zu meinem persönlichen Soundtrack in Japan, vor allem das Lied *Only Love Can Conquer Hate*. Als ich die Szene im Park drehte, hatte ich immer ein traumartiges, schwebendes Bild vor Augen. Rodrigo und Joey bauten ein Traversensystem an der Schaukel auf, weil ich die gesamte Sequenz mit einer Geschwindigkeit von dreißig Einzelbildern filmen und ihr die Perspektive und den Rhythmus eines ekstatischen Gemütszustands geben wollte. Ich fühlte immer, dass dieser im Drehbuch vorgesehene einfache Wechsel von einer Seite zur anderen eine großartige Gelegenheit bot, Einblick in Chiekos Kopf und ihre Welt zu erhalten. Ich brauchte eine Art Adagio, das in einem Staccato explodieren würde. Erst im Schnittraum bemerkte ich, dass *Only Love Can Conquer Hate* genau das Lied war, das Chieko vermutlich hören würde, wenn sie wie Sakamoto die Klänge der Stille vernehmen könnte.

Seite 236

Wenn ich einen Film plane, mache ich keine Fortschritte, so lange ich ihn nicht klar in einen musikalischen Rahmen eingebettet habe. Mit zwanzig Jahren hatte ich eine Radiosendung in Mexiko-City, in der ich täglich drei Stunden lang und über fünf Jahre lang alles tat, sagte und spielte, was ich wollte. Ich schrieb und produzierte provokante Geschichten und Figuren, die ich mit eklektischer Musik kombinierte. Mit diesen Elementen schuf ich ein Ambiente, das die musikalische und akustische Fantasie anregte. So lernte ich, die Leute drei Stunden lang zu unterhalten. Die verfügbaren Mittel unterschieden sich nicht sehr von denen des Films.

Eine Woche vor dem Drehbeginn in Tokio besuchte ich einen Club, um Shinichi Osawa zu treffen, der heute einer der prominentesten japanischen Produzenten und DJs ist. Ich wusste, dass ich das Lied *September* (von Earth, Wind and Fire) für die Einleitung der Diskothekensequenz verwenden wollte, denn ich nutze gerne bestimmte Lieder aus dem kollektiven Gedächtnis. Gleichzeitig suchte ich nach einem etwas aktuelleren Lied, um Zeiträume und Atmosphären zu kombinieren. Ich strebte einen Kontrast aus warmen und aggressiven Tönen an, um Chiekos dramatischen Moment zu schildern. Shinichi forderte mich auf, mich hinter sein Pult zu stellen. Als er *The Joker* von Fat Boy Slim auflegte, wusste ich sofort, dass es genau das war, was ich gesucht hatte. Die Jugendlichen hörten auf zu existieren und verloren sich in einem Wirbel aus Ekstase und Schweiß. Mit ihren geschlossenen Augen sahen sie aus, als würden sie einem Guru huldigen, der sie in ein mantrisches, erotisches Land führt.

Am nächsten Tag lud mich Shinichi in sein Studio ein, um das lange Intro von Earth, Wind and Fire zu bearbeiten, das ich für die Eingangsszene in der Diskothek brauchte, und Fat Boy Slim meisterhaft mit einem großartigen Beat zu mischen. Ich filmte die Szene mit dieser Hintergrundmusik und fühlte später im Schnittraum zusammen mit Stephen Mirrione ein starkes Herzklopfen, ähnlich dem Trip der Jugendlichen.

Seite 239

Die Geschichte von Chieko dreht sich nicht um perversen Sex, sondern um das Bedürfnis nach Zuwendung. Wenn uns keine Worte zur Verfügung stehen und wir nicht in der Lage sind, mit Sprache zu berühren oder von ihr berührt zu werden, wird der Körper zu unserem einzigen Ausdrucksmittel.

Um Chiekos vielschichtige Vergangenheit in wenigen Szenen anzudeuten, bedurfte es einer ebenso vielschichtigen, jedoch tief menschlichen und empathischen Figur. In einer Welt, in der die Schauspielkunst zur Übertreibung neigt, war es ein Vergnügen, einen Schauspieler zu finden, dessen Persönlichkeit, Können und Eleganz sich in einer Sparsamkeit der Bewegungen ausdrücken, die nur wenige beherrschen. Die Disziplin und die menschliche Wärme Koji Yakushos verhalfen Chiekos Geschichte zu Gewicht und Tiefe. Seine minimalen Bewegungen, die von einem Augenaufschlag bis zu einer ausgestreckten Hand reichen, machen den Unterschied. Auf die gleiche Weise besitzt Satoshi Nikaido, der die Rolle des Kenji spielt, die nötige Größe, um genau das zu tun, was er mit Chieko tat: einer Person Würde zu schenken, auch wenn sie selbst glaubt, keine zu besitzen.

Seite 240

Beim Filmen gibt es nichts Traurigeres als den letzten Drehtag. Nostalgie ergreift das Set, und man verspürt eine Art postnatale Depression, die einige Zeit anhält.

An dem Tag, als wir Chiekos einsamen Spaziergang vor den kaiserlichen Gärten filmten, geschah etwas, das ich zunächst für einen Scherz der Art Direction unter Brigitte Brochs Leitung hielt. Alle Bäume rund um die Gärten waren mit ineinander verschlungenen marokkanischen und japanischen Flaggen geschmückt. Insgesamt entsprachen die Farben dieser beiden Flaggen dem Grün-Weiß-Rot der mexikanischen Flagge. Auf diese Weise nahmen die drei Länder, in denen wir gedreht hatten, an einem kalten, wunderschönen Herbsttag von uns Abschied. Was aber hatte eine marokkanische Flagge an diesem Tag – unserem letzten Drehtag für einen Film, der eben diese beiden Länder behandelt – und an genau dieser Stelle in Japan zu suchen? Und dann der Zufall, dass beide Flaggen zusammengenommen die Farben der mexikanischen Flagge ergeben? Ganz einfach: König Mohammed VI. von Marokko war zu Besuch im Palast. Allerdings gibt es weder Schicksal noch Zufall – alles ist vorbestimmt.

Die Fundamente für *Babel*

Ein Gespräch zwischen Rodrigo García und Alejandro González Iñárritu

Welchem Bild oder welcher Idee entsprang das Projekt? Und wie hast du das Drehbuch, ausgehend von diesem Keim, entwickelt?

Wie du weißt, ist ein Drehbuch nur die technische Umsetzung einer Geschichte. Diese ist das Ergebnis einer Idee, die wiederum dem Unterbewusstsein, der Intuition und der Irrationalität entspringt.

Vielleicht war es der ästhetische und kulturelle Eindruck, den meine erste Reise nach Marokko im Alter von achtzehn Jahren (umgeben von einer Wolke aus Existenzialismus und Haschisch) bei mir hinterließ, oder auch die vielen Nöte und Entbehrungen im Exil; im Grunde entstand *Babel* jedoch aus dem moralischen Bedürfnis, Dinge zu klären und auszusprechen, die mein Herz und mein Denken erfüllten. Ich meine die unglaublichen und schmerzhaften globalen Paradoxa, die sich überall auswirkten und schließlich in persönliche Tragödien mündeten. Zunächst reifte die Idee, die ich seit langem in mir trug; später entstand das Konzept, das die mit *Amores perros* und *21 Gramm* begonnene Trilogie mit sich kreuzenden Geschichten abschließen sollte.

Nach Abschluss von *Amores perros* unternahm ich sehr viele Reisen durch die ganze Welt, auch nach Japan, und zog für mein neues Projekt sogar nach Los Angeles. Meine Familie und ich kamen vier Tage vor dem 11. September in die USA, und die Welt um uns herum veränderte sich.

Es war keine leichte Erfahrung, in dem „Imperium" unter einem paranoiden Regime mit einem verschärften Nationalismus zu leben. Man konnte keine hundert Meter gehen, ohne auf eine nordamerikanische Flagge und einen misstrauischen Blick zu stoßen. Es war eine schwierige, quälende Zeit, und ich fiel in eine schwere Depression. Ich denke aber, dass ich, ohne Mexiko, mein Zuhause, meine bekannte Umgebung zu verlassen, nie das Bedürfnis oder den Hunger verspürt hätte, mich dieser Herausforderung zu stellen.

Die Idee zu *Babel* kam mir, als ich gerade in Memphis mit den Dreharbeiten zu *21 Gramm* beginnen wollte. Zum ersten Mal führte ich bei einem Film außerhalb meines Landes und in einer anderen Sprache als in meiner Muttersprache Regie. Erneut handelte es sich um drei parallele Geschichten von Eltern und Kindern, eingebettet in eine übergreifende Struktur mit dem zentralen Thema „Verlust". Der bloße Gedanke, die Theorie der parallelen Realitäten nicht nur außerhalb meines Landes, sondern auf globaler Ebene umzusetzen, raubte mir den Schlaf.

Ich fing an, mit dem Drehbuchautor und Regisseur Carlos Cuarón an diesem Konzept zu arbeiten. Ursprünglich handelte es sich um fünf Geschichten in fünf Sprachen, die sich auf fünf verschiedenen Kontinenten

ereignen. Carlos und ich beschäftigten uns kurz mit einigen möglichen Handlungen. In allen sollte eine Entscheidung in einem fernen Land radikale Auswirkungen auf das Leben von Menschen haben, die nie deren Ursache erfahren würden. Während wir uns damit befassten, gab eine mexikanische Zeitung bekannt, dass Carlos und ich zusammen an einem Projekt mit globaler Thematik arbeiteten. Obendrein erfuhr ich durch Zufall, dass der brasilianische Regisseur Fernando Meirelles ein ähnliches Projekt vorbereitete. Ich sprach mit ihm und stellte fest, dass es stimmte.

Carlos Cuarón beschloss damals, sich auf ein anderes Drehbuch, mit dem wir uns in der Vergangenheit beschäftigt hatten, zu konzentrieren und selbst Regie zu führen. Nach einiger Zeit wechselte Fernando zu einem anderen Projekt, und ich bat Guillermo Arriaga, wieder mit mir zusammenzuarbeiten.

Guillermo schlug mir fünf Handlungen vor, von denen dann zwei übrig blieben: die wunderschöne, homogene Geschichte der marokkanischen Kinder und der Anfang der Geschichte des Paares Richard und Susan, die auf natürliche und einfache Art mit der vorherigen verbunden war. Damals war dieser Gedanke allerdings noch nicht ausgereift. Ich entwickelte die Figur des mexikanischen Kindermädchens, das die amerikanischen Kinder hütet, weil ich nicht nur von meinem Land, sondern auch von den Immigranten und der tragischen Situation an der Grenze erzählen wollte. Hinzu kam die Figur in Tokio, ein taubstummes japanisches Mädchen, das bei einem allein erziehenden Mann aufwächst.

Die Figur der Amelia war für mich stets eine Verkörperung von Julia, der Mexikanerin, die in unserem Haus in Los Angeles arbeitet. Sie erzählte mir, dass sie die Wüste sechsmal durchquert hat und jedes Mal von den Kontrollstreifen erwischt wurde. Julia verbrachte drei Tage und drei Nächte in der Wüste, ohne auch nur eine Spur von Zivilisation zu sehen.

Bei mehr als einem Grenzgänger setzte aus Wassermangel und wegen der Hitze die eingeatmeten Luft die Lungentätigkeit aus. Erst beim siebten Versuch schaffte es Julia, die Grenze zu überqueren. Ihr zwanzigjähriger Sohn sitzt im Gefängnis, und sie kann ihn nicht besuchen, weil die Immigrationsbehörde sie nach Mexiko abschieben würde. Es gibt keine traurigeren Geschichten als die, die sich an der Grenze abspielen. Ich reise alle sechs Monate mit meinen Kindern nach Tijuana, um mein Visum zu verlängern. An der Grenze hat sich eine Ritual der Erniedrigung institutionalisiert. Die entsprechende Szene in *Babel* ist eine getreue Wiedergabe der Schikanen und Kontrollen, die ich selbst mitunter ertragen musste.

Die Idee zu der japanischen Geschichte kam mir mit einem einzigen Bild, das jedoch viele Emotionen in mir weckte. Ich spazierte gerade durch Hakone, einen etwa eineinhalb Stunden von Tokio entfernt liegenden Ort mit Schwefelwasser-Quellen, vertrockneten Bäumen, Dauernebel, schwarzen, flughundähnlichen Raben und einem Boden voller schwarzer Eierschalen, welche die Menschen nach dem Kochen ihrer Eier in den heißen Quellen dort zurücklassen. Es schien mir wie ein Bild aus einem Kurosawa-Film.

Als ich den Berg hinabstieg, vernahm ich schreckliche gutturale Laute. Aus dem Nebel tauchte ein geistig zurückgebliebenes Mädchen auf, das sehr langsam ging und von einem etwa sechzigjährigen Mann begleitet wurde. Alle Passanten, besonders die Kinder, mieden das Mädchen furchtsam. Der Mann aber hielt sie sehr zärtlich, liebevoll und würdevoll am Arm.

Dieser Anblick berührte mich. Monate später, als ich noch immer unterwegs war und mit meiner Familie nach Stockholm reiste, traf ich auf viele taubstumme Menschen. Sie waren überall und fielen mir wegen ihrer Gestik und der Dramatik ihrer Kommunikation auf. Für mich war dies eine fremde Sprache, welche die meisten von uns, die wir mit der Fähigkeit gesegnet sind, zu hören und zu sprechen, nicht kennen. In der gleichen Nacht hatte ich einen erotischen Traum über eine junge Frau in einer Zahnarztpraxis. All diese scheinbar zusammenhanglosen Bilder boten mir einen Grund, in einer meiner Lieblingsstädte zu filmen, die ich für ihren mysteriösen Charakter und ihre Widersprüchlichkeiten bewundere. Ich hatte die Idee, die Geschichte eines Vaters und seiner Tochter zu erzählen, die auf verschiedene, jedoch gleichermaßen schreckliche Weise an Einsamkeit leiden. Ich rief Guillermo Arriaga aus Stockholm an. Ihm gefiel meine Idee, und wir beschlossen, vier statt fünf Geschichten zu verfilmen. Dem folgten zwei Jahre schwieriger, intensiver Zusammenarbeit. Obwohl Guillermo weder Japan noch Marokko kennt, schrieb er dank seines Talents ein Drehbuch, das als Entwurf für die erste Arbeitsphase zu *Babel* diente.

Nach Fertigstellung des Drehbuchs, als es für das Projekt noch keine Schauspieler-Crew und keine gesicherte Finanzierung gab, lud ich Jon Kilik und Steve Golin ein, den Film gemeinsam mit mir zu produzieren. Ich selbst finanzierte das Projekt, und die beiden waren die ersten, die an den Film glaubten und das Abenteuer als Partner bis zum Schluss wagten. Im Dezember 2004 stiegen wir drei in ein Flugzeug und flogen zusammen mit Brigitte Broch, meiner Freundin und Art Directorin des Films, nach Tunesien und Marokko. Damit begann die Erkundungstour und die wahre Reise *Babel*.

Du wolltest immer einen globalen Rahmen für deinen Film, eine Leinwand, auf der ein vom Baum fallender Apfel zwei Kontinente entfernt wirtschaftliche, politische und menschliche Konsequenzen zeigt. Zu welchem Zeitpunkt wandte sich die Geschichte *Babel* von der Globalisierung ab und befasste sich stärker mit den drei Familien?

Der einzige Grund, diese drei Filme als Trilogie zu betrachten, außer dass sie eine gemeinsame Struktur und sich überschneidenden Geschichten aufweisen, ist, dass es sich letztendlich um Geschichten von Eltern und Kindern handelt. Dies war bei *Amores perros* und *21 Gramm* der Fall. Obwohl *Babel* implizit soziale und politische Themen auf globaler Ebene behandelt, ist es dennoch ein Quartett aus sehr intimen Geschichten.

Der Teil mit den marokkanischen Kindern, der sich ursprünglich in Tunesien abspielen sollte, war für mich eher eine Tragödie über den moralischen Zusammenbruch einer höchst spirituellen moslemischen Familie als eine Geschichte über Kinder, die von der Polizei verfolgt werden. Für den Vater der Kinder ist die Tatsache, dass Yussef seiner Schwester nachspioniert und diese sich nackt auszieht, mindestens genauso bedeutend wie ihr Schuss auf einen Bus. Wenn die Werte schwinden, wird alles sinnlos. Wenn ein Kettenglied zerbricht, geht nicht nur das Glied, sondern die ganze Kette entzwei.

Auf dieser Geschichte, die stets die solideste war, bauten die anderen Geschichte auf. Die Erzählung rund um das Paar Richard und Susan, das durch Marokko reist, war zunächst eher auf den politischen als auf den familiären Aspekt ausgerichtet und behandelte die Politik der Regierungen, nicht die menschliche Politik, die am vielschichtigsten ist. Dazu zählten Szenen mit Botschaftern, stellvertretenden Ministern und Fernsehsendern. Wir brauchten sehr lange um festzustellen, dass in dieser Geschichte kein Platz für archetypische Figuren war.

Wenngleich ein Großteil dieser marokkanischen Geschichte aus der Sicht von Susan gefilmt wurde, war es für mich am schwierigsten herauszufinden, wie sich Richards Perspektive darstellen ließe. Auf einmal begriff ich, dass mir die Einbettung von Richards Blickwinkel in eine hyperrealistische Perspektive ermöglichte, die Situation einer Figur zu beschreiben, die nie bemerkt, was in der Welt passiert oder in den Nachrichten erzählt wird oder welchen Druck sein Land ausübt bzw. welche paranoiden Anschuldigungen seine Regierung gegen die marokkanische Regierung erhebt. Nur über ein Transistorradio, das Meldungen in einer unbekannten Sprache sendet, und durch den Telefonanruf eines Freundes erfährt Richard kurz von den Geschehnissen, die sich ringsum zutragen. Ich überlegte, dass eine Figur mit derart reduzierten Zügen dem Publikum nicht mehr Informationen liefern sollte, als sie selbst besaß. Wann haben wir Normalbürger die Gelegenheit, an einem Gespräch der Politiker und ihrer Vertreter teilzunehmen? Dies geschieht nur im Film, doch ich wollte nicht, dass man diese Geschichte als Film empfände. Ich wollte beim Publikum ein Gefühl für die politischen Fehler und Fehlinterpretationen der Medien wecken.

Für mich handelt die Geschichte von Richard und Susan nicht nur von einem amerikanischen Paar, das gemeinsam ankommt und sich hoffnungslos in der Wüste verirrt. Es ging mir vielmehr um zwei Personen, die einander verloren haben und in die Wüste gehen, um einander zu finden. Der Schlüssel zum Verständnis dieser Figuren liegt im Verlust eines Sohnes sowie in dem Schmerz und den Schuldgefühlen, die dieses Unglück bei ihnen hervorruft.

Chieko, das japanische Mädchen, leidet nicht nur unter der Abwesenheit einer Mutter, sondern auch unter dem Fehlen der Sprache. Wenn wir nicht in der Lage sind, mit Sprache zu berühren oder von ihr berührt zu werden, wird der Körper zum Instrument, zur Waffe, zur Einladung.

Dies ist auch in Amelias Geschichte der Fall, die eine unsichtbare Bürgerin und zugleich eine nicht anerkannte Mutter ist.

Babel bewegt sich mit bewundernswerter Gewandtheit von Land zu Land und von Sprache zu Sprache und zeigt dabei großes Einfühlungsvermögen in die Menschen, ungeachtet ihrer Lebensumstände. Ich habe allerdings den Eindruck, dass deine Zuneigung im Mexiko-Teil überschäumt. Warst du dir dessen bewusst?

Die Mexiko-Geschichte zu drehen, war sehr schwierig, nicht nur wegen des komplizierten Grenzthemas, sondern auch wegen der widrigen Witterungsbedingungen. Wir filmten in den heißesten Wüsten der Erde und hatten Kinder dabei. Da es sich um mein Heimatland handelte, konnte ich leicht die Kontrolle verlieren und würde später strenger beurteilt werden. In die Subkultur des von mir früher gemiedenen und abgelehnten Grenzgebietes einzudringen und sie zu untersuchen, war ein echtes anthropologisches Abenteuer.

Meine erste Entscheidung, um dem Film gegenüber treu und kohärent zu bleiben, war, aus dem Drehbuch (und später im Schnittraum) ganze Blöcke mit Stereotypen und Gemeinplätzen zu streichen, die dramatisch nichts leisteten und dieses idealisierte, heitere Mexiko darstellten, das es nicht mehr gibt, vor allem nicht in einer Gegend wie an der Grenze zu den USA, wo die Menschen wortkarger und hinterhältiger sind.

Meine zweite Entscheidung war, Mexiko – zumindest anfangs – aus dem Blickwinkel der amerikanischen Kinder zu betrachten. Diese machten zum ersten Mal die Erfahrung, über die Grenze von San Jacinto nach Mexiko einzureisen – vermutlich wird es den meisten Zuschauern auf der Welt ähnlich gehen. Wie ich bereits erwähnt habe, überquere ich die Grenze alle sechs Monate mit meinen Kindern. Obwohl sie Mexikaner sind, faszinieren die Farben, die Süßigkeiten, die Esel, der Schlamm, die Huren, das fehlende Gras und die staubige Luft ihres Landes sie noch immer. Wo ein Erwachsener Elend und Armut sieht, erblicken Kinderaugen Farben und Freude. Wer einmal die Grenze der USA nach Tijuana überquert hat, weiß, dass die Luft dort wie geladen ist und man fast absurde Gegensätze verspürt. Manche Menschen bezeichnen Tijuana als die Achsel Lateinamerikas. Für mich ist es der Ort, an dem sich der kühnste Traum mit dem traurigsten Ende kreuzt.

In dem Ort Carrizo, eine Stunde von Tijuana entfernt, filmte ich die Hochzeit von Luis, Amelias Sohn. Im Rahmen unserer Erkundungstour besuchten wir viele Hochzeiten, von denen manch eine in einer Messerstecherei endete. Abgesehen von der folkloristischen Komponente bot mir diese Hochzeit die einzige Möglichkeit, Amelia und ihre Welt kennen zu lernen. Ich wusste, wenn ich in diesem Moment beim Publikum keine Empathie für Amelia erzeugen konnte, war diese Figur praktisch tot. Sie würde wenig mehr als ein ungebildetes Dienstmädchen sein, das die Kinder auf unverantwortliche Weise in Gefahr bringt.

Deshalb entschied ich, eine filmische Luftblase in einer imaginären Zeit zu schaffen, eine Art Kapsel, mit deren Hilfe ich Amelia als Mutter, Freundin, Geliebte und vor allem als Ersatzmutter für die amerikanischen Kinder darstellen konnte. Chavela Vargas' Lied im Hintergrund legt einen Hauch von Melancholie über die Szene. Wie viele Mexikaner befindet sich auch Amelia in der paradoxen Situation, dass sie ihre eigenen Kinder vernachlässigen muss, um für fremde Kinder zu sorgen. So geht es vielen in den USA lebenden Mexikanern, die Autos reparieren, aber kein Recht auf einen Führerschein haben, und den Amerikanern Häuser bauen, jedoch nicht genug Geld für ihre eigene Miete verdienen.

Meine Dreharbeiten an der mexikanischen Grenze waren von sehr viel Liebe, aber auch von sehr viel Schmerz gekennzeichnet, denn diese beiden Gefühle beherrschen diese Region.

Dein Umzug von Mexiko in die USA, um dort *21 Gramm* zu drehen, war eine große persönliche wie auch berufliche Herausforderung. Welche neuen Herausforderungen boten sich dir als Regisseur bei dieser Gelegenheit? Was hast du erreicht, was du zuvor nicht erreicht hattest?

Es gab große physische und logistische, aber vor allem intellektuelle und emotionale Herausforderungen. Ich bin sicher, dass jeder mit drei Orangen gleichzeitig jonglieren kann. Ich wette aber, dass dir beim Versuch mit vier Orangen die Früchte zigmal herunterfallen, bevor du die Sache in den Griff bekommst. *Babel* enthält vier Geschichten statt drei wie die Filme *Amores perros* und *21 Gramm*, so dass der Film für mich von dem gewohnten Schema abweicht. Außerdem war ich wegen der Dreharbeiten auf drei Kontinenten und in drei verschiedenen Kulturen gezwungen, das Drehbuch den jeweiligen Umständen entsprechend anzupassen und umzuschreiben.

In diesem Film erlaubte ich mir mehr dichterische Freiheit; ich fühlte mich viel ungezwungener und sicherer als bei den vorherigen Projekten. Ich versuchte neue Dinge im Vergleich zu den anderen Filmen, beispielsweise eine Koexistenz von Realismus und Hyperrealismus mit der Welt der Fantasie, mit der Kohärenz und Logik des Stummfilms, jedoch mit der Anarchie der Musik und dem Ton als Erzähler im Vordergrund.

Ich verwandelte eine Drehbuchzeile in eine zehnminütige Sequenz, die aus der inneren Sicht einer Figur erzählt wurde. Dies hat zur Folge, dass das Publikum anhand der Bilder, Klänge und Metaphern in die Figur und ihre Situation eintaucht. Bei den Szenen, die Chieko im Park oder in der Diskothek zeigen, versuchte ich, dem Publikum die Klänge der Stille genau so zu vermitteln, wie sie Chieko in ihrem Kopf und aus ihrer Perspektive erlebt. Denn die Stille kann bisweilen geradezu ohrenbetäubend sein. In der Sequenz, in der Richard und Susan per Hubschrauber geborgen werden, wollte ich mit dem Bild einen fliegenden Wal andeuten, der in das Wüstenmeer gelangt und ein Aufeinandertreffen von Kulturen und großen sozioökonomischen Unterschieden symbolisiert.

Für mich ist Kino sehr viel mehr als eine Handlung oder eine bebilderte Anekdote. Kino ist das, was zwischen zwei Dialogen geschieht und was man nur mit der Stille der Bilder ausdrücken kann. Über die Identifikation mit den Figuren, ihren Geschichten und Lebensumständen hinaus wollte ich eine emotionale Verbindung zum Publikum schaffen und bediente mich der Montage, der

Musik, der Dialektik und der Nebeneinanderstellung von visuellen und emotionalen Bildern. Das heißt, dass ich auf alle Mittel des Kinos zurückgriff, was ich in meinen beiden vorherigen Filmen nicht getan hatte. In der gesamten Komposition müssen mein Team und ich unsichtbar bleiben, wir dürfen für das Publikum während der Erfahrung, die mit dem Betrachten des Films verbunden ist, nie erkennbar sein. Wenn meine Arbeit auf der Leinwand offensichtlich ist, habe ich versagt, und alle meine bisherigen Erklärungen sind nutzlos.

Kino ist lebendig und wird phasenweise umgesetzt, wobei diese Phasen nie zu enden scheinen. Wie du weißt, kommt die Filmmontage einer Neufassung gleich. In diesem Sinne gestaltete sich die Montage des Films *Babel* aufgrund seiner Beschaffenheit besonders schwierig. Ich kann mir nicht vorstellen, mit einem anderen Cutter als Stephen Mirriones zu arbeiten. Sein Talent und seine Klarheit waren von großer Bedeutung, um diese vier Orangen in der Luft zu halten, und die Eleganz seiner Schnitte machte die Übergänge harmonischer. Wir schnitten ganze Blöcke heraus, welche die ursprüngliche Struktur des Drehbuchs verunklärten, und wieder bearbeitete ich den Stein, um seine wahre Form zu enthüllen.

Ich erinnere mich insbesondere, wie wir den Epilog für die Geschichte von Yussef und Ahmed fanden. Eines Tages, als wir die Berge von Ouarzazate passierten, kam ein ungewöhnlich starker Wind auf. Wir mussten uns fast festhalten, um nicht umgeweht zu werden. Ich gab Anweisungen, die Kameras aus dem Lieferwagen zu holen, und bat Yussef und Ahmed, am Rande der Schlucht mit dem Wind zu spielen. Das Bild hatte keinerlei dramatische Bedeutung, barg jedoch für mich eine wunderschöne Ästhetik und Poesie. Aus dem gleichen Grund ließ ich ein altes, herrenloses Boot in die Mitte eines riesigen, felsigen Wüstentals bringen, um die Präsenz des Meeres in jener Region anzudeuten. Bei der Erkundungstour in Tunesien stießen wir auf hunderte Meeresfossilien, und ich weiß, dass man mitten in der Sahara Walskelette gefunden hat. Dieser Gedanke erschütterte mich und erregte mit der Zeit Schwindel in mir. Für mich war das Boot in der Wüste eine Metapher für die Arche Noah, für die Anwesenheit des Menschen in den unermesslichen Wüsten der Zeit.

Ebenfalls am letzten Tag filmten wir von einem Kamerawagen eine Nahaufnahme von Yussef, der den Tod seines Bruders beweinte. Eigentlich wollte ich dieses Bild mit dem der Arche Noah zusammenschneiden, in der sein Bruder und sein Vater langsam in der Ferne verschwinden, um mit diesem Bild den Tod des Bruders vorwegzunehmen. Als ich aber den ersten Schnitt sah, bemerkte ich, dass die Geschichte von Yussef und Ahmed sehr früh und damit weit vor dem Filmende abschloss. Es schien, als wäre Ahmeds Tod völlig bedeutungslos. Noch schlimmer war, dass dieser Moment für den Zuschauer so weit vor dem emotionalen Höhepunkt des Films lag, dass er in Vergessenheit zu geraten drohte.

Wir brauchten einen Epilog, genau wie in den drei anderen Geschichten. Heute scheint es klar und leicht, diese kleinen zusammenhanglosen Momente zu schneiden und im Film unterzubringen, doch es erforderte viel Zeit und Arbeit. Jetzt ist diese Szene nicht nur ein großartiger Epilog der Geschichte, sondern auch einer der emotionalsten Momente des Films, denn es ist der einzige Flashforward in der Filmstruktur und lässt die Wüsten Marokkos und Mexikos metaphorisch miteinander verschmelzen: Der Wind in Amelias Haar, als sie ihren Sohn an der Grenze umarmt, ist der gleiche Wind, der auch die Kinder in Marokko schüttelt, oder der, den der zu Susans und Richards Bergung eingeflogene Hubschrauber erzeugt. Dieser Abschnitt und die Szene, die Chieko im Park und in der Diskothek zeigt, sind meine Lieblingssequenzen, bei denen Mirrione mit seinem Talent und seiner Genauigkeit eine Schlüsselrolle gespielt hat.

Eine weitere große Herausforderung bei der Montage bestand darin, von einem Land ins nächste überzuleiten, ohne einen allzu abrupten Wechsel zu erzeugen, der den Zuschauer ablenken könnte. Hier spielt die Musik eine grundlegende Rolle, und Gustavo Santaolalla war einmal mehr der Dreh- und Angelpunkt. Er reiste nicht nur in jedes einzelne Land, in dem wir drehten, um dort aufzunehmen und Nachforschungen anzustellen, sondern er entschied auch, einen *Oud*, ein sehr altes arabisches Instrument, das als Mutter der Gitarre gilt, zu verwenden und damit den musikalischen Leitfaden des Films zu gestalten. Wegen seiner harten Saiten ist der *Oud* ein schwer zu spielendes Instrument. Gustavo lernte, es zu spielen, um es für die Filmmusik zu verwenden.

Ich wollte der Musik eigentlich mehr Platz als in meinen vorherigen Filmen einräumen, doch Santaolallas Fingerkuppen schafften es auf minimalistische Weise, unser Herz mit einer einzigen Note zu brechen. Der Klang des *Oud* bietet nicht nur den Vorteil seines afromediterranen Ursprungs, sondern erinnert auch an das Wehklagen der Flamenco-Gitarre – und damit der mexikanischen Gitarre – mit einem Anflug der japanischen *Koto*. In einem einzigen Instrument vermochte es das Genie Santaolalla, drei Kulturen zu vereinen, ohne auf die folkloristischen Instrumenten jedes Landes zurückgreifen zu müssen, was undenkbar gewesen wäre.

All dies entdeckte ich erst während der Arbeit; letztendlich mache ich Filme, um das Filmemachen zu lernen: Immer, wenn ich einen Film beginne, scheint es, als hätte ich alles vergessen, was ich im vorherigen gelernt habe. Es ist, als würde ich vorzeitig an Alzheimer leiden. So bezeichne ich mich selbst nicht als Regisseur, sondern als einen Typen, der drei Filme und ein paar Kurzfilme gemacht hat und außerdem ein frustrierter Musiker ist.

Ich träume davon, in meinem Leben wenigstens einen großen Film hervorzubringen, fühle aber manchmal, dass mein Ehrgeiz Lichtjahre von meinem tatsächlichen Talent entfernt ist.

Trotz des globalen und vielsprachigen Kontexts wird *Babel* als intimer und persönlicher als deine beiden vorherigen Filme empfunden. Worauf führst du das zurück?

In allen Ländern, in denen ich für *Babel* drehte, versuchte ich, mir selbst auf die Finger zu schauen, um nicht meinen ästhetischen Versuchungen zu erliegen und am Ende ein Dokudrama vom Typ *National Geographic* oder – noch schlimmer – vier zusammenhanglose, aus der Sicht eines Touristen gedrehte Kurzfilme zu schaffen. Ich musste gegensätzliche und bisweilen widersprüchliche Entscheidungen fällen: Zum einen musste ich die Geschichten trennen und abgrenzen, zum anderen galt es, sie zu verknüpfen. Was *Babel* am Ende zu einem einzigen Film werden ließ, war die Möglichkeit, eine einzige Note zu finden, die den ganzen Film durchzieht.

Über den formalen Teil, über den ich später sprechen möchte, hinaus, betrachte ich meine Figuren mit viel Liebe und Empathie. Diese Sichtweise durchdringt den ganzen Film und ermöglichte, dass trotz der verschiedenen visuellen Stile ein einziger Tonfall und eine einzige Stimmung vorhanden sind. Ich versuchte, mich in jeder Szene obsessiv darauf zu konzentrieren, die Intimität und die winzigen Details der Innen- und Außenwelt der Figuren zu filmen. Auch wenn es selbstverständlich klingen mag, ich dachte auf lokaler Ebene, um universelle Gültigkeit zu erreichen.

Der Kern (die Seele des Films) ist die gleiche Geschichte, die viermal erzählt wird und auf den zwei großen Tragödien des Menschen aufbaut: seine Unfähigkeit, zu lieben und geliebt zu werden, sowie die Verletzlichkeit der von uns geliebten Menschen. Immer, wenn ich eine Geschichte begann, war es, als würde ein neuer Film anfangen. Am Ende liebte ich meine Figuren, litt und weinte mit ihnen und merkte, dass es der gleiche Film war, den ich ein weiteres Mal drehte.

Das Beste an den Dreharbeiten zu *Babel* war, dass ich zunächst einen Film über die Unterschiede zwischen den Menschen (und das was uns trennt: die physischen Barrieren und die Sprache) drehte, mir jedoch nach und nach bewusst wurde, dass der Film eigentlich die Dinge behandelt, die uns vereinen, uns verbinden und uns zu einer Einheit werden lassen. Diese Dinge sind die Liebe und der Schmerz: Einen Japaner oder einen Marokkaner können ganz unterschiedliche Dinge glücklich machen, doch das Leid hat für alle dieselben Ursachen.

Was das Äußere – die Form und die Ästhetik – betrifft, so entschieden mein Freund, der hervorragende Kameramann Rodrigo Prieto, und ich, das Risiko einzugehen und *Babel* als eine bunte Mischung zu gestalten: Jedes Land sollte in verschiedenen Stilen, Texturen und Formaten gefilmt werden. Theoretisch sollte jede Geschichte einen eigenen Charakter besitzen; jeder Stil und jedes Format sollten sich den dramatischen Bedürfnissen der Figuren und ihren Lebensumständen unterordnen. Meine begabte Freundin und Art Directorin Brigitte Broch schlug uns wiederum vor, diese Länder nach Rottönen zu unterteilen: Burgunderrot für Marokko, Blutrot für Mexiko und Violett für Japan. Marokko wurde in 16 mm mit ausgebleichten Farben gefilmt, Mexiko in 35 mm mit leuchtenden Farben und Japan – dank Rodrigos brillantem Vorschlag – im Breitbildverfahren mit Anamorphoten, welche die Figur hervorragend isolieren und für die Thematik dieser Geschichte geeignet sind.

Dass diese Collage funktionierte, liegt daran, dass hinter jeder dieser scheinbar willkürlichen Entscheidungen ein tieferer Beweggrund sowie eine sehr enge Zusammen- und Teamarbeit lagen. Rodrigo Prieto und Brigitte Broch sind meine rechte und meine linke Hand. Ihre Unterstützung ist für meine Arbeit sehr wichtig, und das Verständnis, das wir füreinander entwickelt haben, ist eine enorme Bereicherung für das Endergebnis.

Ich strebte stets nach einer mit den Figuren kohärenten Filmsprache und wollte erreichen, dass, obwohl der ganze Film mit der Handkamera gedreht wurde, meine visuelle Grammatik und mein Stil einen einheitlichen Atem, einen inneren Rhythmus im Dienste der Emotionalität der Inszenierung enthalten sollten.

Allem Anschein nach waren die Dreharbeiten selbst wie ein Turmbau zu Babel. Wie war es, mit Laienschauspielern zu arbeiten, die nicht deine Sprache sprachen?

Schauspieler zu lenken ist schwierig. Schauspieler in einer anderen Sprache als deiner eigenen zu lenken, ist noch viel schwieriger. Doch Laienschauspieler in einer Sprache, die ich nicht verstehe, zu lenken, war meine bisher größte Herausforderung als Regisseur. Noch siebzehn Tage vor Drehbeginn in Marokko hatte ich keine anderen Schauspieler als Brad Pitt und Cate Blanchett.

Für die Rollen der Kinder Yussef und Ahmed und ihre Hirtenfamilie sowie für alle Figuren rund um die Geschichte von Richard und Susan wollte ich eigentlich professionelle Schauspieler aus dem marokkanischen Dorf und den moslemischen Gemeinden in Paris. Doch niemand hatte das Aussehen, das ich brauchte. Ich dachte an eine gegerbte Haut, wie man sie nur südlich des Atlas und tief in der Sahara findet. Die meisten professionellen Schauspieler aber besaßen eine glatte Haut und hatten die schlechten schauspielerischen Angewohnheiten der Telenovelas angenommen. Auch wenn wir sie noch so sehr schminkten, sahen sie aus wie Schauspieler aus einem Hallmark-Film.

Dann entschied ich zusammen mit Alfonso Gómez, Hervé Jakubowicz, Marco Robert und meinem Casting-Team, die schier hoffnungslose Suche in allen kleinen Orten rund um Tamnougalt und Ouarzazate anzutreten, um dort die richtigen Personen für *Babel* zu finden. Von den Minaretten der Moscheen wurde mit schallenden Megafonen die frohe Botschaft verkündet, dass Schauspieler für den Film *Babel* gesucht wurden. Es erschienen hunderte Menschen, die wir auf Video aufnahmen. Abends prüfte ich diese Videos und suchte die Personen aus, die mich äußerlich interessierten. Zusammen mit Hiam Abbass, einer wunderbaren Schauspielerin und Freundin, die weniger mein Dialog-Coach als mein Schutzengel war, führten wir am nächsten Tag mit den ausgewählten Personen Proben und Übungen durch, mit denen ich mich jeweils für ihre emotionale Bandbreite sensibilisiere.

Für mich war dies die erste Erfahrung mit Laienschauspielern, also ganz normalen Menschen. Es war einfach unglaublich, und ich werde das wiederholen, wann immer es geht. Obwohl das Verfahren frustrierend und die Kenntnislosigkeit wie auch die technischen Einschränkungen ein Nachteil sein können, ist und bleibt die Unbefangenheit ausdrucksstärker als die Erfahrung. Die Unschuld, Reinheit und Ehrlichkeit einer Person, die sich selbst spielt, ist unvergleichlich. Ein Beispiel ist Abdullah, der Vater der marokkanischen Kinder, der als Schreiner am Stadtrand von Fes lebt, mich jedoch mit seiner Disziplin und seiner dramatischen Bandbreite verblüffte. Beispielsweise in den Szenen, in denen er seine Kinder schlägt oder sein Sohn Ahmed stirbt (und die von mir in drei Tagen gedreht wurden), behielt er die Intensität in allen Aufnahmen und jederzeit bei. Sobald ich ihm die Körperbewegungen der Sequenz vorgeführt hatte, wiederholte er sie mit Rhythmus und Präzision. Solche Szenen sind selbst für professionelle Schauspieler von Weltrang schwierig.

So geschah es auch mit Hassan oder mit Yussef. Von Anfang an zeigten mir ihre Augen, wie tief ihr Gefühlsleben war. Wenn man sich nur einige Minuten mit einer Person unterhält und ihr in die Augen schaut, kann man leicht erkennen, ob jemand viel erlebt hat oder nicht und ob er emotional geladen genug ist, um Gefühle aus seinem Inneren auf die dargestellte Figur zu übertragen.

Die Schauspieler mit den Laienschauspielern zu mischen, gestaltete sich dagegen etwas schwieriger. In der Geschichte von Yussef und Ahmed handelte es sich nur um Laienschauspieler; in der Geschichte von Richard und Susan war dies aber nicht der Fall. Scheinbar einfache Szenen wie die mit Cate Blanchett und Sfia, der alten Frau, die sich um die blutende Susan kümmert, oder die Szene mit dem Tierarzt, der Susans Wunde in Richards Beisein näht, waren ganz und gar nicht einfach. Sfia war eine fünfundachtzigjährige Berberin, die noch nie in ihrem Leben eine Kamera gesehen hatte. Sie stammte aus Taguenzalt, einem Dorf, in dem wir ohne Strom drehten, und wohnte in dem Haus neben dem Drehort. Sfia sprach nur Berberisch. Der Tierarzt war tatsächlich der Tierarzt des Dorfes und sprach nur Arabisch. Eine einfache Anweisung wie „wenn du ‚what' hörst, stehst du auf und schließt das Fenster" wurde für Sfia zu einer dreistündigen Odyssee. Es war ein echter Erfolg, dass sie es schaffte – zweimal auf die gleiche Weise –, und vor allem, dass sie sich nicht zur Kamera umdrehte und lächelte.

Ich lernte, dass wenn ein Regisseur jemanden auswählt, der äußerlich auf den ersten Blick das Wesentliche einer Figur zum Ausdruck bringt, und wenn die betreffende Person auch nur ein einziges Merkmal mit der Figur gemeinsam hat, der Regisseur nach der Entdeckung dieser Person und einer klaren Darstellung seiner dramatischen Absichten jeden Menschen auf der Welt zum Schauspieler machen kann.

Wie war die Erfahrung, mit einem Weltstar wie Brad Pitt inmitten dieses Ensembles aus Laienschauspielern und unter derart widrigen Umständen zu arbeiten? Was hat dich bewogen, ihn und Cate Blanchett auszuwählen?

Die Arbeit mit den professionellen Schauspielern von *Babel* war eine ebenso wertvolle Erfahrung wie die Zusammenarbeit mit den Laienschauspielern. Auch wenn sich Fiktion und Realität während der Dreharbeiten einige Male überschnitten und schwierige Umstände und Arbeitsbedingungen (das Klima, die Drehorte, die verschiedenen Sprachen) herrschten, erfuhr ich stets Unterstützung vonseiten der Schauspieler, die mir großes Vertrauen entgegen brachten.

Obwohl die Rolle des Richard auf den ersten Blick nicht zu einem Schauspieler wie Brad Pitt passt, hat mich seine magnetische Wirkung, die über seine Popularität hinausgeht, immer beeindruckt. Er hat die Ausstrahlung einer Person, die mit sich selbst zufrieden ist. Als ich ihn vor vier Jahren kennen lernte, fiel mir von Anfang an sein Mut auf. Wir drehten zusammen eine Werbekampagne für japanische Jeans, die aus einer Reihe von absurden Bildergeschichten bestand, die ich mir spontan ausdachte. Brad bestand darauf, bei der Arbeit bis an seine physischen Grenzen zu gehen, und brachte sich damit sogar in Gefahr. Die Produktionsfirma wurde angesichts unseres Vorgehens nervös, setzte ein Schreiben auf, dass sie nicht für mögliche körperliche Schäden bei Brad haften würde, und bat ihn, dies zu unterschreiben. Sein Agent war blass und erschrocken und bat Brad, den Unfug zu unterlassen und dieses Dokument auf keinen Fall zu unterschreiben. Brad würdigte ihn keines Blickes, unterschrieb die Papiere und machte weiter, was er wollte. Wir drehten noch ein paar Stunden und hatten sehr viel Spaß. In der letzten Bildergeschichte sieht man, wie Brad auf einem Surfbrett das schmale Geländer einer riesigen Treppe hinabfährt.

Als ich ihm vier Jahre später die Rolle des Richard in *Babel* anbot, nahm er sie ohne Einwände an. Es ist nicht leicht, Schauspieler und Stars von seinem Kaliber dazu zu bringen, solche Rollen zu spielen. Schließlich ist mit jedem Independent- und Low-Budget-Film auch ein gewisses Risiko verbunden, und gute Vorsätze bringen nicht immer gute Resultate hervor.

Für mich bestand die Herausforderung darin, den Star Brad Pitt hinter der Figur zum Verschwinden zu bringen, um nicht nur den Schauspieler, sondern auch den Menschen hinter diesem Image hervorkommen zu lassen. Wenn die Leute am Ende vergessen würden, wer er war, und er sich mit den anderen Figuren vermischen konnte, ohne herauszustechen, wäre dies nicht nur ein Erfolg für Brad Pitt, sondern auch für den Film selbst. Es gab viele Risiken, doch Brad nahm alle Herausforderungen mutig an. Er stellte sich vor allem der größten Gefahr, die den Schauspielern immer droht: Er gab sich in meine Hände und schenkte mir sein Vertrauen. Dieser Prozess war nicht leicht, denn Brad hatte private Probleme zu meistern; trotzdem vermischte er nie sein Privat- mit seinem Berufsleben.

Die Ursache des Konflikts zwischen Richard und Susan lag im Drehbuch ursprünglich bei einem von Richard in der Vergangenheit verübten Seitensprung. Einige Wochen vor Drehbeginn schlug ich ein tiefer liegendes Drama vor, nämlich den plötzlichen Tod eines Kindes. Brad erfuhr von der Änderung erst bei seiner Ankunft in Marokko. Es war eigentlich schon schwierig genug, eine Figur anhand einer nur dreißig Seiten langen Geschichte zu entwickeln. So war es nicht leicht, auf einmal dieses neue dramatische Element im Drehbuch zu verarbeiten: Wer war Richard? Warum handelte er auf diese Art und Weise? Tagtäglich musste die verletzliche Figur, die Brad auf der Leinwand umsetzte, unter anstrengenden physischen Bedingungen erforscht, gefunden und mit Leben gefüllt werden.

Aufgrund der körperlichen Erschöpfung und der stetigen Gefühlsintensität, die seine Rolle erforderte, wurde Brad wie die von ihm verkörperte Figur immer zerbrechlicher und empfindlicher, bis zu jener Szene, in der er eine große Selbstbeherrschung und Sensibilität ausstrahlt und die mir persönlich so gut gefällt: Richards letztes Telefongespräch mit seinem Sohn, das uns am Ende auf universelle Weise die Machtlosigkeit des Menschen enthüllt und bei dem sich Brad völlig verausgabte.

Mit Cate Blanchett war es anders: Sie war lange Zeit eine meiner Lieblingsschauspielerinnen, und ich habe sie buchstäblich angefleht, die Rolle der Susan zu übernehmen. Sie weigerte sich, und zwar aus gutem Grund. Im Drehbuch wurde Susan als eine Frau beschrieben, die die meiste Zeit des Films blutend und halb bewusstlos auf dem Boden liegt. Meiner Meinung nach gewannen die Ereignisse jedoch erst aus Susans Sicht an Intensität und Bedeutung, was ich Cate auch so erklärte. Um beim Publikum innerhalb von fünfundzwanzig Minuten Zuneigung und Verständnis für eine Figur zu erzielen, die sich anfangs die Hände mit Desinfektionsmittel reinigt, die Coca Cola nach ihrem Mann wirft und sich mit jedem Zentimeter ihres Lebens und ihres Körpers als höchst unangenehme Person erweist, bedurfte es einer Schauspielerin von Cates Format. Jeder Moment ihrer Auftritte – ganz gleich ob sie steht, schläft oder sitzt – steckt voller Emotion. Von der ersten Szene an bestimmt sie die Regeln und das Niveau des Spiels.

Mich verblüfft noch immer der Moment, in dem sie Pfeife raucht, obwohl ich diese Szene schon so oft gesehen habe. Es scheint leicht zu sein, doch was sie tut, sagt und dich mit ihren Augen fühlen lässt (und nur mit den Augen, weil sie keinen anderen Körperteil bewegen kann), ist einfach unglaublich.

Selbst wenn sie aus den zuvor genannten Gründen fünfundzwanzig Aufnahmen in ein und derselben Position wiederholen musste, damit der Tierarzt oder Sfia ihre Zeile bzw. ihren Rhythmus finden konnten, bot mir Cate jedesmal die gleiche intensive Ausstrahlung. Ihre Großzügigkeit und Professionalität erleichtern die Arbeit jedes Regisseurs.

Wie wirkte es sich auf dein Leben aus, um die halbe Welt zu reisen und mit Menschen derart unterschiedlicher Herkunft und Gewohnheit zusammenzuleben? Inwiefern veränderte *Babel* deine Sichtweise der Dinge?

Ich denke, dass dich alle Filme verändern; doch dieser Film hat mich aus vielen Gründen am meisten verändert. Es war eher eine Lebensentscheidung als eine berufliche Wahl. Ich wusste, dass damit Opfer und Veränderungen im Alltag meiner Familie, die mein Lebensmittelpunkt und mein Ausgangspunkt ist, verbunden waren. Ich wusste, dass wir – meine Kinder, meine Frau und ich – menschlich von dieser Erfahrung profitieren würden, aber auch, dass viele Opfer gebracht werden mussten. Man kann nicht mehr derselbe sein, nachdem man mit so vielen Personen zusammen war und sich auf sie eingelassen hat. Wenn ich vor Drehbeginn eine zynischere und pessimistischere Haltung gegenüber dem Leben hatte, war ich am Ende hoffnungsvoller und optimistischer hinsichtlich des Menschen, denn alle diese Vorurteile und inneren Barrieren können tatsächlich in sich zusammenbrechen, wenn wir uns einfach berühren. Ich bemerkte, dass das Aufeinanderprallen der nordamerikanischen und der moslemischen Kultur nicht auf einer radikalen Gegensätzlichkeit, sondern auf ihrer unglaublichen Ähnlichkeit beruht. Ihr Fanatismus, ihr extremer Nationalismus und die Art und Weise, wie sie die Frau zum Objekt machen, sind sich sehr ähnlich, auch wenn sie unterschiedlich scheinen mögen.

Während der Dreharbeiten zu *Babel* stellte ich fest, dass die Menschen im Grund gut und umso reiner und glücklicher sind, je weniger sie besitzen.

Ich weiß, dass du ein tief religiöser und spiritueller Mensch bist. Doch obwohl deine Filme jüdisch-christliche Themen wie den Sündenfall, die Erlösung oder die Schuld behandeln, steht die Religion nicht im Mittelpunkt deiner Geschichten, nicht einmal in *Babel*, wo es um Menschen aus verschiedenen Kulturen geht. Warum trafst du diese Entscheidung und noch dazu in einer Zeit, in der die Flagge der Religion hochgehalten wird?

Für mich findet Religion eher auf intellektueller als auf moralischer Ebene statt. Anders als in *21 Gramm*, als ich mit der Figur von Benicio del Toro das Phänomen des religiösen Fanatismus ergründete, war in *Babel* kein Platz für das Thema Religion. Dieser Film behandelt gerade die Verletzlichkeit und Zerbrechlichkeit des Menschen bzw. der Tierchen, die wir im Grunde sind. Dass wir selbst beim Urinieren noch lieben und des Mitmenschen bedürfen. Dass uns die Einsamkeit tötet und uns der Liebesentzug vernichtet, ebenso wie der Verlust eines Liters Blut. In einer Szene beobachtet Richard, wie Anwar in Richtung Moschee betet, und schaut ihn an, als wolle er einen Glauben finden, den er selbst unglücklicherweise nicht besitzt.

Im biblischen Babel stiftete Gott die Verwirrung, und der Mensch muss heute die Lösung finden. Gott ist nicht in dieser Gleichung enthalten.

Du hast während deiner Karriere als Filmregisseur meist mit den gleichen Personen gearbeitet: Rodrigo Prieto, Brigitte Broch, Guillermo Arriaga, Martín Hernández. Wie war die Erfahrung, sich mit ihnen zu entwickeln, mit ihnen zu wachsen? Inwiefern haben ihre Stile und Talente deine Filme beeinflusst?

Ich lernte Rodrigo Prieto als Kameramann kennen, als ich noch Werbespots drehte und wir bei verschiedenen Kampagnen zusammenarbeiteten. Ich werde nie vergessen, wie ich ihn – nachdem ich ihm das Drehbuch zu *Amores Perros* geschickt hatte – zum Essen einlud, um unsere Gedanken zur visuellen Gestaltung des Projekts auszutauschen. Ich nahm eine Reihe von Fotobüchern als Illustrationen für meine Vorstellungen mit, und Rodrigo holte genau die gleichen Bücher aus seinem Koffer. In diesem Moment war mir klar, dass wir uns gut verstehen würden und wir eine gemeinsame Sicht der Dinge besaßen. Die Aufnahmen mit Rodrigo zu planen oder mit ihm am Set zu arbeiten, ist eine wahre Freude;

ihn die Kamera führen zu sehen, ist ein Erlebnis; geradezu unglaublich ist es jedoch, später im Schnittraum in allen Einzelheiten zu sehen und zu entdecken, in welch unvergleichlicher Manier er mit der Kamera selbst kleinste emotionale Details wiedergibt.

In *Babel* gab es nur drei Szenen, für die wir einen Kamerawagen verwendeten, darunter die letzte Szene und eine Nahaufnahme von Yussef, der den Tod seines Bruders beweint. Alles andere filmte Rodrigo mit geschulterter Kamera. Von *Amores perros* bis *Babel* habe ich eine unglaubliche Weiterentwicklung bei ihm festgestellt. Sein Umgang mit dem Licht und seine professionellen Kenntnisse sind großartig und werden nur noch von seinen eleganten Umgangsformen übertroffen. In einem Film steht mir niemand so nahe wie er. Wir kennen uns so gut, dass uns eine einzige Geste oder ein einfacher, unverständlicher Laut genügt, um eine ganze Filmstrategie zu bestimmen. In über zwölf Jahren, die wir uns nun schon kennen und zusammenarbeiten, gab es nicht einen einzigen unerfreulichen Moment zwischen uns.

Brigitte Broch lernte ich fast zur gleichen Zeit wie Rodrigo kennen; wir arbeiteten zum ersten Mal im Rahmen einer Werbekampagne zusammen, die viele internationale Preise gewann (und bei der ich interessanterweise auch erstmals mit Gael García Bernal arbeitete). Brigitte ist die Lebensbejahung in Person: Wenn sie eine Atmosphäre schafft, spricht jeder Gegenstand und jedes Detail, und seien sie noch so geringfügig, und tragen zu einer tiefgründigen Beschreibung der Figuren bei. Wir drehen gerne im Freien, und Brigitte hat stets ein besonderes Gespür für die besten Drehorte – nicht etwa wegen ihres Erscheinungsbilds, sondern wegen ihrer Seele und der Energie. Bei unseren ständigen Gesprächen rund um Farben, Texturen, Gerüche und Formen während der endlosen Erkundungstouren in aller Welt reden wir im Grunde über das Leben. Meine Filme und mein Leben wären ohne sie nicht dasselbe.

Martín Hernández und ich studierten zusammen an der Universität. Unser erstes gemeinsames Projekt entstand, als wir etwa zwanzig Jahre alt waren: Ich war Regieassistent und Filmkomponist bei einem Kurzfilm eines gemeinsamen Freundes; Martín war der Tontechniker. Später fingen wir gemeinsam bei einem Radiosender an und hatten jeder eine dreistündige Sendung. Er war fünf Jahre lang der meistgehörte Radiosender in Mexiko-Stadt. Ich begann, freche, provozierende Geschichten, Figuren und Episoden zu erfinden, die Martín fürs Radio produzierte. Heute, zweiundzwanzig Jahre später, arbeiten wir noch immer zusammen, und nicht nur unsere Zuneigung ist gewachsen. Martín besitzt wie kein anderer diese sonderbare Fähigkeit, dich die Haut des Klangs sehen und spüren zu lassen.

Pelayo Gutiérrez, der Regisseur des Kurzfilms, bei dem ich Martín kennen lernte, stellte mir Guillermo Arriaga vor. Ich hatte damals in irgendeiner Zeitung erklärt, dass die Professoren an den mexikanischen Universitäten ein überaus schlechtes Niveau hätten; Guillermo war zu dieser Zeit Hochschullehrer. Als er zu dem Essen kam, bei dem uns unser Freund Pelayo einander vorstellen wollte, war er bereits schlecht auf mich zu sprechen. Doch im Laufe dieses Treffens fanden wir

viele Gemeinsamkeiten, und am Ende bat ich ihn, ein Szenario auszuarbeiten, das ich damals entwickelte und das Sinn und Zweck unseres Geschäftsessens war. Unsere Freundschaft wuchs, und jenes erste Treffen brachte mehrere gemeinsame Träume und Projekte hervor. Damit begann eine erfolgreiche Beziehung, aus der *Amores perros* entstand. Guillermo ist ein großartiger Drehbuchautor: Seine Erzählkunst und die Fähigkeit, komplizierte Situationen in zwei Zeilen zusammenzufassen und unerwartete Lösungen für große Probleme zu finden, sind einzigartig. Er ist ein fabelhafter Partner mit einer eigenen Welt, der gleichzeitig flexibel genug ist, seine Arbeit in Teamarbeit umzusetzen, und daher die Geschichte und die Figuren in den Dienst des Films zu stellen vermag.

Lynn Fainchtein dagegen war unsere „Feindin". Sie hatte eine Radiosendung bei einem Konkurrenzsender und wurde von uns immer in der Luft zerrissen, auch wenn sie dies bestreitet. Ganz im Ernst, sie hatte einen tadellosen Musikgeschmack, und ihre Sendung war die einzige, die ich mich außerhalb meines Senders zu hören traute – ohne dass irgendjemand davon wusste. Heute sind wir dicke Freunde. Ihr Musikgeschmack ist noch immer der gleiche: eklektisch und erlesen. Da wir derselben Generation angehören, haben wir einen ähnlichen Musikgeschmack, so dass sie meine Filme zum Tanzen bringt. Sie war es auch, die mich auf Gustavo Santaolalla aufmerksam machte, indem sie mir eine Platte von Ron Rocco vorspielte, als ich auf der Suche nach einem Musiker für *Amores perros* war.

Ich erinnere mich, dass ich mit einer VHS-Videokassette und einem Ausschnitt aus *Amores perros* nach Los Angeles flog, um ihn Santaolalla vorzuspielen. Er wollte die Filmmusik nur dann übernehmen, wenn ihm der Film gefiel. Während er ihn sich ansah, ging ich in den Garten und rauchte eine Packung Zigaretten. Zwei Stunden später kam er mit verweinten Augen heraus. Eine innige Umarmung besiegelte eine Freundschaft fürs Leben. Niemand ist wie er in der Lage, dir mit einer einzigen Note eines beliebigen Instruments das Herz zu brechen. Aníbal ist sein Partner und Seelenverwandter. Diese beiden Halunken waren grundlegend für meine Filme.

Davon abgesehen gibt es am Set einen einzigen Guru, einen Typ, dessen Gegenwart alle suchen. Wo immer er geht und steht, verbreitet er Ausgeglichenheit und gute Laune und ist wie ein Therapeut. Er wird *el Tiburón* – „der Hai" – genannt und heißt eigentlich José Antonio García. Er ist nicht nur ein hervorragender Tontechniker, sondern dank seiner Freundschaft und menschlichen Eigenschaften für mich einzigartig.

Ebenfalls von größter Bedeutung für *21 Gramm* und *Babel* war Alfonso Gómez Rejón. In *21 Gramm* war er mein persönlicher Assistent und half mir bei einer äußerst wertvollen Studie zu den Figuren. Diesmal, bei *Babel*, leitete er das Casting, war Ermittler und Second Unit Director. Sein Material war unentbehrlich, und seine Hilfe beim Casting auf der Straße einfach unglaublich.

Ich könnte dir noch stundenlang erzählen, wie wichtig mir noch andere Personen sind und waren, wie beispielsweise Tita Lombardo, Line Producer bei *Amores*

perros und auch bei *Babel*. Ich sehe sie als meine Patin im Filmwesen an. Corinne Weber, die schon seit fünf Jahren meine Assistentin ist und Co-Produzentin von *Babel* war. Robbie und Joey, die Rodrigos Oberbeleuchter und Kabelträger sind und seit *21 Gramm* verblüffende technische Kunststücke vollbracht haben, um den Bedürfnissen des Films gerecht zu werden; sie gehören mittlerweile zur Familie. Oder Batan Silva, der diesmal erstmals mein Regieassistent war und in Japan für einen krönenden Abschluss sorgte.

Am unglaublichsten war jedoch das Privileg und die Gelegenheit, zum ersten Mal mit Jon Kilik, Steve Golin und Ann Ruark zu arbeiten. Bei einer Produktion von diesem Kaliber ist es nicht leicht, die Vision des Films stets aufrechtzuerhalten und gleichzeitig die unzähligen logistischen und finanziellen Probleme zur Umsetzung des Films zu lösen. Unglaublich, aber wahr: Wir behielten stets und bis zuletzt eine gute Kommunikation sowie viel Solidarität und Respekt bei. Der Film wurde wie geplant gut abgeschlossen, und alle leisteten hervorragende Arbeit im finanziellen, technischen und menschlichen Bereich.

Ann Ruark, Co-Produzentin und Line Producerin, ist einer der wenigen Menschen, die alle Tricks rund ums Filmemachen verstehen und beherrschen und dabei auch noch Klasse haben.

Wer hätte gedacht, dass mein guter Freund und Agent John Lesher, der mir anfangs bei der Entwicklung und Fertigstellung des Projekts half, nun *Babel* ins Kino bringen würde?

Ich hatte das Glück, Brad Grey zur rechten Zeit zu treffen, als er gerade seinen Traum verwirklichte, Paramount Pictures zu verändern. Vom ersten Augenblick an vertraute er uns und dem Projekt hundertprozentig und unterstützte uns mit großem Respekt und der nötigen Freiheit, diesen Film zu machen.

Wenn die Arbeit im Rahmen einer Familie wie der unseren verrichtet wird, ähneln die Dreharbeiten eher einer Rockgruppe auf Tournee als einem Filmteam beim Drehen. Die engen und gleichzeitig flüchtigen Beziehungen, die beim Filmdreh entstehen, sind nicht leicht zu verarbeiten, da man über längere Zeit und meist an fernen Orten mehr mit dem Team als mit der eigenen Familie zusammenlebt. Wenn die Dreharbeiten zu Ende sind, weißt du, dass du eine Person, die du so sehr geliebt hast, möglicherweise nie wieder siehst. In meinem Fall ist es anders, denn ich kannte alle Mitglieder meiner kreativen Familie bereits lange Zeit, bevor ich Filmemacher wurde. Daher bin ich gleich zweifach gesegnet: Ich habe eine Arbeit, die mir gefällt, und verrichte sie im Kreise meiner Freunde.

La mémoire des blessures

Préface par Eliseo Alberto

*Sans doute n'est-il pas d'autre mémoire
que la mémoire des blessures*

Czeslaw Milosz

Un livre de photographies peut ou doit aussi être une fenêtre. Il s'ouvre à la lumière et se referme à l'ombre.

Toute image se fixe dans le clair-obscur de la mémoire. Elle s'imprime par le biais d'un larcin nécessaire aussi bien qu'impuni.

Un œil l'a vue et saisie au vol : ensuite, des milliers de pupilles se l'approprient, ou encore la recréent sans demande d'autorisation.

Ni de pardon.

Ceux qui s'approchent de ce livre ne pourront que céder au désir de l'explorer avec la longue-vue de l'émotion, ce sentiment d'esprits troublés qui surprend l'homme chaque fois qu'il se sait participer à une expérience créative – qu'il s'agisse de la sienne propre ou de celle d'autrui.

Dans *Babel*, le livre, l'émotion frémit à mi-chemin entre les extrêmes de la passion et de la raison.

Chaque page renferme un paysage humain, portrait du temps qu'elle nous lègue en héritage.

Qu'elle s'arrête sur le désert d'un visage au beau milieu du désert même du Maroc ou dans la plaine du regard errant dans les éternités de Tijuana tel un oiseau aveugle qui ne trouve de nid nulle part.

Dans quel coin de l'univers se trouve cette mer de rochers où flotte une barcasse abandonnée sans timonier ni poissons ni hameçons ? Qui a bien pu l'abandonner là ? Est-ce de ce fantôme que nous nous inquiétons aujourd'hui ?

Le cosmos s'arrête un moment sur la douleur d'un père qui embrasse sa fille nue au sommet d'un gratte-ciel de Tokyo : assurément, c'est Dieu lui-même qui les abrite.

Il a oublié un moment sa superbe et souffle sur eux comme sur nous son silence.

Le silence explique presque toute chose.

Le vent a ses raisons de fouetter. Nous ne l'entendons pas dans les œuvres des maîtres photographes Patrick Bard, Graciela Iturbide, Mary Ellen Mark et Miguel Rio Branco. Et elle est muette, la musique dans cet antre de Tokyo où une adolescente désemparée se cherche elle-même au point qu'elle finira par se trouver dans la pureté de son intacte nudité.

Si ce n'était par le silence de l'image, comment s'expliquerait la désespérance gelée de cette femme perdue dans le désert qui sent peser sur elle le fardeau d'une tristesse imméritée ? Les enfants dont elle est responsable se déshydratent au soleil, perdus en plein néant. Ici, le seul espoir est la flaque d'ombre d'un arbuste.

Pourquoi écoutons-nous le tremblement silencieux des petits bergers marocains tourmentés par l'écho d'un tir de fusil ?

Elle est sourde la balle qui traverse la vitre de l'autobus et qui s'enfonce au plus près du cœur d'une femme trop belle pour mourir si jeune, et sourde la douleur convulsée de son mari qui réalise à quel point ils ont tous deux besoin de l'autre, à présent que l'amour se vide de son sang et s'écoule en un filet d'aveux.

S'il suffit d'une seconde pour mourir, pourquoi ne suffirait-elle pas à changer notre vie ?

Le monde tient dans l'éternité de la seconde.

Toujours prétentieuse, la mort se soustrait au portrait.

L'âme de la photographie, comme de presque tout dans cette vie, est la paix. La paix n'est pas docile, mais héroïque. Tôt ou tard elle s'impose, n'importe le prix.

Elle le savait très bien, María Eladia Hagerman, quand elle réunit quatre génies de l'art contemporain pour leur faire rejoindre la troupe qui allait suivre le cinéaste Alejandro González Inarritu (et ses fidèles compagnons de voyage) dans l'aventure d'un tournage et d'un tour du monde, dans la poursuite rêvée d'un long métrage qui paraissait alors une folie aussi insurmontable que son antécédent biblique : inventer les miradors de Babel, symbole du passé de l'homme sur terre. Jamais González Inarritu ne s'était lancé un tel défi. Le résultat est tout simplement extraordinaire, un chef-d'œuvre du cinéma. Il y a bien longtemps que je n'ai plus peur des adjectifs : la perfection narrative de *Babel*, le film, nous montre que les fragilités et les forces humaines s'équilibrent en chacun de nous. C'est pourquoi, quand nous quittons la salle obscure, il semble inévitable que nous finissions par penser à nous-mêmes, aux douleurs qui nous gouvernent et aux illusions qui pourraient nous sauver de ce mal que nous appelons la solitude. J'ose affirmer que rarement dans l'histoire du cinéma et de la photographie, autant de talent a pu être réuni au sein d'une seule et même aventure artistique.

Babel, le livre, est et n'est pas le témoignage graphique de cette expérience. Les regards des photographes ne se bornent pas à scruter les drames de l'histoire qu'on se propose de filmer avec rigueur, professionnalisme et inspiration. La faculté d'observation tout à fait unique de chacun d'eux sonde l'espace environnant, entre la scène et l'horizon, avec une tendresse et une sagacité infinies, preuve irréfutable que l'intelligence est sans doute possible une exigence incontournable de l'art.

J'écoutais récemment ce cri peint à la main sur un mur de Mexico : « Assez de réalités : nous voulons des promesses ! » Et j'ai eu peur soudain d'habiter moi aussi ce monde d'illusions désespérées.

Les livres et les films comme ceux de *Babel* rendent une âme au corps.

Si dure que devienne la vie, si abrutissant que soit le pessimisme, si noire que soit la longue nuit qui nous attend, la vie est un exploit qui vaut la peine d'y participer.

Le silence sonore du film parcourt tout le livre. L'image elle aussi se lit. Les mots deviennent superflus.

Ouvrez grands les deux battant de cette fenêtre de *Babel* : il se pourrait bien que de l'autre côté, vous vous trouviez vous-même.

Chasseurs de papillons

Introduction d'Alejandro González Iñárritu

Il m'est arrivé de rêver que les paupières puissent conserver ou graver en elles les labyrinthes sans fin des images qui passent par la rétine, et que ces paupières, imprégnées comme un papier calque, puissent ensuite être exprimées de manière à recueillir tous les souvenirs de notre vie. Mais pour leur immense majorité, toutes ces images s'évanouissent, et rares sont celles qui survivent à la dissolution. Ainsi, de même que le présent n'est qu'une angoissante tranche de temps constamment dévorée par le passé, pour moi, comme réalisateur de cinéma, il est tout aussi angoissant de voir passer à travers la vitre de ma voiture des centaines ou des milliers d'images et de personnes qui défilent de gauche à droite sur ma rétine pour disparaître ensuite de ma mémoire, bien qu'elles aient été capables, en une seule seconde, de susciter en moi des questions infinies et de m'inspirer des multitudes d'idées. C'est ainsi qu'il y a trois ans, une seule image entrevue dans la station thermale de Hakone, au Japon, a pu déclencher en moi le désir et la nécessité de filmer toute une histoire dans la capitale des idéogrammes.

Le maître Akira Kurosawa a dit : « Les plus belles chauses ne sont jamais captées sur film. » Il semble que cette réalité vaille pour tous les décors de cinéma du monde. Le livre que vous tenez entre vos mains n'est rien d'autre qu'une tentative de libérer l'instant de sa condamnation : la fugacité.

Babel est le dernier film de la trilogie que j'ai commencée avec *Amours chiennes* et *21 Grammes*. Il s'agit d'un triptyque d'histoires qui explorent à un niveau local, étranger et pour finir global les rapports profonds et complexes entre parents et enfants. L'idée de réaliser *Babel* m'est venue d'un concept que seuls peuvent produire en nous l'exil et la conscience d'être un immigrant. Il est difficile de vivre dans un pays du premier monde quand on vient d'un pays du tiers monde. Cela dit, le champ de vision s'élargit et l'on acquiert une nouvelle perspective. Aujourd'hui, je me demande plutôt « où vais-je ? » que « d'où viens-je ? ».

J'ai commencé le tournage de *Babel* avec la ferme conviction que j'allais réaliser un film sur les différences entre les êtres humains et sur leur incapacité à communiquer, pas seulement à cause des barrières linguistiques, mais aussi à cause des frontières physiques, politiques et émotionnelles. Je m'étais proposé de le faire à partir d'une perspective complexe et universelle pour arriver finalement au plan le plus intime – entre deux personnes.

Dès le départ, l'équipe a été formée de Mexicains, d'Américains, de Français, d'Italiens, d'Arabes, de Berbères et d'Allemands, et pour finir de Japonais. Parallèlement au sujet central du film, je sentais que malgré tous les outils que nous avons développés pour améliorer la communication entre les êtres, la réalité s'avère en fin de compte très différente. Le problème, ce ne sont pas les nouveaux outils infinis dont nous disposons pour communiquer les uns avec les autres, mais le fait que personne n'écoute. Quand il n'y a rien à écouter, il n'y a rien à comprendre, et si nous cessons de comprendre, notre langage devient inutile et finit par nous diviser. Travailler en cinq langues différentes et inconnues avec des acteurs reconnus, mais aussi – pour la plupart – avec des non acteurs qui, comme dans le cas des humbles communautés marocaines, n'avaient jamais vu une caméra, a exigé de moi un travail patient d'observation et d'assimilation.

Comme des gitans avec un grand cirque itinérant, ma famille de substitution – à savoir mes amis et collaborateurs de toujours, sans lesquels cette aventure n'aurait pu aboutir –, ma famille de sang et moi-même avons voyagé sur trois continent pendant presque toute une année.

Au fil des semaines, des mois, des visages, des géographies et des saisons, le choc produit par l'observation de tant de cultures, mais aussi l'impact physique et psychologique du voyage ont fini par nous transformer, moi-même et tous ceux qui ont réalisé ce film avec moi. Au long du périple, il y a eu des morts, des naissances, des situations intenses de joie et de souffrance, et de nombreuses occasions de fraternité et de communion : à être exposés et à vivre aussi profondément tant d'humanité, nous avons été transformés, mais le film lui aussi l'a été. L'orgie de culture à laquelle nous avons participé a fait que le processus créatif s'est modelé peu à peu de manière à devenir quelque chose de très différent, voire d'opposé à l'objectif initial, ce qui montre une fois de plus qu'un film n'est en définitive rien d'autre qu'un prolongement de soi-même.

Dans une grande partie de la planète, les frontières et les aéroports se sont transformés aujourd'hui en un carnaval de méfiance et de dégradation où la sécurité se substitue à la liberté, où les armes sont les rayons X et le délit l'altérité.

Et pourtant, en filmant *Babel*, j'ai pu constater que les vraies frontières se situent à l'intérieur de nous et que plus encore que dans l'espace physique, c'est dans le monde des idées que se dressent les barrières. Je me suis rendu compte que les choses qui nous rendent heureux comme êtres humains pouvaient être très différentes, mais que celles qui nous rendent misérables et vulnérables au-delà de notre culture, de notre race, de notre langue ou de notre position économique, sont les mêmes pour tous les hommes. J'ai découvert que la grande tragédie humaine se réduit à l'incapacité de pouvoir aimer ou être aimé, à l'impossibilité de toucher ou d'être touché par ce sentiment, qui est ce qui donne son sens à la vie et à la mort de tout être humain. De ce fait, *Babel* s'est peu à peu transformé en un film sur ce qui nous unit et non sur ce qui nous sépare.

Pour moi, ce tournage est devenu un voyage non seulement extérieur, mais intérieur, et comme toute œuvre qui vient des tripes, ce film – comme les deux précédents – est un témoignage de mon expérience vitale, avec mes qualités et mes multiples limitations. Pendant le tournage d'*Amours chiennes* et de *21 Grammes*, du fait de la concentration du travail et des objectifs précis imposés par l'histoire qu'il s'agissait de filmer, j'ai ressenti douloureusement l'impossibilité de fixer non seulement la beauté de tel ou tel instant, mais aussi les multiples scènes ou images qui surgissaient autour de moi en marge du tournage. Où sont passés ces visages et la texture des bas quartiers de Memphis où nous avons filmé *21 Grammes*, où sont ces arbres harassés et ces corbeaux suspendus comme des sphères dans les matins brumeux, sur les rives du Mississipi ? Où sont passés les yeux furibonds des enfants qui nous ont agressés, un pistolet à la main, lors des repérages d'*Amours chiennes*, et qui plus tard, pendant le tournage, allaient nous servir le café avec des visages d'enfants pris sur le fait ? Qu'est devenu le geste du propriétaire de la maison que nous avons louée pour le personnage de Benicio del Toro dans *21 Grammes*, quand nous lui avons appris que nous avions découvert un cadavre en décomposition sous un matelas de la chambre ? Ces images et ces moments n'ont existé qu'une fraction de seconde pour se perdre ensuite dans l'oubli, sans pouvoir être documentés dans la mémoire collective.

La réalité d'un film est beaucoup plus que ce qui entre finalement dans le rectangle de l'écran, et cette réalité s'incruste inexorablement en tous ceux qui participent à la réalisation du film. Ce livre est une tentative de sauver ces images fugaces d'humanité partagée, de tout ce qui a fait que *Babel* a commencé à être une chose pour finir par en être une autre, les images des visages, des formes, des vents et des horizons qui ont frappé et transformé comme des chutes de pierres tous ceux qui ont cheminé ensemble depuis le début.

Chaque film pourrait en générer un autre. Quand on est en train de filmer, les yeux et les sens sont tellement éveillés qu'on tombe un peu partout sur des personnages potentiellement plus intéressants que le personnage du film lui-même. Cela dit, la curiosité en a déjà tué plus d'un, et elle peut aussi être la mort du réalisateur. En théorie, cette curiosité pourrait être satisfaite au moyen d'un simple appareil photo. Ce n'est pas compliqué que cela : un simple « clic » – et voilà. En pratique, c'est autre chose.

Un fier entomologiste peut bien nous montrer des centaines de papillons épinglés dans leurs coffrets de bois et nous captiver avec les multiples et fascinantes couleurs de leurs ailes. Mais ces coffrets ne sont rien d'autre que des sarcophages avec un couvercle en verre, et ces papillons, si jolis par leurs formes et leurs couleurs, manquent de la chose la plus fascinante que possède un papillon : la grâce de voler. De la même manière, même si une photographie a pu fixer un corps à un moment donné, tout comme le papillon, si elle ne possède en même temps la faculté de voler, elle est morte. La raison pour laquelle le scintillement léger que nous envoie la vitre d'une voiture, ou la raison pour laquelle quelques secondes d'une image entrevue dans un parc peuvent faire naître toute une histoire ou tout un film dans l'esprit d'un artiste, c'est que ces images, si brèves soient-elles, sont vivantes. Leur vie ne dépend pas de la durée de l'observation, mais de leur vérité et du point de vue de celui qui les reçoit. La seule chose qui sépare l'objet de celui qui le regarde est le regard ; et lui – le regard – est ce qui fait que l'art existe et qu'il est un miracle individuel.

Tout comme le regard de Rodrigo Prieto a su capter et dessiner dans *Babel* la vérité et la poésie des corps et des figures en mouvement, quatre maîtres de la photographie fixe ont fait de même avec les mondes parallèles du temps congelé.

La raison pour laquelle les pages de ce livre battent comme des ailes de papillons, avec des images encore vivantes qui semblent vouloir s'envoler du papier, c'est que ceux qui les ont captées n'ont pas capturé des papillons, mais que, sans même les effleurer, ils ont su en extraire l'esprit et la vérité. Les regards tout à fait uniques de Mary Ellen Mark, Graciela Iturbide, Miguel Rio Branco et Patrick Bard ont permis que ces images deviennent des histoires sans son. C'est leur regard qui fait que leurs photographies sentent le Sahara, le désert de Sonora – et même le désert de Tokyo. Leur curiosité à l'égard du visage humain, de l'animal, du mur et des ombres de ce que personne ne voit est la même que celle des enfants. Seule l'humanité, le génie et l'universalité propres de ces quatre photographes pouvaient faire que des cultures et des géographies aussi lointaines et aussi différentes deviennent quelque chose d'aussi proche et d'intime, montrant ainsi une fois de plus que l'image et la musique sont les expressions les plus proches de l'espéranto. Leurs méthodes de travail, si différentes, parviennent pourtant au même effet : mettre la poésie au service du rêve et subordonner la beauté à la vérité de l'instant.

L'émotion et la grande dignité que montrent les personnages des photographies de Mary Ellen Mark est une chose qui n'a cessé de m'impressionner depuis de nombreuses années. Mary Ellen Mark a fait le portrait de ceux que la société ignore, transcendant à sa manière et à travers son univers esthétique le document journalistique. Curieusement, l'impact émotionnel de ses photographies dans *American Odyssey* a été une source d'inspiration pour Brigitte Broch, Rodrigo Prieto et moi-même lors de notre travail pour *Amours chiennes*.

Également au Maroc, Patrick Bard a laissé les images voler en toute liberté avec sa manière de les documenter : grâce à ses contacts profonds et humains avec les natifs du pays et en extrayant d'eux une honnêteté et une naturalité rarement atteintes. Dans chaque image, ce photographe-romancier nous fait éprouver tout le poids de la vie ordinaire.

D'un autre côté, l'esprit de Graciela Iturbide, dont les photographies m'ont également fait grandir, est si pur et si subtil qu'il semble toujours en suspension. Derrière ses yeux étincelants se cachent une grande sagesse et une grande noblesse. La limpidité de ses images font de mon pays quelque chose d'idyllique en même temps que véridique. Véridique parce qu'elle le voit et nous le révèle dans son travail et que cela suffit pour qu'on la croie et le célèbre avec elle. Ses photographies dans ce livre ont le parfum de mon pays. Ouvre ton cœur et tu verras que c'est vrai.

Pour finir, je crois que nul ne manie la couleur comme Miguel Rio Branco. Les livres de sa première période m'a inspiré tout comme de nombreux autres cinéastes. Sa célèbre photographie du chien mort reste à jamais gravée dans l'esprit de celui qui y a été exposé. Peintre, cinéaste, photographe, artiste multimédia et surtout poète conceptuel, Rio Branco se maintient dans un perpétuel état de réinvention et d'évolution. Les triptyques qui apparaissent dans ce livre semblent avoir capté de manière abstraite L'ADN complexe de Tokyo. Personne ne voit ce qu'il voit. Dans le coin le plus oublié, les objets dialoguent avec leurs ombres.

Les avoir eu tous les quatre dans l'environnement de *Babel* a toujours été un honneur et un privilège.

L'idée de ce livre est venue de ma femme María Eladia. Seule une personne ayant sa sensibilité pouvait choisir parmi tant de papillons pour réunir une gamme de couleurs, d'odeurs et de textures aussi variées et pourtant faire coexister dans un unique livre quatre visions puissantes sur trois continents et deux réalités. Ses heures interminables de travail, pendant des mois, ont fini par donner corps au livre qu'elle a visualisé et rêvé. En incorporant aussi quelques photographies additionnelles de Murray Close, Eniac Martinez, Yvonne Venegas, Junko Kato et Tsutomu, qui ont joliment complété par leur talent et leur sensibilité les éléments de ce voyage auquel ils ont eux aussi participé, ce livre a pu remplir pleinement son propos. Dès l'origine, il avait été décidé que les photographies s'attacheraient non à la nature du film, mais à sa réalité parallèle. L'expérience qui sous-tend ce propos est de vérifier que la fiction ressemble autant à la réalité que la réalité s'infuse dans la fiction. Notre intention a été d'explorer cette frontière. Il y a là les communautés, les visages, les villes verticales ou enclavées dans la boue qui nous ont entourées, qui se sont intégrées et qui nous ont inspirés pendant le tournage. Ce sont les mondes tangibles et poétiques derrière celui de *Babel*.

En fait, certaines des plus belles chauses peuvent bien être captées sur film.

Maroc

Page 28

À dix-huit ans, j'ai traversé l'Atlantique à bord d'un cargo sur lequel j'ai travaillé comme mousse. Je suis parti avec trois amis et j'ai survécu pendant un an avec trois mille dollars. Après avoir passé la frontière à Ceuta, nous avons pris un car jusqu'à Marrakech. Pour l'écrivain Paul Bowles, la différence entre un touriste et un voyageur réside dans le fait que le second n'a pas de billet de retour. Au cours de cette année, j'ai pu vérifier la véracité de cette observation.

La chaleur dans le car était infernale. J'avais sur moi une bouteille d'eau tiède à moitié pleine ; en face de moi, un enfant brun avec de beaux yeux verts n'arrêtait pas de me fixer. Il avait un fruit dans la main et me l'offrit. Je lui fis signe que je n'en voulais pas et que je le remerciais ; il insista et je déclinai à nouveau. Il me dit quelque chose en arabe que je ne compris pas. Sa mère et quelques passagers se retournèrent. Je dus accepter le fruit à moitié rogné. À peine avais-je pris le fruit qu'il me demanda ma bouteille d'eau. Je regardai tour à tour ma bouteille et l'enfant. Je pesai le pour et le contre et lui dis que non. Il dit alors quelque chose à sa mère et celle-ci me dit à son tour quelque chose. Tout à coup, tous les passagers du car me regardaient comme pour voir si j'aurais le culot de refuser de l'eau à l'enfant. Je lui tendis ma bouteille à contrecœur. L'enfant commença à rire et à boire. Soudain, tout le car riait : l'enfant offrit à boire à tout le monde et tous riaient aux éclats de mes amis et de moi. Ensuite, l'enfant demanda à manger aux autres passagers et commença à répartir la nourriture entre tous. Les gens n'arrêtaient pas de rire. Mes amis et moi ne rions qu'à demi, comme quand on cherche à comprendre une blague. C'était comme si c'était la première fois que les passagers voyaient un étranger. L'enfant m'apporta quelques morceaux de biscuits et se présenta. Il s'appelait Abdullah : il avait une grâce et un charme incomparables. En descendant du car au Maroc, des milliers d'enfants comme Abdullah commencèrent à nous entourer et à courir derrière nous. Le bruit qu'ils faisaient était fabuleux.

Je me rappelais le Maroc enveloppé d'un halo de mystère et d'un nuage de haschich. Ce pays a eu sur moi un formidable impact esthétique et culturel. Vingt-deux ans après ce voyage, j'ai voulu tourner à Marrakech parce que je sentais un lien qui me remontait de ma mémoire. Une fois de plus, les enfants magiques ne tardèrent pas à se montrer.

Page 49

Quand j'étais enfant, ma mère me rapporta un jour de New York un petit plâtre de la *Pietà* de Michel-Ange. Pendant toute mon enfance, je me suis endormi et réveillé avec cette figurine derrière mon oreiller. J'ai voulu que Richard porte Susan comme une métaphore de cette image de la douleur. Brad a porté Cate plus de cinquante fois dans de longues ruelles ; Rodrigo Prieto, le directeur de la photographie, courait toujours derrière

eux avec une caméra de cinquante kilos sur les épaules. Quelques jours plus tard, quand je voulus refaire cette scène, ce furent les acteurs et Rodrigo qui implorèrent ma pitié.

Page 50

Dans le scénario original, le conflit entre Richard et Susan naissait d'une infidélité commise autrefois par Richard. Quelques semaines avant le tournage, j'ai proposé de porter le drame à un niveau plus profond – comme l'est l'accouchement d'un enfant mort-né. Brad a appris ce changement du scénario en arrivant au Maroc. En fait, il était déjà difficile de construire un personnage seulement à partir de trente pages d'histoire. Et il n'a pas été facile d'encaisser le choc de ce nouvel élément dramatique dans l'intrigue. Qui était Richard ? Pourquoi fit-il ce qu'il fit ? Chaque jour, dans des conditions physiques exténuantes, Brad a dû creuser, découvrir et inventer le personnage vulnérable qu'il a lui-même construit à l'écran.

Page 53

Même si le rôle de Richard pouvait à première vue ne pas sembler évident pour un acteur comme Brad Pitt, le construire a été une aventure aussi excitante pour lui que pour moi. Il n'est pas facile que des acteurs de sa stature acceptent d'interpréter ce genre de personnages. Pour moi, le défi était d'arriver à ce que Brad Pitt, la célébrité, disparaisse derrière le personnage pour laisser le champ libre non seulement à l'acteur, mais aussi à l'être humain derrière l'image. Il m'a toujours semblé que Brad possède une présence magnétique qui va au-delà de sa popularité. Il y avait un gros risque pour lui et il a relevé tous les défis avec un grand courage. Il a surtout accepté le risque suprême auquel s'exposent toujours les acteurs : celui de se mettre entre les mains du réalisateur et de se lancer dans le vide.

Page 56

Si l'expérience du tournage a été pour tous très proche des thèmes du film, dans le cas de Cate, la fiction et la réalité se sont superposées de manière très radicale. Pendant qu'elle était au Maroc, son fils d'un an subit une brûlure du second degré aux deux jambes. Cate a dû parer à la première urgence dans un humble hôpital marocain et s'envoler sans tarder pour Londres afin de lui faire donner les soins nécessaires. Deux jours plus tard, ayant reçu l'assurance que son fils s'en sortirait, elle nous donna une leçon de professionnalisme comme je n'en avais jamais vue et revint pour jouer Susan, une femme qui perd son sang par une blessure physique autant qu'émotionnelle.

Page 61

Dix-sept jours avant le tournage, je n'avais encore aucun acteur. Nous nous sommes mis à rechercher des acteurs dans tous les villages. Nous allions dans les mosquées et annoncions par haut-parleurs que le film était arrivé et que nous cherchions des gens pour jouer dedans.

Sfia (page opposée) est une femme berbère de Taguenzalt qui vivait dans la maison attenante à celle où nous tournions. La profondeur de son regard m'a amené à lui donner le rôle sans la moindre hésitation. Il a été extrêmement difficile de réussir les scènes où elle joue. Quand nous en étions à la vingtième prise et que Cate Blanchett continuait à me donner toute son intensité, la vieille femme oubliait où elle devait aller et se tournait vers la caméra en souriant.

Mohamed a débarqué un jour au bureau pour trouver du travail comme technicien informatique. Il s'autodéclarait *hacker*. J'ai été frappé par la noblesse de son visage où se lisait en même temps la douleur : le visage de quelqu'un qui cherche à se dépasser, mais à qui la vie ne prête pas grande attention. Il m'a semblé qu'il était très proche de la nature du personnage d'Anouar.

Page 62

J'ai demandé à Cate Blanchett d'accepter d'interpréter Susan. Au début, elle était réticente, non sans raisons : dans le scénario, Susan n'était qu'une femme allongée par terre, en sang, à moitié inconsciente. Mais je savais que seule Cate pouvait donner au personnage la gravité et la consistance nécessaires et qu'elle élèverait le niveau de jeu pour tous les participants. Et c'est ce qui s'est passé. Et chaque fois que je la voyais jouer, non seulement elle m'émouvait, mais je ne cessais de rendre grâce qu'elle eût accepté le rôle.

Si elle avait su qu'elle allait être enduite de miel rouge et gluant mêlé d'odeurs fécales pour attirer les mouches, par une température de quarante degrés dans une pièce sans air conditionné, je crois bien qu'elle n'aurait pas accepté.

Page 70

Je ne peux concevoir plus grande générosité au monde que celle que nous avons vue dans les humbles villages du sud du Maroc. Quand nous passions devant une maison, immanquablement, on nous offrait du thé, des amandes, des dattes, du lait de chèvre, des sourires et le traditionnel *salâm alaïk*, les gens se touchaient le cœur et lançaient au ciel un baiser de la main. Il m'est apparu clairement que le consumérisme occidental est une course au néant spirituel. Il est certain que les femmes travaillent plus que les hommes et que ceux-ci prennent un peu trop le *five o'clock* social. Cinq fois par jour cependant, tous consacrent quelques minutes à prier et à se relier à leur partie spirituelle.

Page 72

Pour la communauté de Taguenzalte, *Babel* a été un cirque divertissant pendant treize semaines. Le dernier jour de tournage, il y a eu bien des pleurs de part et d'autre. Les premiers à croire en ce projet et à joindre leurs forces aux miennes ont été Jon Kilik et Steve Golin, mes coproducteurs, dont l'amitié, l'expérience et le soutien ont été inappréciables. Avec Ann Ruark, ils ont travaillé passionnément et inlassablement pour orchestrer ce « cirque itinérant » global pendant presque

un an, fournissant toujours le nécessaire pour nous permettre de réaliser le film.

Nous avons tous passé des moments extraordinaires avec l'humble communauté de Taguenzalte, de sorte que le dernier jour de tournage, bien des larmes ont coulé des deux côtés. Nous nous sommes tous cotisés pour faire venir l'électricité jusqu'à Taguenzalt. Quelques mois plus tard, l'un d'entre nous est retourné sur place et nous a raconté que les terrasses étaient déjà équipées d'antennes paraboliques. Je n'ai pu m'empêcher d'éprouver un sentiment de tristesse et de confusion.

Page 85

J'ai voulu filmer dans un désert qui ne soit pas trop romantique : un désert dur, rocailleux, pas un désert de dunes. Trouver un lieu dans les immenses étendues du Sahara est incroyablement difficile. C'est un espace tellement ouvert qu'on se demande sans cesse pourquoi tel lieu serait meilleur que tel autre.

Page 88

Cette scène montre le moment de l'effondrement moral de la famille musulmane ; elle demandait une haute intensité physique et émotionnelle. Quand le langage est une barrière entre le réalisateur et les acteurs, la mimique devient un outil incontournable. Hiram Abbass a été mon interprète et mon ange gardien : le pont émotionnel entre les acteurs marocains et moi.

Page 90

Un jour, sur la place principale de Tamnougalt, Alfonso Gómez m'a appelé pour que je vienne voir un enfant très spécial. C'était Boubker. Je lui expliquai que j'allais lui faire faire un bout d'essai et lui dire quelques phrases, et que je ne voulais pas qu'il me réponde avec des mots, mais qu'il me dise ce qu'il éprouvait avec les yeux. « Ta mère vient de mourir. » Ses yeux s'emplirent de larmes et nous restâmes tous abasourdis par son expression. Ce fut un moment unique. Je sus que j'avais trouvé mon acteur pour le personnage de Youssef. Ensuite, j'ai appris que sa mère était morte sept ans plus tôt et que son père était un homme qu'il ne voyait jamais. Sans le savoir, j'avais touché en lui une blessure très profonde. Rien n'est plus puissant que la réalité, et elle ne peut être contrefaite.

Page 92

Après avoir vu un premier montage de *Babel*, mon ami l'écrivain Eliseo Alberto me dit qu'il semblait qu'Abdullah et Hassan étaient descendus du ciel pour interpréter leurs rôles et qu'ils étaient ensuite remontés. Quand j'ai aperçu leurs visages parmi les centaines d'hommes qui s'étaient groupés à l'extérieur des mosquées pour le casting, j'ai pensé la même chose. Le visage de ces hommes est proprement biblique : le visage même de l'humanité telle qu'elle est décrite dans les testaments musulman, juif et chrétien. Abdullah, comme Joseph dans la Bible, travaille comme charpentier dans la banlieue de Fès.

Page 93

La plupart des durs visages des Marocains sont doux quand ils sourient. Ils n'ont pas la malignité que nous leur attribuons si souvent. Pourtant, le visage de Hassan a été difficile à dompter. Il fallait que son personnage se montre vulnérable face à l'intimidation policière, mais il était bloqué. La communication par mimiques était insuffisante, et Hiam, en parlant avec lui dans sa langue, a trouvé les mots pour le relier à ses émotions. Hassan nous a dit que jamais il n'avait rendu visite à sa mère morte, de sorte que le tournage a été pour lui comme une thérapie, et pendant plus de six heures, il n'y a eu personne qui ait pu retenir ses larmes. À la fin, il nous a remerciés, et moi, j'ai remercié Hiam.

Page 94

Au Maroc, notre équipe a compté cent vingt personnes : des Italiens, des Français, des Américains, des Mexicains et des Marocains parlant arabe ou berbère. L'existence de six langues au sein d'une équipe de travail a été la source de bien des problèmes par manque de compréhension. Plus encore que les différences de langue, c'est le point de vue qui posait problème. Nous avons été soumis à une chaleur accablante et à des conditions extrêmes. De nombreuses scènes extérieures ont dû être filmées par des températures très élevées, nous avons dû gravir des côtes et supporter beaucoup de poussière. Pour certains d'entre nous, qui venions du tiers monde, il a été un peu plus facile de supporter ces conditions. La réalité d'un berger marocain ne diffère pas tellement de celle d'un berger mexicain. Rodrigo Prieto autant que moi-même et les membres mexicains de l'équipe avons été heureux de pouvoir comprendre leurs conditions de vie et leurs limitations.

Page 104

Said et Boubker sont devenus comme des frères. Comme dans la fiction, Saïd était rebelle, actif, intuitif et anticonformiste, et Boubker passif, introspectif, rationnel et mélancolique. Avec le cachet du film, Said s'est acheté une moto et Boubker un ordinateur.

Le dernier jour du tournage au Maroc, nous avons filmé la scène de fin de journée où Youssef, filmé en gros plan, pleure et imagine son frère qui vient de mourir marchant avec leur père le long d'une mer de désert rocailleux. C'est là que j'ai fait installer une barque vide. Cette scène leur a été pour eux une charge émotionnelle très lourde. Un peu plus tôt pendant le tournage, j'avais filmé spontanément, comme un cadeau des montagnes, une scène dans laquelle les enfants jouaient avec le vent. Prises ensemble, toutes ces scènes sont finalement devenues l'épilogue de leur histoire. Le dernier jour, le tournage achevé, Said et Boubker ne pouvaient s'arrêter de pleurer. Nous, qui étions devenus leur famille, nous partions le lendemain. Je leur ai promis à tous les deux que nous nous reverrions un an plus tard au cours d'un festival. Heureusement j'ai pu tenir ma promesse : nous nous sommes revus à Cannes.

Mexique

Page 114

À Tijuana, les gens ne sont pas d'ici ou d'ailleurs : tout le monde est de passage. Il n'y a que dans un lieu comme celui-ci qu'on peut trouver une géante en plâtre comme celle qu'un amoureux construisit pour que sa femme puisse apercevoir d'en haut la terre promise qu'elle ne pourrait jamais atteindre.

La première chose qui frappe dans cette ville, c'est le mur qui la longe. On l'appelle « la plaie » : une blessure ouverte qui s'étire sur plusieurs kilomètres, construite avec les déchets des clôtures métalliques utilisées pour la construction qu'un aéroports construisit en préfabriqué de la guerre du Vietnam. La chose la plus aberrante est que ce mur se prolonge jusque dans l'océan, au cas où un terroriste voudrait passer la frontière en sous-marin ! On y voit accrochées des milliers de croix portant les noms des hommes, des femmes et des enfants qui ont été engloutis par le désert ou qui ont disparu entre le Mexique et les États-Unis, la frontière la plus passée au monde. Une fois achevé, le mur deviendra le plus grand monument à l'intolérance de l'histoire de l'humanité.

Page 120

Un jour, j'ai appris qu'on réalisait une performance à la frontière (page précédente). Un homme devait voler de l'autre côté et être arrêté par la police américaine dans un acte spectaculaire impliquant la critique. En fin de compte, ce fut un échec retentissant. Il s'agissait seulement d'un « homme balle » américain qui n'avait pas la moindre idée ni le moindre intérêt pour la portée symbolique de son acte et qui avait seulement été payé pour accomplir cet exploit. Mais même ainsi, la puissance onirique de cet acte représente le rêve de bien des gens qui vivent ici. Si seulement nous avions des ailes…

Page 121

Je suis musicologue et j'aime les bonnes choses dans tous les genres, mais pour une raison ou une autre, la musique du nord ne m'avait jamais *parlé*. J'éprouvais à son égard un sorte de rejet *a priori*. Après avoir vécu plus de deux mois à Tijuana et à Sonora et avoir exploré et tenté par la force des choses de me connecter avec cette musique, à la fin, elle m'est apparue sous un autre jour. Les tubes qui passaient à la radio et les paroles des chansons, ajoutées à mon expérience personnelle, ont fait que pour la première fois j'ai pu y trouver un sens émotionnel. La douleur et la frustration des paroles et des mélodies simples et sirupeuses plongent leurs racines non dans ce que les gens possèdent, mais dans le manque de ce que l'on n'a jamais eu ou ne pourra jamais avoir. Avoir capitulé face à cette musique a été un des meilleurs cadeaux que j'ai retirés de cette expérience.

Page 131

Dans ma maison à Los Angeles travaillait une femme qui s'appelle Julia. Elle est née dans l'État de Oaxaca, et c'est seulement après six tentatives infructueuses qu'elle a réussi à traverser le désert sans être rattrapée. Elle a un fils de vingt ans qui est en prison et à qui elle n'a pas pu rendre visite une seule fois en deux ans parce qu'elle serait immédiatement renvoyée dans son village natal. Julia vit constamment dans la peur. Comme des millions de Mexicains qui vivent aux États-Unis, Amelia est une citoyenne invisible. Ironiquement, tout comme elle, des milliers de femmes latino-américaines ont affronté les mêmes dangers en franchissant la frontière mexicaine, une entreprise qui peut s'avérer plus dure et plus risquée que de franchir celle des États-Unis.

Pour moi, le travail d'Adriana Barranza a donné un nouveau sens au mot « incarnation » en ceci qu'avec chaque mouvement du corps, des mains et des yeux, elle a incarné avec tendresse et subtilité l'esprit d'un personnage qui aurait aisément pu tomber dans le stéréotype. Son jeu a été tout simplement sublime. Dès le début, j'ai songé à Gael pour *Babel*. Personne n'aurait pu incarner comme lui un personnage ayant autant de comportements contradictoires en un temps aussi court. Dans *Amours chiennes*, Adriana était la mère de Gael, dans *Babel*, elle était sa tante. Dans les deux cas, comme fils et comme neveu, il lui a causé de grandes peines et l'a plongée dans différents enfers. La seule chose que j'ai pu promettre à Amelia et à Gael, c'est que je ne referais plus un film dans lequel Gael conduit une voiture. Chaque fois qu'il en conduit une, cela se termine en tragédie.

Page 136

Dès les premiers repérages, j'ai été attiré par la communauté d'El Carrizo, une rancheria située à une heure de Tijuana : sobre, fruste, mais aimable et un cœur gros comme ça. Dans *Babel*, une histoire parallèle se déroulait dans cette maison (à gauche), celle de la fiancée enceinte qu'Amelia persuadait de se rendre à son propre mariage. Pour finir, j'ai décidé de supprimer cette histoire, mais d'une manière ou d'une autre, son atmosphère a laissé une empreinte dans le film. Le petit gros qu'on voit dans cette photo est un enfant qui lors des trois visites que j'ai faites dans sa maison, n'a pas bougé une seule fois de son fauteuil. En face de lui, il y avait un énorme téléviseur et une assiette de chips vide.

Page 148

Au nord de mon pays, les mariages sont très différents de ceux du sud. À Tijuana, les cérémonies sont dures, poussiéreuses, sans rites ni traditions enracinées. Dans le cadre de mes recherches pour *Babel*, j'ai assisté à plusieurs mariages et j'ai tenté de filmer celui du fils d'Amelia la manière la plus fidèle possible concernant tout ce que je voyais : verres et assiettes en plastique, absence totale de fleurs ou de tout autre ornement, chaises bigarrées posées sur l'omniprésente poussière. Brigitte Broch, mon amie et designeuse de production, dont chaque décision donne vie au décor, a accompli un merveilleux travail.

Toutes les personnes qui apparaissent dans la scène du mariage (page suivante) font partie de la communauté d'El Carrizo. Je n'ai jamais vu de gens plus vivants et joviaux. Bien que j'aie filmé pendant de nombreuses journées et jusqu'à six heures du matin, jamais il n'y a eu la moindre plainte de leur part. Rien que des sourires et des danses sans fin. Pour moi, pour eux et pour toute l'équipe, le mariage a été une vraie fête. Les gens se connaissaient déjà et cela se ressent dans cette scène.

Page 150

De même que Gustavo Santaolalla et moi nous sommes enfermés dans un studio pour enregistrer différents groupes de musique gnawa au Maroc, de même, à Tijuana, je me suis enfermé avec Lynn Fainchtein pour écouter et enregistrer de très nombreux groupes du nord. Les gens du nord écoutent uniquement de la musique du nord. C'est comme une religion. Leurs thèmes expriment une douleur et des motifs qu'on ne peut comprendre si on ne les écoute en adoptant leur point de vue. De par leur sincérité, leur charme et leur contact avec le public, les « Incomparables » font honneur à leur nom.

Page 155

Quand j'ai rencontré Bernie, j'ai immédiatement changé d'idée par rapport à celle qui avait été écrite pour le personnage de Luis, le fils d'Amelia. Je l'ai connu à Tijuana lors du casting et j'ai parlé avec lui pendant à peu près une heure. Il m'a dit qu'il avait tout fait dans la vie : Casanova, truand, videur, musicien, pompier, tout. Comme on dit, un gars qui veut « aller de l'avant ». Malgré tous ses efforts pour faire croire à ses mauvais penchants, sa noblesse le trahissait. Sa coupe de cheveux hip hop à la tijuanienne et ses yeux sauvages, pourtant pleins de tendresse, m'ont semblé très intéressants. Comme lui, des millions de jeunes frontaliers ressentent le passage de la frontière américaine comme une humiliation.

Page 165

Tous les six mois au cours des cinq dernières années, j'ai dû passer la frontière entre Tijuana et les États-Unis avec mon épouse et mes enfants. Bien que je l'aie franchie si souvent, je suis toujours affecté par le contraste et la disparité entre les deux pays. Toutes les voitures qui viennent des États-Unis pour entrer dans mon pays passent sans la moindre fouille ni le moindre ennui. En revanche, toutes celles qui entrent du Mexique aux États-Unis sont scrupuleusement fouillées, ce qui transforme ce passage en rite d'humiliation et de suspicion. Pour moi, l'acte violent et inopiné de Santiago ne vient pas d'une fouille, il est une réaction aux années d'abus de pouvoir et aux procédés employés.

Pendant trois jours de tournage, je me suis efforcé de reproduire les impressions que j'ai maintes fois vécues personnellement. Nous avons construit une guérite semblable à celle de Tecate, en plein désert de Sonora, et Rodrigo Prieto, Batan Silva et moi inspections le matériel de la seconde unité lors de ses allées et venues pour présenter le matériel.

Page 166

C'est incroyable comme les enfants comprennent parfois bien mieux les choses que les acteurs éprouvent. Ils n'ont pas d'autre prétention que d'obéir. Pour Nathan Gamble et Elle Fanning, qui interprètent les enfants du couple américain, il y a eu des moments pénibles pendant le tournage : la chaleur du désert de Sonora était beaucoup plus forte qu'au Maroc. Quand la nuit tombait, ils devenaient irritables et somnolents. En plus de la chaleur et de la fatigue, les enfants ont vécu d'autres moments difficiles. Nous filmions dans une zone où il y avait des serpents. Une fois, pendant une prise, Nathan en a vu un sortir d'un trou dans le sable. Il était réellement terrifié. Cette prise est restée dans le film.

Page 168

Adriana Barranza a eu deux micro-infarctus. Pour cette scène, elle a dû porter pendant bien des jours et de nombreuses fois une fillette de 30 kilos et courir dans le désert par une chaleur de quarante degrés. Un jour que la chaleur était particulièrement accablante, cinq membres de l'équipe ont dû aller se faire soigner à l'hôpital pour cause de déshydratation. Adriana a commencé à éprouver des malaises. Elle était au bord de l'évanouissement et m'a demandé de lui donner une heure pour se rétablir. Je lui ai dit d'aller se reposer à l'hôtel. « Non, m'a-t-elle répondu, je sais bien ce que c'est qu'une heure de retard et qu'on perd beaucoup d'argent. Donne-moi seulement une heure. » Elle a pris une douche dans son trailer et au bout d'une heure, elle est sortie fin prête pour continuer de travailler sur la même scène. Je n'avais jamais assisté à un tel niveau d'engagement et d'effort physique. Nous avons encore tourné pendant deux heures quelques-uns des moments les plus durs. Peut-être Adriana a-t-elle pensé que si les émigrants n'avaient pas le choix de pouvoir se reposer pendant la traversée du désert, pourquoi Amelia l'aurait-elle ?

Page 172

Rodrigo Prieto n'est pas seulement mon frère, mais mon bras droit. Son rapport presque obsessionnel avec l'éclairage est presque aussi intense que sa capacité à raconter une scène et à dessiner un personnage avec le pinceau de sa caméra. En bon chasseur de papillons, même quand il filme caméra à l'épaule, parfois à quelques centimètres des acteurs, jamais il n'interrompt le processus. Il vogue et respire avec.

En filmant dans le désert du Maroc, il a dû quitter le tournage les sept derniers jours parce que ses parents fêtaient leur soixantième anniversaire de mariage. Il allait à cette fête avec un bonheur enfantin. Quelques mois plus tard, à Tijuana, Rodrigo a reçu un appel en pleine nuit : sa mère venait de mourir soudainement. Le lendemain matin, comme un soldat, il a voulu travailler le temps de lui trouver un remplaçant. Avant de commencer à tourner, nous avons accompli une petite cérémonie avec toute l'équipe. Rodrigo a parlé de sa mère comme je n'avais jamais entendu quelqu'un le faire. Il nous a arraché des larmes à tous et jamais le désert ne m'a paru si désert. Quand il est revenu, la

paix se lisait sur son visage. Il m'a dit qu'il avait échangé quelques mots avec un colibri.

Page 174

Au moment où nous filmions la scène d'Amelia arrêtée par la police des frontières, tous les médias étaient pleins de l'histoire d'un jeune de dix-sept ans originaire d'Oaxaca qui avait tenté de traverser le désert de l'Arizona avec sa mère. Tous deux étaient partis avec un groupe de gens. Sa mère a eu les jambes paralysées et la gorge serrée et elle n'avait pu continuer de marcher. Les autres l'avaient abandonnée sur place. Au bout de trois heures, la mère avait dit à son fils d'aller chercher de l'aide, sans quoi lui aussi mourrait. Le jeune avait marché seul pendant deux jours sans une goutte d'eau avant d'être rattrapé et renvoyé au Mexique. Quand il raconta ensuite à son grand-père ce qui s'était passé, celui-ci, un homme de soixante-dix ans, se rendit en Arizona et lança une campagne avec l'aide d'une station de radio pour pouvoir récupérer le corps de sa fille. Dix jours plus tard, on ne retrouva rien d'autre que ses chaussures blanches en cuir verni, deux fémurs et la serviette à carreaux jaune dont le fils avait couvert le visage de sa mère avant de partir. Les hommes de cette camionnette avaient été arrêtés quelques jours plus tôt aux États-Unis et nous leur avons demandé s'ils voulaient jouer dans un film. Leurs histoires n'étaient pas moins terribles que celle-ci.

Japon

Page 202

Une seule image a suffi à faire naître en moi l'idée qui sous-tend ce qui allait ensuite devenir l'histoire japonaise de *Babel*, une image qui aujourd'hui encore fait résonner en moi de nombreuses émotions.

Je marchais à Hakone, un endroit situé à une heure et demie de route de Tokyo et formé de fumerolles sulfureuses, d'arbres secs, d'un constant brouillard, de corbeaux noirs comme des roussettes et d'un sol recouvert de coquilles d'œufs noirs jetées par les gens après avoir été cuits dans les eaux thermales. L'atmosphère était digne d'un film de Kurosawa.

En descendant des hauteurs, j'entendis des sons gutturaux terribles. De la brume apparut une jeune fille handicapée mentale marchant très lentement et accompagnée d'un homme d'une soixantaine d'années qui prenait soin d'elle. Tous ceux qui descendaient, particulièrement les enfants, l'évitaient avec une certaine terreur. Mais cet homme la soutenait de son bras avec une grande tendresse, amour et dignité. Cette image m'a profondément ému. Pendant le même voyage, quelques mois plus tard, alors que j'étais à Stockholm avec ma famille, je n'ai cessé de rencontrer des sourds-muets. J'étais interpellé par leur gestuelle et par le caractère dramatique de leur communication. Tout cela m'est apparu comme un langage inconnu et ignoré de presque tout le monde – de nous qui avons

la grâce de toucher et d'être touchés par la parole. « Le langage du silence », pensai-je. La même nuit, j'eus un rêve érotique sur une adolescente dans un cabinet de dentiste. Toutes ces images apparemment sans lien m'ont fourni les raisons de tourner dans une de mes villes préférées – à cause de son mystère et de ses contradictions. Plus tard, Guillermo a écrit une belle histoire sur deux genres de manques, absences, solitudes, différentes mais également terribles. Parfois, les villes me font sentir plus seul que les déserts.

Page 207

Depuis *Amours chiennes*, à la manière d'un rituel, je célèbre une bénédiction collective les premier et dernier jour du tournage. J'aime les bénédictions. Comme l'indique l'étymologie, elles viennent en effet du latin *benedicere*, « bien dire », dire du bien de quelque chose ou de quelqu'un. Je crois fermement au pouvoir et à l'énergie des paroles, qui ne sont parfois rien d'autre que ce dont le cœur est plein. J'utilise des roses rouges pour le premier jour et des roses blanches pour le dernier. Le dimanche 6 novembre 2005 à 5h30 du matin, face au Tsukiji, le plus grand marché aux poissons du monde, les quelque quatre-vingt « Japoaméricamexicains » que nous étions nous sommes pris la main, avons formé un cercle, prié, gardé une minute de silence et décapité les roses rouges. Au cri d'« Abba Eli », nous avons lancé les pétales de sang dans le ciel bleu pâle qui recouvrait la ville des kimonos et des idéogrammes. C'était un matin d'automne froid, passif et romantique, idéal pour commencer la quatrième et dernière partie de *Babel*. À 6h30, la police de Tokyo nous recherchait et nous poursuivait rageusement dans les rues de la ville pour arrêter le responsable et interrompre le tournage. À trois heures de l'après-midi commença à tomber une averse capable d'anéantir l'île de Mishima. C'est ainsi qu'a débuté le premier jour de tournage à Tokyo.

Page 208

Comme c'est aussi le cas pour les personnages de leurs films, au Japon, les gens sont ce qu'ils font, pas ce qu'ils disent.

Par exemple, il ne viendrait jamais à l'idée d'un père de dire à sa fille « je t'aime ». Comme dans une bonne prestation théâtrale, au Japon, les sentiments doivent être implicites dans les actes, pas dans les mots.

Pour moi, dans une scène, les mots sont la chose la moins importante. Une scène bien écrite ou bien mise en scène devrait pouvoir être comprise silencieusement, sans paroles, et le personnage être défini par l'action. De là la grandeur du cinéma muet – le cinéma pur.

Les mots ne sont que de petites barques qui flottent sur le grand fleuve des émotions.

Un an avant le début du tournage, lors du casting au Japon, j'ai fait la connaissance de Rinko Kikuchi. Elle s'est présentée silencieusement. Nous avons fait une première lecture et je suis resté abasourdi. J'avais cru qu'elle était sourde-muette. Quand j'ai appris qu'elle ne l'était pas, j'ai eu des doutes. J'étais obsédé par l'idée de trouver une actrice sourde-muette pour le rôle de Chieko. Je l'ai revue le jour suivant. Sa générosité,

son esprit et son intensité étaient parfaits, mais elle n'était pas sourde-muette. Je suis rentré à Los Angeles avec Rinko dans ma tête, mais sans pouvoir encore me décider.

Durant les neuf mois suivants, pendant que nous tournions au Maroc et au Mexique, de sa propre initiative, sans informer personne et sans que le rôle lui eût été attribué, Rinko a décidé de prendre des cours de langage des sourds-muets à ses propres frais. Quand je suis retourné au Japon pour filmer, il m'a été impossible de distinguer Rinko d'une vraie sourde-muette. Jamais je n'avais vu une telle force de conviction, une telle discipline ni une telle nécessité de jouer un rôle. Une semaine à peine avant de commencer le tournage, je lui ai dit qu'elle avait le rôle. Son émotion et ses larmes furent infinies, profondes et silencieuses.

Page 220

Dans le film, tous les amis et toutes les amies de Chieko sont sourds-muets. Les trouver et les convaincre de jouer n'a pas été facile, mais il a été encore moins facile de leur faire passer un casting ou de tenter une scène. La chose se passait à peu près comme ceci : dans un salon, en face de moi, s'asseyait une jeune sourde-muette. À côté de moi, j'avais une interprète anglais-japonais et à côté d'elle, une interprète du japonais en langage des sourds-muets. Quand je demandais quelque chose à la jeune fille, par exemple : « T'est-il arrivé d'imaginer ou de rêver le son de quelque chose ? », la première interprète traduisait en japonais à la seconde, et celle-ci faisait parvenir ma question à la sourde-muette. La jeune femme réfléchissait pendant quelques minutes, puis donnait sa réponse en langage des sourds-muets, laquelle était ensuite traduite en japonais par son interprète ; pour finir, l'interprète d'anglais m'a dit : « En juin. » Tel a été Babel à son sommet.

Page 222

Tous les jours, pendant le trajet en voiture entre les lieux du tournage et chez moi, j'écoutais sans cesse le même disque : CHASM de maître Riyuchi Sakamoto. Ce disque est devenu ma bande-son au Japon, spécialement la chanson « Only Love Can Conquer Hate ». Au moment de filmer la scène de Chieko dans le parc, j'ai toujours imaginé quelque chose d'onirique, de flottant. Rodrigo et Joey ont monté un système de riggs sur la balançoire, car je voulais filmer toute cette séquence à trente images par seconde et lui donner le point de vue et la cadence de quelqu'un qui est en *ecstasy*. J'ai toujours senti que ce qui n'était dans le scénario qu'une simple transition d'un côté vers l'autre pouvait fournir une opportunité unique de se mettre dans la tête et dans le monde de Chieko. Il me fallait une sorte d'adagio explosant en staccato. C'est seulement au montage que j'ai découvert que cette musique était précisément « Only Love Can Conquer Hate », le morceau qu'entendrait sûrement Chieko si elle pouvait, comme Sakamoto lui-même, entendre les sons du silence.

Page 236

Quand je conçois un film, je ne peux avancer tant que je ne l'ai pas clairement situé au sein d'une palette musicale. À vingt ans, j'ai animé une émission radiophonique à Mexico. Trois heures par jour, je faisais, disais et passais sur les ondes ce que je voulais, et cela pendant cinq ans. J'écrivais et produisais des histoires et des personnages provocateurs que je combinais avec une musique éclectique. Avec ces éléments, je créais un espace qui stimulait des idées musicales et sonores. C'est ainsi que j'ai appris à divertir les gens pendant trois heures de temps. Il s'agissait d'outils qui ne différaient guère de ceux du cinéma.

Une semaine avant de commencer le tournage à Tokyo, je suis allé dans un club voir Shinichi Osawa, qui est aujourd'hui un des producteurs et DJs les plus prestigieux du Japon. Je savais déjà que j'utiliserais la chanson d'Earth Wind and Fire « September » pour l'intro de la séquence dans la discothèque, car j'aime utiliser certaines chansons de la mémoire collective. Mais je voulais aussi une chanson plus récente pour combiner les temps et les atmosphères ; quelque chose de chaud contre quelque chose d'agressif, qui dessinerait un moment dramatique de Chieko. Shinichi m'a invité à venir derrière sa console. Quand il a commencé à passer « The Joker » de Fat Boy Slim, j'ai su que c'était exactement ce que je cherchais. Les adolescents cessèrent d'exister et se perdirent dans un voyage d'ecstasy et de sueur. Les yeux fermés, ils semblaient adorer un gourou qui les conduisait vers un pays mantrique et érotique. Le jour suivant, Shinichi m'a invité dans son studio pour faire la longue introduction d'Earth Wind and Fire dont j'avais besoin pour l'entrée dans la discothèque, et il a magistralement mixé Fat Boy Slim avec une énergie d'enfer. J'ai filmé la scène avec cette musique, et dans la salle de montage, Stephen Mirrione et moi avons ressenti une palpitation proche du voyage des adolescents.

Page 239

L'histoire de Chieko ne parle pas de sexualité pathologique mais du besoin d'affection. Quand les mots sont hors d'atteinte et que nous ne pouvons les toucher ni être touchés par eux, le corps devient notre seul instrument d'expression.

Pour pouvoir suggérer et étayer le passé complexe de Chieko à l'appui de seulement quelques scènes, il me fallait une présence tout aussi complexe, mais aussi : tout aussi profondément humaine et empathique.

Dans un monde où les styles de jeu semblent se précipiter vers les cris de l'exagération, nous avons eu le bonheur de trouver un acteur dont l'esprit, la solidité et l'élégance se présentaient à travers une économie gestuelle que très peu maîtrisent sur terre. La discipline et la chaleur humaine de Koji Yakusho a donné consistance et gravité à l'histoire de Chieko. Ses micromouvements, qui vont d'un mouvement de paupière au maintien de la main, ont fait toute la différence. De la même manière, Satoshi Nikaido, qui interprète le rôle de Kenji, possède cette noblesse d'esprit qui lui a permis de faire ce qu'il a fait avec Chieko : rendre sa dignité à une personne qui croyait ne pas en avoir.

Page 240

Dans la réalisation d'un film, rien n'est plus triste que le dernier jour de tournage. La nostalgie inonde toute l'équipe et l'on commence à sentir comme une dépression postnatale qui s'étire dans la durée.

Et pourtant, le jour où nous avons filmé Chieko marchant seule devant les jardins impériaux, il s'est passé une chose que j'ai d'abord prise pour une farce du département artistique dirigé par Brigitte Broch : tous les arbres entourant les jardins étaient ornés de drapeaux marocains et japonais entremêlés. Les couleurs cumulées des deux drapeaux donnaient les vert, blanc et rouge du drapeau mexicain. Les trois pays dans lesquels j'avais filmé nous faisaient leurs adieux par une froide et belle journée d'automne. Que faisait donc là le drapeau marocain en ce jour et à cet endroit précis du Japon, le dernier jour du tournage d'un film qui parlait de ces deux mêmes pays et dont les couleurs réunies étaient celles du drapeau mexicain ? Le roi Mohammed VI était venu en visite officielle au palais impérial. Mais il n'y a pas de hasards ni de coïncidences. Tout est destin.

Les ciments de *Babel*

Conversation entre Rodrigo García et Alejandro González Iñárritu

Quelle est l'image ou l'idée qui a été à l'origine du projet ? Et comment as-tu développé le scénario à partir de ce germe ?

Comme tu le sais, un scénario n'est rien d'autre que l'application technique d'une histoire, laquelle est le résultat d'une idée qui a elle-même son origine dans le monde subconscient, dans le monde de l'intuition et de l'irrationnel.

Peut-être est-ce l'impact esthétique et culturel de mon premier voyage au Maroc à l'âge de 18 ans (dans un nuage d'existentialisme et de haschich), ou l'accumulation des absences pendant l'exil – mais au début, *Babel* est né d'une nécessité morale de purger et de parler des choses dont mon cœur et mon esprit étaient pleins : les incroyables et douloureux paradoxes globaux dont les effets se font sentir sur des territoires proches ou lointains et qui aboutissent en dernier lieu à des tragédies individuelles. Tout cela a commencé à cuire en moi à partir de quelque chose que je portais confusément dans mes entrailles comme une oppression et plus tard comme un concept qui allait clore le triptyque d'histoires croisées que j'ai commencé avec *Amours chiennes* et *21 Grammes*.

Après avoir terminé *Amours chiennes*, j'ai énormément voyagé dans le monde – jusqu'au Japon – et je me suis même installé à Los Angeles pour monter mon nouveau projet. Ma famille et moi sommes arrivés aux États-Unis quatre jours avant le 11 septembre et nous avons vu le monde changer autour de nous.

L'expérience de vivre dans l'Empire sous un régime paranoïaque, avec un nationalisme exacerbé, n'a en rien été facile. On ne pouvait faire cent mètres sans croiser un drapeau américain et un regard de suspicion. Ça a été une étape difficile et intense. J'ai sombré dans une profonde dépression.

Cela dit, je crois que si je n'étais pas parti du Mexique, si je n'avais pas quitté mon petit *home* et ma zone de confort, je n'aurais jamais éprouvé la nécessité ou la soif de relever ce défi.

L'idée de *Babel* m'est venue au moment où j'allais commencer le tournage de *21 Grammes* à Memphis. C'était la première fois que je me lançais dans la réalisation d'un film hors de mon pays et dans une langue qui n'était pas la mienne. Une fois de plus, il devait s'agir de trois histoires parallèles de parents et d'enfants, résolues dans le cadre d'un exercice structurel intéressant dont le thème central serait la perte.

La seule idée de porter la théorie des réalités parallèles non plus seulement à l'étranger, hors de mon pays, mais à un niveau global, était quelque chose qui m'empêchait de dormir.

J'ai d'abord commencé à travailler sur ce concept avec le scénariste et réalisateur Carlos Cuarón. À l'origine, il devait s'agir de cinq histoires en cinq langues se déroulant sur cinq continents différents. Carlos et moi avons travaillé pendant une très courte période sur une série de scénarios possibles. Dans chacun, une décision prise dans un pays lointain affectait radicalement la vie d'êtres humains qui jamais ne se douteraient de l'origine des événements. Nous en étions là quand un grand quotidien mexicain annonça que Carlos et moi travaillions sur un projet commun autour d'un thème global. Pour couronner le tout, je découvris par hasard que le réalisateur brésilien Fernando Meirelles préparait un projet similaire. J'en parlai avec lui et pus vérifier que c'était vrai.

Carlos Cuarón décida alors de concentrer ses efforts sur un autre scénario sur lequel nous avions travaillé précédemment – pour le réaliser lui-même. De son côté, Fernando s'est lancé plus tard dans un autre projet, et c'est alors que j'ai invité Guillermo Arriaga à travailler de nouveau avec moi.

Guillermo m'a proposé cinq scénarios, dont deux allaient survivre, même s'ils étaient encore très embryonnaires : la sublime et solide histoire des enfants marocains et le début de l'histoire du couple de Richard et Susan, laquelle venait s'entrelacer naturellement et physiquement avec la précédente. De mon côté, je mis sur la table le personnage de la nounou mexicaine qui s'occupe d'enfants américains – du fait de la nécessité que j'éprouvais de raconter quelque chose non seulement sur mon pays, mais aussi sur les émigrés et la tragique situation frontalière –, et le personnage de Tokyo : une adolescente sourde-muette dont s'occupe un homme seul.

Pour moi, le personnage d'Amelia a toujours été une incarnation de Julia, la femme mexicaine qui travaille avec ma famille dans notre maison de Los Angeles. Elle m'a raconté comment elle a tenté six fois la traversée du désert et comment elle a été rattrapée par les véhicules de surveillance. Julia a passé trois nuits et trois jours dans le désert sans voir l'ombre d'une trace de civilisation.

Plus d'une personne qui a passé la frontière est morte d'une déficience pulmonaire, à cause de la déshydratation et de l'air brûlant qui passe par la gorge. C'est seulement à la septième tentative que Julia a pu passer. Son fils de vingt ans est en prison et elle ne peut lui rendre visite parce que les autorités la renverraient au Mexique. Il n'y a pas d'histoires plus tristes que celles de la frontière. Je vais moi-même à Tijuana tous les six mois avec mes enfants pour renouveler mon visa. C'est une ligne où s'est institutionnalisé un rite d'humiliation. La scène qui traite de ce sujet dans *Babel* est une restitution fidèle des formes mécaniques d'inspection que j'ai subies en plusieurs occasions.

L'idée de l'histoire japonaise m'est venue d'une seule image qui a déclenché en moi de nombreuses émotions. Je marchais à Hakone, un endroit situé à une heure et demie de Tokyo, avec des sources d'eaux sulfureuses, des arbres racornis, un constant brouillard, des corbeaux noirs comme des roussettes et un sol couvert de coquilles d'œufs noires que les gens jettent après les avoir bouillies dans les eaux thermales. Cela m'a semblé une image digne d'un film de Kurosawa.

En redescendant des hauteurs, j'ai entendu des sons gutturaux terribles. De la brume est apparue une jeune fille handicapée mentale, marchant lentement et accompagnée d'un homme d'une soixantaine d'années qui prenait soin d'elle. Tous ceux qui descendaient, particulièrement les enfants, l'évitaient avec une certaine terreur. Mais cet homme la soutenait de son bras avec une grande tendresse, amour et dignité.

Cette image m'a profondément ému. Pendant le même voyage, quelques mois plus tard, alors que j'étais à Stockholm avec ma famille, je n'ai pas cessé de rencontrer des sourds-muets. Il y en avait partout. J'étais interpellé par leur gestuelle et par le caractère dramatique de leur communication. Tout cela m'est apparu comme un langage inconnu et ignoré de presque tout le monde – de nous qui avons la grâce de toucher et d'être touchés par la parole. La même nuit, j'eus un rêve érotique sur une adolescente dans un cabinet de dentiste. Toutes ces images apparemment sans lien m'ont fourni les raisons de tourner dans une des villes que je préfère – à cause de son mystère et de ses contradictions. J'ai eu l'idée de raconter l'histoire d'un père et d'une fille avec deux genres de solitude très différentes, mais tout aussi terribles. J'ai appelé Guillermo de Stockholm, il a aimé l'idée et à partir de là, nous avons décidé qu'il y aurait trois histoires au lieu de cinq. Les deux années de collaboration qui ont suivi ont été difficiles et intenses. Bien que Guillermo ne connaisse ni le Japon ni le Maroc, son talent lui a permis d'écrire un scénario qui a servi de *blueprint* pour démarrer la première étape de l'aventure de *Babel*.

Une fois le scénario au point, alors que je n'avais encore aucun acteur pour ce projet, et moins encore de financement assuré, j'ai invité Jon Kilik et Steve Golin à produire le film avec moi. J'autofinançais encore le projet et ils furent les premiers à croire au film et à être prêts à tenter l'aventure comme associés – jusqu'à la fin. En décembre 2004, nous avons pris l'avion tous trois avec Brigitte Broch, mon amie et designeuse de production, et nous nous sommes rendus à Tunis et au Maroc pour commencer les premiers repérages et le vrai voyage de *Babel*.

Pour ce film, tu as toujours voulu un cadre global : une trame dans laquelle une pomme tombant d'un arbre aurait un impact économique, politique et humain à deux continents de distance. À quel moment *Babel* est-il devenu une histoire moins sur la globalisation que sur trois familles ?

La seule raison pour laquelle les trois films peuvent être considérés comme une trilogie, hormis le fait qu'ils ont en commun une structure d'histoires croisées, c'est qu'il s'agit en définitive d'histoires sur les rapports entre parents et enfants. Cela vaut pour *Amours chiennes* aussi bien que pour *21 Grammes*. Même si *Babel* aborde implicitement des thèmes sociaux ou politiques à une échelle globale, le film n'en reste pas moins un quartette d'histoires intimes.

Pour moi, l'histoire des enfants marocains, qui devait initialement se dérouler à Tunis, était moins une histoire sur des enfants poursuivis par la police qu'une tragédie sur l'effondrement moral d'une famille musulmane éminemment spirituelle. Pour le père des enfants, il est tout aussi grave que Youssef épie sa sœur et que celle-ci se dénude, que le fait qu'ils aient tiré sur un autobus. Quand les valeurs se perdent, tout perd son sens ; quand un maillon se rompt, ce n'est pas seulement un maillon qui se rompt, mais toute la chaîne.

C'est à partir de cette histoire, qui a toujours été la plus solide, que se sont construites les autres. Au début, l'histoire de Richard et Susan, le couple qui voyage à travers le Maroc, s'attachait beaucoup plus aux aspects politiques qu'à l'aspect familial : elle touchait à la politique des gouvernements et non à la politique de l'humain, qui est beaucoup plus complexe. Elle comportait des scènes avec des ambassadeurs, des vice-ministres et des chaînes de télévision. Il nous a fallu longtemps avant de comprendre qu'il n'y avait pas de place dans cette histoire pour des personnages archétypaux.

Bien qu'une grande partie de l'histoire marocaine soit filmée depuis le point de vue de Susan, le plus difficile pour moi a été de trouver la manière de raconter la perspective de Richard. Et puis à un moment donné, j'ai compris que si je soumettais le point de vue de Richard à une approche hyperréaliste, je pourrais décrire la situation d'un personnage qui ne réalise jamais ce qui se passe dans le monde, ni ce qui se dit aux nouvelles, ni les pressions et les accusations paranoïaques de son gouvernement à l'encontre du gouvernement marocain. C'est seulement par une station de radio émettant dans une langue inconnue et par l'appel téléphonique d'un ami que Richard se rend brièvement compte de ce qui se passe autour de lui. J'ai considéré que si le personnage disposait d'aussi peu d'éléments d'information, je ne devais pas en fournir au public plus qu'il n'en avait lui-même. En tant que civils, quand avons-nous l'opportunité de prendre part aux débats des politiciens et de leurs représentants ? Cela n'arrive qu'au cinéma, et je ne voulais pas que cette histoire soit perçue comme un film. Je voulais que le public perçoive les erreurs politiques et les fausses interprétations des médias de manière intuitive.

Pour moi, l'histoire de Richard et Susan, plus qu'une histoire sur un couple d'Américains qui arrivent ensemble dans le désert pour s'y perdre sans espoir, est l'histoire de deux êtres perdus l'un par rapport à l'autre, qui arrivent dans le désert pour se rencontrer. La clef pour comprendre qui ils sont réside dans le fait qu'ils ont perdu un enfant et dans la douleur et la culpabilité que ce drame a produites en eux.

Dans le cas de Chieko, l'adolescente japonaise, en plus de l'absence d'une mère, elle souffre de l'absence de la parole. Quand nous ne pouvons toucher ou être touchés par les paroles, le corps se transforme en outil, en arme, en invitation.

C'est la même chose dans l'histoire d'Amelia qui, en plus d'être une citoyenne invisible, est aussi une mère non reconnue.

***Babel* passe avec une admirable fluidité d'un pays à l'autre et d'une langue à l'autre, avec une grande empathie pour l'être humain, indépendamment des circonstances. Cela dit, mon sentiment est que ton amour déborde plus qu'ailleurs dans la partie mexicaine. Est-ce quelque chose dont tu as été conscient ?**

Il a été très difficile pour moi de filmer l'histoire mexicaine, pas seulement à cause de la complexité de la question frontalière, mais aussi en raison de l'extrême rudesse des conditions climatiques. Nous avons tourné dans le désert le plus chaud du monde et avec des enfants. Comme il s'agissait de mon pays natal, je pouvais facilement déraper et j'allais être jugé plus rigoureusement. Pénétrer et examiner à la loupe la subculture frontalière qu'autrefois je fuyais et refusais a été toute une aventure anthropologique.

Ma première décision pour rester fidèle et cohérent avec le film, a été d'exclure du scénario – et plus tard au montage – des pans entiers de stéréotypes et de lieux communs qui n'apportaient rien sur le plan dramatique et qui dessinaient ce Mexique idéal et charmant qui n'existe plus aujourd'hui – et moins encore dans une zone comme la frontière avec les États-Unis, où les gens sont plus durs et retors.

Ma seconde décision, du moins au début, a été de considérer le Mexique du point de vue des enfants américains, qui vivent pour la première fois l'expérience d'entrer au Mexique par la frontière de San Jacinto – comme ce sera d'ailleurs le cas pour une grande partie du public tout autour du globe. Comme je te l'ai dit, je passe la frontière tous les six mois avec mes enfants. Bien qu'ils soient mexicains, ils continuent d'être interpellés par les couleurs, les sucreries, l'âne, la boue, les putes, l'absence de gazon et l'air poussiéreux de leur pays. Ce qui n'est que misère et pauvreté pour un adulte, aux yeux d'un enfant, c'est de la couleur et de la joie. Tous ceux qui ont passé la frontière des États-Unis vers l'État de Tijuana savent qu'il y a une certaine électricité dans l'air et un contraste presque absurde.

Certains disent que Tijuana est l'aisselle de l'Amérique latine [à cause de sa situation à l'articulation du « bras » californien. (ndt). Pour moi, c'est un endroit où se côtoient les rêves les plus nobles et les fins les plus tristes.

Dans la communauté d'El Carrizo, à une heure de Tijuana, j'ai filmé le mariage de Luis, le fils d'Amelia. Nous avons souvent assisté à des mariages, et certains se sont terminés à coups de couteaux. Au-delà de l'aspect folklorique, pour moi, ce mariage a toujours représenté la seule possibilité de connaître Amelia et son univers. J'ai eu conscience que si je ne parvenais pas à établir l'empathie du public avec elle à ce moment-là, le personnage était mort. Elle ne serait rien d'autre qu'une servante qui risque la vie de ses enfants de manière irresponsable.

C'est la raison pour laquelle j'ai décidé de construire une bulle cinématographique de temps imaginaire : une capsule qui me permettrait de dessiner Amelia comme mère, comme amie, comme amante, et surtout comme mère postiche d'enfants américains. La chanson de Chavela Vargas flotte en toile de fond pour accompagner les airs de la mélancolie.

Amelia, comme beaucoup de Mexicains, se trouve dans la situation paradoxale de devoir négliger ses propres enfants pour s'occuper d'enfants étrangers. De la même manière, beaucoup de Mexicains qui vivent aux États-Unis réparent des voitures des Américains mais n'ont pas le droit d'avoir un permis de conduire ; ils construisent les maisons des Américains mais n'ont pas assez d'argent pour payer leur propre loyer.

J'ai filmé la frontière mexicaine avec beaucoup d'amour, mais aussi avec beaucoup de souffrance parce que ce sont les deux sentiments qui prédominent dans cette région.

Ton installation du Mexique aux États-Unis au moment de filmer *21 Grammes* a été un immense défi personnel et professionnel. Quels sont les nouveaux défis auxquels tu as été confronté cette fois-ci en tant que réalisateur ? Qu'as-tu atteint que tu n'avais pas encore atteint avant ?

Il y a eu de grands défis d'ordre physique et logistique, mais surtout intellectuel et émotionnel. À mon avis, n'importe qui peut jongler avec trois oranges, mais je te parie que si tu essaies avec quatre, elles vont tomber une centaine de fois avant que tu n'arrives à les maîtriser. *Babel* comporte quatre histoires au lieu de trois comme dans *Amours chiennes* et *21 Grammes*, et le film est différent du schéma auquel j'avais déjà commencé à m'habituer. De plus, du fait que *Babel* a été filmé sur trois continents et dans trois cultures différentes, j'ai dû adapter et réécrire le scénario selon les circonstances.

Dans ce film, je me suis permis davantage de licences poétiques ; je me suis senti beaucoup plus libre et plus sûr que dans mes films précédents. J'ai tenté des choses que je n'avais pas faites dans mes autres films : par exemple, parvenir à faire cohabiter le réalisme et l'hyperréalisme avec le monde de l'imaginaire ; tout cela avec la cohérence et la logique du cinéma muet, mais avec l'anarchie de la musique et de la bande-son comme narrateurs de premier plan.

J'ai transformé une ligne de scénario en une séquence de dix minutes racontée du point de vue du monde intérieur d'un personnage, de manière à ce que le public, par le truchement des images, des sons et des métaphores, soit immergé dans le personnage et dans sa situation. Concernant les séquences qui se déroulent dans le parc et dans la discothèque, j'ai cherché à faire éprouver au public les sons du silence, telle que Chieko les éprouve elle-même depuis sa tête et son point de vue, parce que dans certains cas, c'est le silence qui peut s'avérer vraiment assourdissant. Dans la scène du sauvetage de Richard et Susan par hélicoptère, je voulais que l'image suggère une baleine volante débouchant dans la mer du désert pour représenter un choc des cultures et de profondes différences socio-économiques.

Pour moi, le cinéma n'est pas seulement un argument ou une anecdote illustrée. Le cinéma est ce qui advient entre deux dialogues ; ce qui peut uniquement se dire avec le silence des images. Au-delà de l'identification avec les personnages, avec leur histoire et leurs conditions, j'ai voulu que le public soit investi émotionnellement à travers le montage, avec la musique, la dialectique et la juxtaposition d'idées visuelles et sensorielles. C'est-à-dire, en exploitant à fond toutes les ressources du cinéma comme je ne l'avais encore jamais fait auparavant. Dans toute cette orchestration, moi et toute l'équipe devons être invisibles et disparaître pendant l'expérience cinématographique du spectateur. Si mon travail apparaît à l'écran, j'ai échoué et tout ce que je t'ai dit n'a aucun sens.

Le cinéma est un animal vivant et se fait au fil d'étapes qui semblent ne jamais devoir finir. Comme tu le sais, monter un film revient à le réécrire. En ce sens, de par la nature même de *Babel*, le montage a été particulièrement difficile. Je ne conçois pas de travailler avec un autre monteur qu'avec Stephen Mirrione. Son talent et sa clairvoyance ont été d'une importance cruciale pour parvenir à jongler avec ces quatre oranges et l'élégance de ses coupes a permis de rendre les transitions plus organiques. Nous avons supprimé des blocs entiers qui déséquilibraient la structure originale du scénario, et une fois de plus, je me suis retrouvé à sculpter la pierre pour parvenir à ce que sa vraie forme se révèle.

Je me rappelle surtout comment nous avons trouvé l'épilogue de l'histoire de Youssef et Ahmed. Un jour que nous changions de lieu de tournage dans les montagnes d'Ouarzazate, un vent insolite a commencé à souffler. Nous étions presque obligés de nous accrocher pour ne pas être emportés. J'ai fait sortir les caméras de la camionnette et j'ai demandé à Youssef et Ahmed de jouer avec le vent au bord du gouffre. L'image n'avait aucune fonction dramatique, mais pour moi, elle avait un merveilleux contenu esthétique et poétique. De la même manière, j'ai fait placer une vieille barque abandonnée au milieu d'une immense vallée désertique et rocheuse pour suggérer l'existence d'une mer dans cette région. Lors des repérages de Tunis, nous avons trouvé des centaines de fossiles marins ; j'ai même appris qu'on avait découvert des squelettes de baleines en plein désert du Sahara. Cette idée m'a ému et au fil du temps, elle a suscité en moi un vertige. Pour moi, la barque dans le désert était une métaphore de l'arche de Noé : le passage de l'homme dans les immensités désertes du temps.

Et le dernier jour du tournage, j'ai filmé sur un *dolly* un gros plan de Youssef pleurant la mort de son frère. Initialement, mon idée était de couper juste sur la scène de la barque de Noé, dans laquelle on voyait s'éloigner son frère et son père, comme une image prémonitoire de la mort du frère. Cela dit, en voyant le premier montage, j'ai trouvé que l'histoire de Youssef et Ahmed se terminait trop tôt, et de ce fait très loin de la fin du film. C'était comme si la mort d'Ahmed n'avait pas d'importance. Pire encore, pour le spectateur, ce moment restait tellement éloigné du climat émotionnel de la fin qu'on risquait de l'oublier.

Il nous fallait un épilogue tel qu'en avaient les trois autres histoires. On pourrait croire qu'il a été facile de trouver la manière de monter ces petits moments et de les placer là où ils devenaient une évidence, mais en réalité, cela a demandé un temps et un travail considérables. Et maintenant, ce n'est pas seulement un grand épilogue pour cette histoire, mais aussi un des moments du film les plus chargés émotionnellement, parce qu'en plus d'être le seul *flashahead* dans le vocabulaire cinématographique du film, ce moment synthétise et fusionne métaphoriquement les déserts du Maroc et du Mexique.

Le vent qui souffle dans les cheveux d'Amelia quand elle embrasse son fils à la frontière est le même qui harcèle les enfants au Maroc, et c'est aussi le même vent produit par l'hélicoptère qui vient sauver Susan et Richard. Cette section et celle de Chieko dans le parc et dans la discothèque sont mes séquences de montage préférées avec celles où Mirrione a joué un rôle crucial avec son talent et sa rigueur.

Un autre défi important du montage était de passer d'un pays à l'autre sans que la transition soit abrupte, sans qu'elle distraie par trop le spectateur. Ici, la musique a été un facteur essentiel, et Gustavo Santaolalla, une fois de plus, en a été la clef.

En plus de voyager et de séjourner dans tous les pays où nous avons tourné pour faire des recherches et des enregistrements, Gustavo a décidé de se servir du oud – un instrument arabe très ancien qui est la mère de la guitare – pour qu'il soit l'ADN musical du film. Avec ses cordes très dures, l'oud est un instrument difficile à jouer. Gustavo a appris à en jouer pour pouvoir interpréter la partition.

Bien que je ne veuille pas faire de la musique un élément plus présent que dans mes autres films, de manière minimaliste, la pulpe des doigts de Santaolalla parvient à nous briser le cœur avec une seule note. Outre le fait qu'il est profondément afro-méditerranéen, le son du oud a la particularité de nous rappeler les pleurs de la guitare de flamenco et donc de la guitare mexicaine, le tout avec un parfum de koto japonais. Dans un seul instrument, le génie de Santolalla a ainsi su réunir les trois cultures sans devoir faire appel aux instruments folkloriques de chaque pays, ce qui aurait été affreux.

Toutes ces choses ont été découvertes en cours de route ; au bout du compte, je fais du cinéma pour apprendre à faire du cinéma. Chaque fois que je commence un film, c'est comme si j'oubliais tout ce que j'avais appris lors du précédent. C'est comme si j'étais atteint prématurément de la maladie d'Alzheimer. De fait, je ne me considère pas comme un réalisateur de cinéma, mais comme un gars qui a fait trois films et quelques courts métrages. Mais aussi comme un compositeur frustré.

Mon rêve est de réaliser au moins un grand film dans ma vie, mais je sens parfois que les choses que je veux faire sont à des années-lumière du talent dont je dispose pour les mener à bien.

Malgré le contexte global et polyglotte, *Babel* semble plus personnel et plus intime que tes films précédents. À quoi cela tient-il à ton avis ?

Dans tous les pays où j'ai tourné *Babel*, j'ai tâché de me lier les mains pour ne pas succomber à mes propres tentations esthétiques et finir par faire un docudrame à la *National Geographic*, ou pire, quatre courts métrages sans lien, filmés du point de vue d'un touriste. Il a fallu faire des choix opposés et même contradictoires : d'un côté, il fallait séparer et délimiter les histoires, et à un autre niveau, il fallait les unifier.

Ce qui fait que *Babel* est finalement devenu un film homogène, ça a été la possibilité de trouver une note commune qui court tout du long.

Au-delà de l'aspect formel, dont je te parlerai après, je regarde mes personnages avec beaucoup de tendresse et d'empathie. Ce regard imprègne tout le film et a permis d'obtenir une unité de ton et d'esprit qui s'impose malgré les différents styles visuels dans lesquels j'ai filmé. Dans chaque scène, j'ai tâché de me concentrer sur le fait de filmer obsessionnellement l'aspect de l'intimité et des microdétails du monde intérieur et extérieur des personnages. Bien que cela puisse paraître évident, j'ai pensé localement pour que cela fonctionne universellement.

La partie interne – l'âme du film – est une même histoire racontée quatre fois, sur les grandes tragédies du mammifère vertical : l'incapacité d'aimer et de recevoir de l'amour, et la vulnérabilité des êtres que nous aimons. Chaque fois que je commençais le tournage d'une histoire, c'était comme si je commençais un autre film. À la fin, j'aimais mes personnages, je souffrais et pleurais avec eux et je me rendais compte que ce n'était rien d'autre que le même film raconté encore une fois.

La meilleure chose dans le tournage de *Babel*, c'est que j'ai commencé par tourner un film sur les différences entre les êtres humains – sur ce qui nous sépare, sur les barrières physiques et linguistiques – mais en cours de route, je me suis rendu compte que je faisais un film sur les choses qui nous unissent, qui nous relient, et qui font que nous sommes un. Ces choses sont l'amour et la souffrance : ce qui rend heureux un Japonais ou un Marocain pourra être très différent, mais ce qui nous rend misérables est la même chose pour chacun.

Pour ce qui concerne l'aspect extérieur – formel et esthétique –, mon ami l'extraordinaire photographe Rodrigo Prieto et moi avons pris le risque de décider de faire de *Babel* un pastiche. Chaque pays devait être filmé dans un style particulier, avec des textures et dans des formats différents. En théorie, chaque histoire devait avoir sa propre personnalité. Chaque style et chaque format devait être subordonné aux nécessités dramatiques des personnages et des situations.

En même temps, ma talentueuse amie Brigitte Broch nous a proposé de distinguer ces pays par différentes gammes de rouges. Rouge marocain pour le Maroc, rouge vif pour le Mexique et un rouge-violet pour le Japon. Le Maroc a été filmé en 16 mm avec des couleurs délavées, le Mexique en 35 mm avec des couleurs vives, et le Japon, suite à une brillante proposition de Rodrigo, en Panavision, avec des lentilles anamorphiques qui isolent le personnage de manière spectaculaire et appropriée pour le sujet de cette histoire.

La raison pour laquelle ce collage fonctionne, c'est que pour tous ces choix apparemment disparates, il y a toujours eu une raison très profonde et un travail de connexion et d'équipe très étroit. Rodrigo Prieto et Brigitte Broch sont ma main droite et ma main gauche. Leur collaboration est très importante dans mon travail et le niveau de compréhension auquel nous sommes parvenus enrichit énormément le résultat final.

J'ai toujours cherché à ce que le langage cinématographique soit cohérent avec les personnages et que ma grammaire et mon style, même si tout le film a été filmé en caméra manuelle, aient une respiration, un *beat* interne au service de l'émotionnalité de la mise en scène.

Apparemment, le tournage a lui-même été une tour de *Babel*. Comment ça a été de travailler avec des gens qui n'avaient jamais joué et qui ne parlaient pas ta langue ?

Diriger des acteurs est une chose difficile. Diriger des acteurs dans une langue qui n'est pas la tienne est beaucoup plus difficile. Maintenant, diriger des non acteurs dans une langue que tu ne comprends pas est le défi le plus grand auquel j'aie jamais été confronté en tant que réalisateur. Il ne restait plus que dix-sept jours avant le début du tournage au Maroc, et je n'avais encore aucun acteur hormis Brad Pitt et Cate Blanchett.

Pour les rôles des enfants Youssef et Ahmed et de leur famille de bergers, et pour tous les personnages autour de l'histoire de Richard et Susan, j'ai d'abord cherché des acteurs professionnels de la communauté marocaine, ainsi que dans les communautés musulmanes de Paris. Cela dit, aucun d'entre eux n'avait l'apparence que je cherchais. Il me fallait ces peaux tannées qu'on ne trouve qu'au sud de l'Atlas et dans l'intérieur du Sahara. La majorité des acteurs professionnels avaient les traits fins, la peau lisse, et ils avaient pris les mauvaises habitudes de jeu des séries télévisées. Nous avions beau les maquiller, ils ressemblaient aux acteurs d'une production Hallmark.

C'est alors qu'avec Alfonso Gómez, Hervé Jacubowicz et Marc Robert, mon équipe de casting, je résolus d'entreprendre une recherche désespérée dans tous les humbles villages des environs de Tamnougalt et d'Ouarzazate pour y trouver les vrais personnages de *Babel*.

Des hauteurs des mosquées et avec des haut-parleurs bruyants, on annonçait la bonne nouvelle que le film *Babel* recherchait des acteurs pour jouer. Des centaines de personnes se sont présentées et nous les avons prises en vidéo. Avec Hiam Abass, une actrice et merveilleuse amie qui, plus que mon *dialogue coach*, est devenue mon ange gardien, le lendemain, nous avons fait des bouts d'essai avec les personnes sélectionnées et quelques exercices que je fais chaque fois pour percevoir leur palette émotionnelle.

C'était la première fois que je travaillais avec des non acteurs, avec des gens courants et ordinaires. Ça a été hallucinant ; je recommencerai chaque fois que je le pourrai et pour toujours. Bien que le processus puisse être frustrant et que l'ignorance et le manque de technique puissent être des inconvénients, l'innocence est et sera toujours plus puissante que l'expérience. La virginité, la pureté et l'honnêteté de quelqu'un qui joue son propre rôle est inégalable.

Un exemple en est Abdullah, le père des enfants marocains. Dans la vie, c'est un menuisier de la banlieue de Fès, et pourtant, sa discipline et son registre dramatique m'ont laissé bouche bée. Dans des scènes comme celle où il frappe ses enfants ou dans celle où son fils Ahmed meurt – qui a nécessité trois jours de tournage – il maintenait l'intensité à chaque prise et à chaque instant. Une fois que je lui avais indiqué les mouvements physiques de la mise en scène, il les répétait avec rythme et précision. Des scènes comme celles-ci sont difficiles à jouer même pour des acteurs professionnels de niveau mondial.

La même chose s'est passée avec Hassan ou avec Youssef. Dès le premier moment, leurs yeux m'ont appris qu'ils possédaient une grande vie intérieure. Rien qu'en parlant quelques minutes avec quelqu'un et en le regardant dans les yeux, il est facile de se rendre compte si la personne possède le bagage émotionnel suffisant pour pouvoir extraire un peu de sentiments de l'intérieur et appréhender métaphoriquement ce qui arrive au personnage qu'il va représenter.

Cela dit, le mélange d'acteurs professionnels et non professionnels est quelque chose de plus compliqué. Dans l'histoire de Youssef et Ahmed, il n'y avait que des acteurs non professionnels. Dans celle de Richard et Susan en revanche, ce n'était pas le cas. Des scènes apparemment simples comme celle de Cate Blanchett et de Sfia, la vieille femme qui soigne Susan quand elle arrive en sang dans la chambre, ou celle du vétérinaire qui recoud la plaie de Susan en présence de Richard n'ont pas du tout été faciles.

Sfia était une femme berbère de 85 ans, et elle n'avait encore jamais vu une caméra de sa vie. Elle était née à Taguenzalte, un village où nous avons dû filmer sans électricité, et elle vivait dans la maison attenante à celle où nous tournions. Sfia parle uniquement berbère. Le vétérinaire est en fait le vétérinaire du village et il parle seulement l'arabe. Pour Sfia, une instruction aussi simple que « quand tu entends crier ‹ What ›, tu te lèves et tu fermes la fenêtre », se transformait en odyssée de trois heures. C'était un tour de force d'arriver à ce qu'elle le fasse bien, plusieurs fois de suite de la même manière et surtout, qu'elle ne se retourne pas chaque fois vers la caméra en souriant.

Ce que j'ai appris, c'est que si le réalisateur choisit quelqu'un qui exprime physiquement ce que le personnage doit exprimer au premier coup d'œil et que si cette personne possède ne serait-ce qu'un seul trait grâce auquel elle peut s'identifier au personnage, une fois que le réalisateur trouve cette personne et qu'il lui indique ses objectifs dramatiques de manière simple et claire, il peut faire jouer n'importe quel être humain de la planète.

Et comment s'est passée l'expérience de travailler avec quelqu'un comme Brad Pitt, qui est une célébrité mondiale, au milieu de cet ensemble de non acteurs et dans des conditions aussi adverses ? Qu'est-ce qui t'a amené à les choisir, lui et Cate Blanchett ?

Travailler avec les acteurs professionnels de *Babel* a été une expérience aussi enrichissante que le travail avec les acteurs non professionnels.

Même quand la fiction, plusieurs fois pendant le tournage, est venue côtoyer la réalité et que les situations et conditions de travail – le climat, les lieux, les différences de langue – ont été difficiles, je me suis toujours senti soutenu par les acteurs et ils m'ont fait l'honneur de m'accorder leur confiance.

Bien que le rôle de Richard puisse à première vue ne pas sembler évident pour un acteur comme Brad Pitt, il m'a toujours semblé que Brad possède une présence magnétique qui va au-delà de sa popularité. Il donne l'impression de quelqu'un qui est à l'aise avec lui-même. Quand j'ai fait sa connaissance il y a quatre ans, ce qui m'a frappé d'emblée, c'est sa bravoure. Nous filmions ensemble une campagne publicitaire pour des jeans japonais qui consistait en une série de vignettes absurdes que j'inventais spontanément au fur et à mesure du tournage.

Brad tenait à pousser les choses jusqu'à un point où il se mettait en danger physiquement. La maison de production a commencé à être nerveuse en voyant ce que nous faisions lui et moi ; ils ont établi un document stipulant qu'ils étaient dégagés de toute responsabilité si Brad se blessait physiquement et lui ont demandé de le signer. Pâle et angoissé, son manager lui a demandé d'arrêter ses frasques et de ne signer en aucun cas ce genre de papier. Brad a signé la feuille sans même y jeter un coup d'œil et a continué de faire ce qu'il voulait. Nous avons encore passé quelques heures à filmer et nous nous sommes beaucoup amusés. Dans la dernière vignette, on voyait Brad sur une planche de surf descendant la mince rampe d'un escalier géant.

Quatre ans plus tard, quand je lui ai proposé le rôle de Richard dans *Babel*, il a accepté sans objection. Il n'est pas facile que des acteurs et des célébrités de sa stature acceptent d'interpréter ce genre de personnage. Après tout, il y a toujours un risque implicite dans tout film indépendant à faible budget, et les bonnes intentions ne suffisent pas toujours à produire de bons résultats.

Pour moi, le défi était d'arriver à ce que Brad Pitt, la célébrité, s'efface derrière le personnage pour laisser le champ libre non seulement à l'acteur, mais aussi à l'être humain derrière l'image. Si à l'arrivée les gens pouvaient oublier qui il était – si lui pouvait se mêler aux autres personnages sans se faire remarquer plus qu'eux, ce serait une victoire non seulement pour Brad Pitt, mais aussi pour le film. Il y avait un gros risque pour lui et il a relevé tous les défis avec courage. Il a surtout accepté le risque suprême auquel sont toujours exposés les acteurs : il s'est mis entre mes mains et m'a accordé sa confiance. Le processus n'a pas été facile. Il passait alors par des moments difficiles dans sa vie ; cela dit, jamais il n'a laissé un domaine empiéter sur l'autre.

Dans le scénario original, le conflit entre Richard et Susan naissait d'une infidélité commise autrefois par Richard. Quelques semaines avant le tournage, j'ai proposé de porter le drame à un niveau plus profond – comme l'est la mort d'un enfant à la naissance. Brad a appris le changement du scénario en arrivant au Maroc. En fait, il était déjà difficile de construire un personnage à partir de seulement trente pages d'histoire. Et il n'était pas facile d'encaisser le choc de ce nouvel élément dramatique dans l'intrigue. Qui était Richard ? Pourquoi fit-il ce qu'il fit ? Chaque jour, dans des conditions physiques harassantes, il a fallu creuser, découvrir et inventer le personnage vulnérable que Brad a construit à l'écran.

Entre l'épuisement physique et l'intensité émotionnelle constante qu'exigeait le personnage, Brad, tout comme son personnage, est devenu de plus en plus fragile et vulnérable jusqu'à parvenir à ce moment où il exsude une grande force et une grande tendresse, et que personnellement je trouve très beau : l'appel téléphonique final de Richard à son fils, qui nous révèle finalement l'universalité de l'être humain face à l'impuissance, et dans laquelle Brad a vraiment tout donné.

Le cas de Cate Blanchett a été différent. Elle est depuis bien longtemps une de mes actrices préférées et je l'ai littéralement suppliée d'accepter d'interpréter le rôle de Susan. Elle éprouvait quelques réticences et ses raisons n'étaient pas sans fondement : dans le scénario, le personnage de Susan était celui d'une femme qui passe les trois-quarts du film allongée par terre, en sang, à moitié inconsciente.

Mais à mon sens, c'était seulement du point de vue de Susan que les événements pouvaient tirer toute leur force et leur pertinence, et c'est ce que je lui ai expliqué. Pour parvenir à ce qu'en 28 minutes, le public parvienne à l'aimer et se sente en empathie avec un personnage qui au début se lave les mains avec un produit désinfectant, qui verse du Coca-Cola sur son mari par terre et se montre très incommode avec le moindre centimètre de sa vie et de son corps, il fallait une actrice de l'envergure de Cate. Chaque moment de son personnage, qu'elle soit debout, endormie ou assise, tourne autour de l'émotion.

Dès la première scène, c'est elle qui fixe les règles et le niveau de jeu.

Bien que je l'aie vue d'innombrables fois, je suis toujours stupéfait par ce moment où elle fume la pipe. Cela peut sembler facile, mais ce qu'elle fait, ce qu'elle dit et fait éprouver avec ses yeux, et seulement avec ses yeux – parce qu'elle ne peut bouger aucune autre partie de son corps – est tout simplement hallucinant.

Et même quand – pour les raisons que je t'ai expliquées – il a fallu faire 25 prises du même plan pour que le vétérinaire ou Sfia puissent trouver leur texte ou leur rythme, Cate, à chaque prise, m'a donné la même intensité. Sa générosité et la maîtrise de ses moyens font que le travail d'un réalisateur est vraiment facilité.

Quel impact cela a-t-il eu dans ta vie de voyager dans la moitié du monde et de vivre avec des gens d'origines et de coutumes aussi différentes ? Comment *Babel* a-t-il changé ta vision des choses ?

Je crois que chaque film te transforme, mais pour moi, celui-ci a été de loin celui qui m'a le plus profondément marqué. Plus qu'un choix professionnel, il a été une décision de vie. Je savais qu'il m'obligerait à un sacrifice et à une transformation dans la vie quotidienne de ma famille, qui est mon noyau et ma base. Je savais que mes enfants, ma femme et moi allions profiter humainement les uns des autres, mais qu'il y aurait aussi à faire beaucoup de sacrifices. On ne peut être le même après s'être connecté et engagé avec autant de personnes. Si avant le tournage, mon attitude à l'égard de la vie était plus cynique et pessimiste, en terminant le film, j'ai eu plus d'espoir et d'optimisme concernant l'être humain, parce qu'assurément ces préjugés et ces frontières intérieures peuvent s'effondrer du seul fait d'être touchés. Je me suis rendu compte que le choc entre la culture nord-américaine et la culture musulmane ne résultait pas du fait qu'elles sont radicalement opposées, mais de ce qu'elles sont incroyablement semblables. Bien qu'apparemment distincts, leur fanatisme, leur nationalisme poussé à l'extrême et l'objectivation de la femme sont de proches parents.

Pendant le tournage de *Babel*, je me suis rendu compte que les gens sont fondamentalement bons, et que moins ils possèdent, plus ils sont purs et heureux.

Je sais que tu es une personne profondément religieuse et spirituelle. Malgré cela, et bien que dans tes films tu abordes des thèmes judéo-chrétiens comme la chute, la rédemption ou la culpabilité, la religion ne joue pas un rôle central dans tes histoires – pas même dans *Babel*, qui traite de gens issus de différentes cultures. Quelles sont les raisons de ce choix – à une époque où la religion se brandit comme un drapeau ?

Pour moi, le débat religieux se situe sur le terrain intellectuel plutôt que moral. Contrairement à *21 Grammes*, dans lequel j'ai exploré le phénomène du fanatisme à travers le personnage de Benicio del Toro, dans *Babel*, il n'y avait pas de place pour la question religieuse.

Le film traite très précisément de la vulnérabilité et de la fragilité de l'être humain : de ces petits animaux qu'en définitive nous sommes, du fait que même si nous urinons, nous aimons et avons besoin de l'autre, du fait que la solitude nous tue, que le désamour nous anéantit – tout comme la perte d'un litre de sang. Dans une scène, le personnage de Richard regarde Anouar faire sa prière vers la Mecque ; il le regarde comme s'il voulait trouver une foi que lui, malheureusement, ne possède pas.

Dans *Babel*, c'est Dieu qui est à l'origine de la confusion, et c'est à l'homme qu'il revient aujourd'hui de trouver la solution. Dieu est absent de cette équation.

Tu as fait toute ta carrière de réalisateur de longs métrages avec beaucoup des mêmes collaborateurs : Rodrigo Prieto, Guillermo Arriaga, Martín Hernandez. Comment est-ce de se développer et de grandir avec eux ? Quelle a été l'influence de leurs styles et de leurs talents sur tes films ?

J'ai connu Rodrigo Prieto comme directeur de la photographie à l'époque où je tournais encore des spots publicitaires. Nous avons travaillé ensemble pour différentes campagnes. Je n'oublierai jamais le jour où après lui avoir envoyé le scénario d'*Amours chiennes*, je l'ai invité à déjeuner pour que nous échangions des idées sur la manière dont nous pourrions aborder le projet visuellement. J'avais avec moi une série de livres de photographie fixe comme référence de ce que je voulais. De sa mallette, Rodrigo a alors sorti les mêmes livres que ceux que j'avais apportés.

Dès cet instant, j'ai su qu'il y avait entre nous une connexion et une vision partagée des choses. Planifier le tournage avec Rodrigo ou être avec lui sur les décors est un bonheur, le voir travailler avec la caméra est une expérience, mais voir et découvrir plus tard dans la salle de montage, dans le détail, sa manière incomparable de raconter avec la caméra les détails émotionnels les plus infimes est une chose impressionnante.

Dans *Babel*, il n'y a que trois scènes pour lesquelles nous nous sommes servis d'un *dolly* : la première, la dernière et le gros plan de Youssef pleurant la mort de son frère. Le reste a été filmé par Rodrigo caméra à l'épaule. D'*Amours chiennes* à *Babel*, je l'ai vu grandir d'une manière hallucinante. Sa maîtrise de l'éclairage et ses connaissances techniques sont immenses, mais plus grande encore est son élégance en tant qu'être humain. Dans un film, personne n'est plus proche de moi que lui. Nous nous connaissons si bien que quand nous sommes sur place, d'un seul geste ou d'un simple son guttural codé, nous pouvons arrêter toute une stratégie de filmage. En plus de douze ans de fréquentation et de travail commun, nous n'avons jamais connu un seul moment désagréable.

J'ai connu Brigitte Broch presque à la même époque que Rodrigo. Nous avons travaillé ensemble pour la première fois pour une campagne publicitaire qui a remporté de nombreux prix internationaux (lors de laquelle, curieusement, j'ai aussi travaillé pour la première fois avec Gael Barcía Bernal). Brigitte est un authentique hymne à la vie. Quand elle conçoit une atmosphère, chacun de ses objets et détails, si infimes soient-ils, parlent des personnages et les décrivent avec une grande profondeur. Nous aimons tourner dans des espaces loués et elle a toujours un flair incroyable pour trouver le meilleur endroit. À parler constamment avec elle de couleurs, de textures, d'odeurs et de formes tout au long des interminables repérages de par le monde, en réalité nous parlons de la vie. Sans elle, mes films et ma vie ne seraient pas ce qu'ils sont.

Martín Hernandez et moi avons fait nos études ensemble à l'université. Nous avons réalisé notre premier projet commun quand nous avions 20 ans : j'étais assistant réalisateur et lui compositeur pour un court métrage réalisé par un ami commun, et Martín en était aussi l'ingénieur du son. Plus tard, nous avons tous deux intégré une station de radio dans laquelle nous avions chacun une émission de trois heures. Pendant cinq ans, la station a été numéro un à Mexico, et à partir de là, j'ai écrit des histoires, conçu des personnages et des séquences transgressives et provocatrices, et Martín les produisait pour la radio. Aujourd'hui, 22 ans plus tard, nous continuons de travailler ensemble et tout n'a cessé de grandir – pas seulement notre amitié. Comme personne, Martín possède la singulière faculté de te faire voir et éprouver l'épiderme du son.

Pelayo Guttiérrez, le réalisateur du court métrage qui nous a permis de nous connaître Martín et moi, est aussi la personne qui m'a présenté Guillermo Arriaga. À l'époque, j'avais déclaré dans un journal que le niveau des professeurs dans les universités mexicaines était désastreux. Guillermo enseignait alors à l'université. Quand il est arrivé au repas où notre ami Pelayo devait nous présenter, Guillermo, sans me connaître, était déjà furieux contre moi. Cela dit, au fil du repas, nous nous sommes trouvé des points communs et pour finir, je l'ai invité à écrire un scénario que je mettais au point à l'époque, et qui était le prétexte de ce repas. Notre amitié s'est renforcée et cette première rencontre a généré différents rêves et projets communs. C'est ainsi qu'a débuté une relation très fructueuse qui a débuté avec *Amours chiennes*. Sa capacité à narrer et à synthétiser les situations les plus complexes en deux lignes et à trouver des solutions inespérées à des problèmes désespérants est tout à fait unique. C'est un collaborateur qui a son univers propre en même temps qu'une grande flexibilité qui lui permet de travailler en équipe pendant qu'il développe son travail, et aussi de subordonner l'histoire et les personnages aux intérêts du film.

En face, Lynn Fainchtein est notre « ennemie ». Elle avait une émission de radio dans une station rivale, et bien qu'elle se refuse à l'admettre, nous n'arrêtions pas de nous démolir. Sérieusement, son goût musical était parfait et son émission était la seule qu'à l'insu de tous, j'osais écouter en dehors de ma propre station. Aujourd'hui, nous sommes de grands amis. Son goût pour la musique n'a pas changé : éclectique et exquis. Étant de la même génération, nous partageons des affinités musicales et c'est elle qui fait danser mes films. C'est aussi elle qui m'a présenté Gustavo Santaolalla en me faisant écouter le disque de Ron Rocco au moment où je cherchais un compositeur pour *Amours chiennes*.

Je me rappelle avoir pris un avion pour Los Angeles avec une cassette VHS contenant un plan d'*Amours chiennes* pour le présenter à Santaolalla. J'avais prévu qu'il ne ferait la bande-son que si cela lui plaisait. Je suis sorti dans le jardin pendant qu'il visionnait la cassette et j'ai fumé un paquet de cigarettes. Deux heures plus tard, il est sorti les larmes aux yeux. Une forte accolade a scellé notre amitié à jamais. Il n'y a personne comme lui pour te briser le cœur d'une seule note de l'instrument qu'on lui met entre les mains. Anibal est son associé et frère d'âme. Ces deux compères ont été des clefs de voûte pour mes films.

D'un autre côté, pour les décors, il n'y a qu'un seul gourou : un type dont tout le monde recherche la présence : où qu'il soit, il transforme les lieux en espaces d'équilibre et de bonne humeur. C'est presque un thérapeute. On l'appelle Le Requin et son vrai nom est José Antonio García. En plus d'être un ingénieur du son hors du commun, son amitié et ses qualités humaines font de lui quelqu'un d'irremplaçable pour moi. Alfonso Gómez Rejón est une autre personne qui a été d'une importance vitale pour 21 *Grammes* et *Babel* : dans 21 *Grammes*, il a été mon assistant personnel et m'a aidé à faire des recherches infiniment précieuses pour les personnages, et là, pour *Babel*, il a aussi été directeur de casting, chercheur et chef de la seconde unité.

Ses matériaux ont été indispensables et son aide pour le casting dans les rues incroyable.

Je pourrais encore continuer longtemps à te raconter combien sont et ont été importantes pour moi des personnes comme Tita Lombardo, producteur exécutif d'*Amours chiennes* et aussi de *Babel* ; je la considère comme ma marraine de cinéma.

Ou comme Corinne Weber, mon assistante depuis cinq ans, qui a aussi été productrice associée pour *Babel*. Et Robbie et Joey, le chef électro et le *key grip* de Rodrigo, qui depuis 21 *Grammes* ont accompli des prouesses techniques inexplicables pour obtenir ce que demandait le film, et qui font aujourd'hui partie de la famille, ou encore Batan Silva, qui a été mon assistant réalisateur pour la première fois à cette occasion, avec l'apothéose finale du Japon.

Mais le plus incroyable, c'est aussi d'avoir eu le privilège et la chance de travailler pour la première fois avec Jon Kilik, Steve Golin et Ann Ruark.

Dans une production de cette envergure, il n'est pas facile de maintenir constamment à flots la vision du film et de résoudre en même temps les problèmes sans fin de logistique et de financement pour pouvoir mener le projet à terme.

Fait incroyable, toujours et jusqu'au dernier jour, il y a eu entre nous une grande communion, une solidarité et un respect indéfectibles.

Le film a pu être mené à bien tel que nous l'avions projeté et ils ont réalisé un travail inouï en termes financiers, techniques et humains.

Ann Ruark, comme productrice associée et producteur exécutif, compte parmi les rares exceptions qui manient et comprennent tous les aspects de la réalisation d'un film, et surtout, qui le font avec classe.

Pour finir, qui aurait pu prévoir que par un jeu du destin, la personne qui m'a aidé dès le début à démarrer et à finaliser le projet, mon grand ami et agent John Lesher, serait aussi celle qui allait lancer et distribuer *Babel* ?

J'ai eu la chance de rencontrer Brad Grey au bon moment, alors qu'il était juste en train de réaliser son nouveau rêve de transformer Paramount Pictures. Il nous a fait confiance dès le début et croyait cent pour cent au projet, nous donnant tout le soutien, le respect et la liberté dont nous avions besoin pour faire le film.

Quand on travaille au sein d'une famille comme celle que nous formons, un tournage ressemble plus à un groupe de rock en tournée qu'à une équipe de cinéma produisant un film. Les relations intenses et en même temps éphémères qui naissent pendant le tournage ne sont pas faciles à vivre dans la mesure où dans des espaces vastes et dans des lieux généralement éloignés, tu vis plus avec une équipe qu'avec ta propre famille. Quand un tournage se termine, on sait qu'il est très possible qu'on ne reverra jamais de sa vie telle ou telle personne qu'on a tant aimée. Mon cas est différent parce que je connais tous ceux qui composent ma famille créative depuis bien avant d'avoir été cinéaste, ce qui représente une double bénédiction : celle de faire un travail qui me plaît et celle de pouvoir le faire avec mes amis.

Biographies / Biografías / Biografien

Alejandro González Iñárritu

Born in Mexico City in 1963, Alejandro González Iñárritu directed and produced his debut feature film in 2000, *Amores Perros*, which was nominated for an Academy Award as Best Foreign Language Film and received over 60 prizes becoming the most awarded film around the world in that year. Iñárritu's follow-up film, *21 Grams* (2003), which he conceived, directed, and produced, starred Sean Penn, Benicio del Toro, and Naomi Watts. Both del Toro and Watts received Oscar nominations for their roles in the film and Penn won the Jury Prize for Best Actor at the Venice Film Festival. In May 2006 Iñárritu completed his third feature film *Babel*, which concluded his trilogy and earned him the Best Director Award at the 59th Cannes Film Festival. Iñárritu also wrote, directed, and produced two short films, *Powder Keg* (2001) and *Darkness* (2002), which was part of the collective feature film 11'09"01. He now lives in Los Angeles with his wife María Eladia Hagerman and their two children, María Eladia and Eliseo.

Nacido en Ciudad de México en 1963, Alejandro González Iñárritu dirigió y produjo en el año 2000 su primer largometraje, *Amores perros*, nominada como mejor película de habla no inglesa en los Oscar; recibió más de 60 premios, lo que le convirtió en la película más galardonada de aquel año. Despúes vendría *21 gramos* (2003), película basada en una idea suya y protagonizada por Sean Penn, Benicio del Toro y Naomi Watts, en la que el cineasta participó como director y productor. Tanto Del Toro como Watts recibieron sendas nominaciones por sus interpretaciones en la película, y Penn obtuvo el Premio del Jurado como mejor actor en el Festival de Cine de Venecia. En mayo de 2006 el director mexicano terminó su tercer largometraje, *Babel*, el filme que cerró su trilogía y que le valió el galardón de mejor director en el 59º Festival de Cine de Cannes. Además, Iñárritu ha escrito, dirigido y producido dos cortometrajes: *Powder Keg* (2001) y *Darkness* (2002), que se inscribe en la película colectiva 11'09"01. Iñárritu vive en Los Ángeles con su esposa María Eladia Hagerman y sus dos hijos María Eladia y Eliseo.

Alejandro González Iñárritu (geb. 1963 in Mexico City) gab sein Debüt als Regisseur und Produzent mit *Amores Perros* (2000). Der Film wurde für einen Oscar als bester ausländischer Film nominiert und erhielt weltweit mehr als 60 Auszeichnungen, mehr als jeder andere Film dieses Jahres. In Iñárritus nächstem Werk, *21 Gramm* (2003), bei dem er Regie führte und das er selbst produzierte, standen Sean Penn, Benicio del Toro und Naomi Watts vor der Kamera. Sowohl del Toro als auch Watts wurden in ihren Filmrollen für einen Oscar nominiert; Penn gewann beim Filmfestival von Venedig den Preis der Jury als bester Schauspieler. Im Mai 2006 vollendete Iñárritu seinen dritten Film, *Babel*, der seine Trilogie abschloss und bei den 59. Filmfestspielen von Cannes den renommierten Preis für die beste Regie gewann. Iñárritu schrieb und produzierte 2001 und 2002 außerdem zwei Kurzfilme, bei denen er auch Regie führte, *Powder Keg* und *Darkness*, der Teil des mehrteiligen Films 11'09"01 war. Iñárritu lebt mit seiner Frau María Eladia Hagerman und ihren beiden Kindern María Eladia und Eliseo in Los Angeles.

Né à Mexico en 1963, Alejandro González Iñárritu a produit et mis en scène en l'an 2000 son premier long métrage, *Amours chiennes*, qui a été nominé aux Academy Awards dans la catégorie meilleur film étranger et a reçu plus de 60 prix internationaux, ce qui en a fait le film le plus primé de cette année. Sur la base d'une idée d'Iñárritu, *21 Grammes* (2003), son film suivant, qu'il a également produit et réalisé, a été interprété par Sean Penn, Benicio del Toro et Naomi Watts. Del Toro et Watts ont tous deux été nominés aux Oscars pour leurs rôles dans ce film et Sean Penn a reçu le prix d'interprétation masculine au Festival de Venise 2003. En mai 2006, Iñárritu a terminé son troisième long métrage *Babel*, qui conclut cette trilogie et lui a valu le prix de la mise en scène au 59ème Festival de Cannes. Iñárritu a aussi écrit, produit et réalisé deux court métrages en 2001 et 2002 : respectivement *Powder Keg* et *Darkness*, qui est une partie du long métrage 11'09"01. Iñárritu vit à Los Angeles avec sa femme María Eladia Hagerman et leurs deux enfants María Eladia et Eliseo.

Mary Ellen Mark

Mary Ellen Mark has achieved worldwide visibility through her numerous books, exhibitions, and editorial magazine work. She is a contributing photographer to *The New Yorker* magazine. For almost three decades, she has traveled extensively to make pictures that reflect a high degree of humanism. Her images of our world's diverse cultures have become landmarks in the field of documentary photography.

Mary Ellen Mark ha logrado un reconocimiento mundial gracias a sus numerosos libros, exposiciones y colaboraciones en revistas. Ejerce regularmente como fotógrafa para el semanario *The New Yorker*. Durante casi treinta años, ha viajado por todo el mundo para captar con su cámara instantáneas que reflejan una gran humanidad. Sus fotografías de las distintas culturas del planeta se han convertido en un hito en el campo de la fotografía documental.

Mary Ellen Mark hat sich durch ihre zahlreichen Bücher, Ausstellungen und die regelmäßigen Beiträge für Zeitschriften wie *The New Yorker* weltweit Beachtung erworben. Seit fast drei Jahrzehnten unternimmt sie ausgedehnte Reisen, um Aufnahmen zu machen, die ihre große Humanität widerspiegeln. Ihre Bilder von den verschiedenen Kulturen unserer Welt sind Meilensteine auf dem Gebiet der Dokumentarfotografie.

Mary Ellen Mark est devenue célèbre dans le monde entier grâce à ses nombreux albums, expositions et reportages pour les magazines. Elle est notamment photographe pour *The New Yorker*. Depuis près de trente ans, elle voyage aux quatre coins du globe et en revient avec des photos marquées par un grand humanisme. Ses images des diverses cultures de notre monde sont devenues de véritables références en matière de photographie documentaire.

Patrick Bard

Patrick Bard, born in France in 1958, is a photographer and a writer. Member of the photographer's agency Editing, based in Paris, he's been focused on the border between Mexico and the United States for years. Patrick's work has been exhibited and published in various countries and his first novel, *The Border*, has been given awards in France and Spain. Working with his wife, Maria Bertha Ferrer, as a team, both travel around the world, from Mongolia to Latin America, all year long.

Patrick Bard nació en Francia en 1958 y es fotógrafo y escritor. Miembro de la agencia de fotógrafos Editing, con sede en París, hace años que centra su trabajo en la frontera entre México y Estados Unidos. La obra de Bard ha sido expuesta y publicada en varios países; además, su primera novela, *La frontera*, ha sido premiada en Francia y España. Junto con su esposa y colaboradora, Maria Bertha Ferrer, viaja durante todo el año por todos los rincones del planeta, desde Mongolia a América Latina.

Patrick Bard (geb. 1958 in Frankreich) ist Fotograf und Schriftsteller. Als Mitglied der Pariser Fotografenagentur Editing beschäftigte er sich jahrelang mit der Grenze zwischen Mexiko und den USA. Patricks Bards Arbeiten wurden in vielen Ländern ausgestellt und publiziert; für seinen Erstlingsroman *The Border* erhielt er Auszeichnungen in Frankreich und Spanien. Zusammen mit seiner Ehefrau Maria Bertha Ferrer reist er das ganze Jahr rund um die Welt, von der Mongolei bis nach Lateinamerika.

Né en France en 1958, Patrick Bard est photographe et écrivain. Membre d'Editing, une agence de photographes basée à Paris, il s'intéresse depuis des années à la frontière qui sépare le Mexique des États-Unis. L'œuvre de Patrick Bard a été exposée et publiée dans plusieurs pays. *La Frontière*, son premier roman, a été primé en France et en Espagne. Travaillant en équipe avec sa femme, Maria Bertha Ferrer, le couple voyage tout au long de l'année, de la Mongolie à l'Amérique Latine.

Graciela Iturbide

Graciela Iturbide has solidified her place as one of the most important contemporary Mexican photographers, whose images reveal her love for her native country and for its people. Most recently, Iturbide has expanded her work to other cultures. Whether at home or in foreign lands, her work explores cultural identity and the ways people adapt to modernization.

Graciela Iturbide se ha consolidado como una de las fotógrafas contemporáneas más importantes de México; su obra refleja el amor por su tierra y su gente. Recientemente, ha integrado otras culturas en la temática de su trabajo. Ya sea que se trate de su país o de otros contextos, las fotografías de Iturbide exploran los matices y expresiones de la identidad cultural, y las formas en que las personas se adaptan a la modernización.

Graciela Iturbide gehört zweifellos zu den bedeutendsten zeitgenössischen Fotografinnen Mexikos. Ihre Bilder zeugen von ihrer Liebe zu ihrer Heimat und deren Menschen. Seit kurzem beschäftigt sich Iturbide in ihrer Arbeit auch mit anderen Kulturen. Doch ob zu Hause oder in fremden Ländern – ihr Werk erkundet kulturelle Identität und die Anpassung der Menschen an die Veränderungen ihrer Gesellschaft.

Graciela Iturbide a gagné sa place parmi les plus importants photographes contemporains du Mexique grâce à des images qui expriment toute sa passion pour son pays natal et ses habitants. Depuis peu, Graciela Iturbide commence à s'intéresser à d'autres cultures. Chez elle comme en terre étrangère, son œuvre explore l'identité culturelle et les différentes façons dont les gens s'adaptent à la modernisation.

Miguel Rio Branco

Miguel Rio Branco was born into a family of diplomats and grew up in Portugal, Brazil, Switzerland, and New York. A ceaseless experimenter in expressive visual arts: Painting, photography, film, and installation have been his medias since the 1960s. He has been awarded several prizes for his work in photography as well as moviemaking. He has published numerous photography books. He has been distributed by Magnum photos since 1980.

Miguel Rio Branco nació en el seno de una familia de diplomáticos y su infancia transcurrió en Portugal, Brasil, Suiza y Nueva York. Branco es un experimentador incansable en el ámbito de las artes visuales expresivas: la pintura, la fotografía, el cine y las instalaciones han sido sus medios de expresión desde los años sesenta. Ha recibido varios galardones por su trabajo tanto en la fotografía como en el cine. También ha publicado numerosos libros de fotografía y, desde 1980, su producción fotográfica es distribuida por Magnum Photos.

Miguel Rio Branco stammt aus einer Diplomatenfamilie und wuchs in Portugal, Brasilien, der Schweiz und in New York auf. Er experimentiert unermüdlich im Bereich der expressiven visuellen Künste: So sind seit den Sechzigerjahren Malerei, Fotografie, Film und Installation sein Metier. Sowohl sein fotografisches Werk als auch seine Arbeit als Filmemacher wurden bereits mehrfach ausgezeichnet. Er hat zahlreiche Fotobücher veröffentlicht. Seit 1980 wird er von Magnum Photos vertreten.

Né dans une famille de diplomates, Miguel Rio Branco a grandi entre le Portugal, le Brésil, la Suisse et New York. Il ne se lasse pas d'explorer les arts visuels : peinture, photographie, cinéma et installations sont les supports qu'il privilégie depuis les années 60. Son travail de photographe et de réalisateur a été distingué par plusieurs prix. Miguel Rio Branco a publié de nombreux albums de photos. Depuis 1980, ses photos sont distribuées par l'agence Magnum.

Eliseo Alberto

Eliseo Alberto is an award-winning author, journalist, and screenwriter. His publications include the novels *Caracol Beach* (Alfaguara award, 1998), *La fábula de José, Informe contra mi mismo* followed by *Dos cubalibres, La eternidad por fin comienza un lunes,* and most recently *Esther en alguna parte.* He has also written several screenplays including *Guantanamera, Cartas del Parque,* and the short film *Contigo a la distancia,* all directed by Tomas Gutierrez Alea. Born and raised in Cuba, he now lives in Mexico City.

Eliseo Alberto ha recibido diferentes reconocimientos como escritor, periodista y cineasta. Entre su producción se cuentan las novelas *Caracol Beach* (premio Alfaguara en 1998), *La fábula de José, Informe contra mí mismo, Dos cubalibres, La eternidad por fin comienza un lunes* y, recientemente, *Esther en alguna parte.* También es autor de varios guiones, como los de *Guantanamera, Cartas del parque* y el corto *Contigo en la distancia,* todos dirigidos por Tomás Gutiérrez Alea. Alberto nació y se formó en Cuba, pero actualmente vive en Ciudad de México.

Eliseo Alberto ist ein preisgekrönter Schriftsteller, Journalist und Drehbuchautor. Zu seinen Veröffentlichungen zählen unter anderem die Romane Caracol Beach (ausgezeichnet mit dem Preis Alfaguara, 1998), *La fábula de José, Informe contra mi mismo,* gefolgt von *Dos cubalibres, La eternidad por fin comienza un lunes* und zuletzt *Esther en alguna parte.* Er lieferte die Drehbücher für *Guantanamera, Cartas del Parque* und für den Kurzfilm *Contigo a la distancia,* alle unter der Regie von Tomas Gutierrez Alea gedreht. In Kuba geboren und aufgewachsen lebt er heute in Mexico City.

Eliseo Alberto a été couronné de nombreux prix en tant qu'écrivain, journaliste et scénariste. Parmi ses publications figurent notamment les romans *Caracol Beach* (Prix Alfaguara 1998), *La fábula de José, Informe contra mi mismo* suivi de *Dos cubalibres, La eternidad por fin comienza un lunes,* et plus récemment *Esther en alguna parte.* Il est aussi l'auteur de plusieurs scénarios, notamment ceux des films *Guantanamera* et *Cartas del Parque* et du court métrage *Contigo a la distancia,* tous réalisés par Tomas Gutierrez Alea. Né à Cuba où il a aussi passé son enfance, Alberto vit aujourd'hui à Mexico.

Rodrigo García

Mexican writer-director Rodrigo García's credits include *Things you can tell just by looking at her* (Fondation Gan Award, Cannes 2000) and *Nine Lives* (Winner Locarno Film Festival, 2005). His credits as director of photography include *Danzón, Mi Vida Loca,* and *Gia.* He is also a regular director on the HBO series *Six Feet Under, The Sopranos, Big Love,* and *Carnivale.*

El escritor y director mexicano Rodrigo García es conocido principalmente por sus producciones *Cosas que diría con solo mirarla* (Premio de la Fundación Gan, Cannes 2000) y *Nueve vidas* (ganadora del Festival de Cine de Locarno, 2005). Como director de fotografía ha firmado de *Danzón, Mi vida loca* y *Gia.* También dirige de forma habitual capítulos de las series de la HBO *A dos metros bajo tierra, Los Soprano, Big Love* y *Carnivàle.*

Der mexikanische Regisseur und Autor Rodrigo García hat unter anderem Filme wie *Things you can tell just by looking at her* (Fondation Gan Award, Cannes 2000) und *Nine Lives* (Sieger beim Filmfestival von Locarno, 2005) gedreht. Als Kameramann war er mit *Danzón, Mi Vida Loca* und *Gia* erfolgreich. Er führt auch regelmäßig Regie bei den Fernsehserien *Six Feet Under, The Sopranos, Big Love* und *Carnivale.*

Parmi les réalisations de l'écrivain et réalisateur Rodrigo García figurent notamment *Things you can tell just by looking at her* (Prix Un Certain Regard – Fondation Gan, Cannes 2000) et *Nine Lives* (Léopard d'or au Festival de Locarno 2005). Ses travaux comme directeur de la photographie incluent *Danzón, Mi Vida Loca* et *Gia.* Il est aussi metteur en scène régulier pour les séries télévisées d'HBO *Six Feet Under, Les Soprano, Big Love* et *Carnivale.*

María Eladia Hagerman

The editor, María Eladia Hagerman, was born and raised in Mexico City, where she received her degree in graphic design. She has designed and collaborated on several book projects, including *Jaime Sabines (Algo sobre su vida)* and other publications.

La editora María Eladia Hagerman nació y creció en Ciudad de México, donde cursó la carrera de diseño gráfico. Ha colaborado como diseñadora en distintos proyectos editoriales, como *Jaime Sabines (Algo sobre su vida).*

Die Herausgeberin María Eladia Hagerman wurde in Mexico City geboren, wo sie auch aufwuchs und ein Grafikdesign-Studium absolvierte. Sie hat bereits mehrere Buchprojekte konzipiert und mitrealisiert, darunter auch *Jaime Sabines (Algo sobre su vida).*

L'éditeur María Eladia Hagerman est née et à grandi à Mexico, où elle a suivi des études de design graphique. Elle a conçu et collaboré à différents projets d'édition de livres, notamment *Jaime Sabines (Algo sobre su vida).*

Film Credits

Paramount Pictures and
  Paramount Vantage present

An Anonymous Content Production
Una Producción de Zeta Film
A Central Films Production

BABEL
Directed and Produced by Alejandro González Iñárritu
Written by Guillermo Arriaga
Based on an Idea by Guillermo Arriaga & Alejandro
  González Iñárritu
Produced by Jon Kilik & Steve Golin
Director of Photography: Rodrigo Prieto, ASC, AMC
Production Designer: Brigitte Broch
Edited by: Stephen Mirrione, A.C.E., & Douglas Crise
Music by: Gustavo Santaolalla
Co-Producer: Ann Ruark
Casting by: Francine Maisler, C.S.A.

Brad Pitt
Cate Blanchett
Gael García Bernal
Kôji Yakusho
Adriana Barraza
Rinko Kikuchi
Said Tarchani
Boubker Ait El Caid
Elle Fanning
Nathan Gamble
Mohamed Akhzam
Peter Wight
Abdelkader Bara
Mustapha Rachidi
Driss Roukhe
Clifton Collins Jr.
Robert Esquivel
Michael Peña
Yuko Murata
Satoshi Nikaido

A film by Alejandro González Iñárritu

Unit Production Manager: Ann Ruark
First Assistant Director: Sebastián Silva
Second Unit Director: Alfonso Gomez-Rejon
Music Supervisor: Lynn Fainchtein
Sound Designer & Supervising Sound Editor: Martín
  Hernández
Production Sound Mixer: José García
Music Mixer & Music Editor: Anibal Kerpel
Costume Designers: Michael Wilkinson, Gabriela Diaque,
  Miwako Kobayashi
Line Producer – Morocco: Ahmed Jimmy Abounouom
Line Producer – Mexico: Tita Lombardo
Line Producer – Japan: Kay Ueda
Casting – Morocco: Geneviéve Akoka, Hervé Jakubowicz,
  Marc Robert

Casting – Mexico: Manuel Teil
Casting – Japan: Yoko Narahashi
Casting Consultant: Alfonso Gomez-Rejon
Acting Coach – Morocco: Hiam Abbass
Interpreter – Japan: Rieko Terai
Sign Language Adviser – Japan: Mariko Takamura

Morocco Cast
Richard: Brad Pitt
Susan: Cate Blanchett
Anwar: Mohamed Akhzam
Tom: Peter Wight
Lilly: Harriet Walter
Douglas: Trevor Martin
Elyse: Matyelok Gibbs
Robert: Georges Bousquet
Jane: Claudine Acs
Walter: Andre Oumansky
James: Michael Maloney
Barth: Dermot Crowley
Tourists: Wendy Nottingham, Henry Maratray, Linda
  Broughton, Jean Marc Hulot, Aline Mowat, Liliane
  Escoza, Lindsey Beauchamp, Michel Dubois, Shirley
  Dixon, Patrick Lebre, John O'Mohoney, Mary
  Mitchell, Edward Lyon, Robert Fyfe
Waiter Casbah: Abdelaziz Merzoug
Bus driver: Omar El Mallouli
Old man in car: El Hassan Ait Bablal
Anwar's grandmother: Sfia Ait Benboullah
Doctor/vet: Hammou Aghrar
Sheik: Mohamed Ait Lahcen
Moukadem: Ali Hamadi
Store owner: Lhacen Znin
Mohammed: Mustapha Amhita
Mohammed's friends: Mohammed Amal El Koussi,
  Mohamed Nait Addi, Mohammed El Bouamraoui,
  Rahmoune Abdelhalim
Yamile: Soukayna Ait Boufakri
Police at Anwar's: Youssef Boukioud, Khouyael Houssein,
  Ken Clifford Alex Jennings
Helicopter pilot: Commandant Mesbah
US Army medics: Timothy Peter Buxton, Dr. Mohammed
  Ourjdal
Reporter US News: Aimée Meditz
Moroccan doctor: Dr. Mohammed Bennani
Yussef: Boubker Ait El Caid
Ahmed: Said Tarchani
Abdullah: Mustapha Rachidi
Alarid: Driss Roukhe
Zohra: Wahiba Sahmi
Yasira: Fadmael Ouali
Jamila: Zahra Ahkouk
Hassan: Abdelkader Bara
Hassan's wife: Ehou Mama
Abdullah's 2-year-old son: Rida Taya
Moroccan police officers: Salah Mezzi, Mohamed Atkliss

Mexico Cast
Amelia: Adriana Barraza
Debbie: Elle Fanning
Mike: Nathan Gamble

Santiago: Gael García Bernal
Lucia: Monica del Carmen
Comadre: Rosa Reyes
Luis: Robert "Bernie" Esquivel
Lucio: Damian Garcia
Amelia's daughters: Barbarella Pardo, Ursula Garcia
Patricia: Cynthia Montaño
Patricia's mother: Maripaz Lopez
Tambora band: Banda El Rosario, Santiago Lizarraga,
  Ismael Gregorio, Pedro Sillas, Enrique Garcia
  Contreras, Fernando Montes Avila, Luis Avila,
  Eugenio Jara Reynoso, Pedro Cuota
Musician: Romeo Echeverria Jimenez "El Gitano"
Wedding band: "Los Incomparables," Guadalupe
  Quintero, Mariano Quintero, Eluterio Higuera,
  Pascual Montaño, Efrain Gonzalez
Patricia's grandmother: Claudia Silvia Mendoza
Patricia's aunt: Norma Samarin, Jacinto Polo Nuño
Amelia's grandfather: Jose Campas Agiñaga
Amelia's father: Miguel Maldonado Tinoco
Amelia's mother: Rosa Campos Maldonado
Emilio: Emilio Echevarria
Officer at border crossing: Clifton Collins Jr.
Officer #2: Aaron Spears
Bill, border patrol: Jamie McBride
John, border patrol: Michael Peña
Helicopter pilot: Ivor Shier
FBI interrogation officer: RD Call

Japan Cast
Chieko: Rinko Kikuchi
Yasujiro: Koji Yakusho
Mitsu: Yuko Murata
Teammates: Kumi Ohkawatsu, Miyuki Tamada
Referees: Hirotaka Nabeya, Kazuya Senzaki, Takanobu
  Imaizumi
Volleyball coach: Koji Yoshida
J-Pop hostess: Saki Kito
J-Pop waitresses: Tomomi Kosugi, Noemi Rika Watanabe,
  Ran Saotome
Kumiko: Sanae Miura
Young man: Kazunori Sasaki
Shocked young man: Ryoji Takiguchi
Young man's friends: Shoushi Nakasone, Jun Tanaka,
  Masayuki Ishii, Yoshiyuki Yagisawa, Hideto Onishi,
  Hiroshi Yazaki
J-Pop special: Zengo Matayoshi, Koji Morisawa
Receptionist: Sumire Matsumura
Mother at dentist: Kyoko Saito
Daughter at dentist: Hazuki Saito
Son at dentist: Yu Tanabe
Patients: Kentaro Tokuhiro, Kiichiro Kawauchi
Dentist: Shigemitsu Ogi
Nurse at dentist's: Tose Fukuda
Kenji: Satoshi Nikaido
Hamano: Kazunori Tozawa
Doorman: Junichi Hayakawa
Haruki: Nobushige Suematsu, Takeshi Shinji Suzuki
Chieko's girlfriends: Reina Makino, Ayako Masagaki, Yurie
  Okada, Erika Okada, Mika Yokoyama, Kimi Unno,
  Kazuma Kazuma Yamane

Haruki's friends: Hideaki Kunieda, Keita Kanegae
Chieko's boyfriends: Tomohiro Higashi, Onbou Miura,
  Daiki Inoue
Club DJ: Shinichi Osawa
Dancers/club: Noriko Yamamura, Motomi Kobayashi
Bartender: Akira Matsuda
Wife: Shizue Yamamoto
Chieko's teammates: Kaoru Mihira Ayaka Kotake,
  Natsumi Hayashida Maki Kuraya, Kana Harada
  Sayaka Shimizu
Babel Volleyball Girls: Ai Takahashi Sumie Kobayashi
  Yoko Iwasaki Eri Terada, Reina Aoki Naoko Kato,
  Ikumi Muramatsu Keiko Nakamichi, Miyuki Kido,
  Fumie Takama Miki Watanuki Aki Yanagisawa,
  Megumi Watanabe Hanako Komatsu Fumie,
  Kikuchi Hotomi Nakajima, Miyuki Aoki Yuko
  Raihou Hosana Ueyama Erika Nakaya, Sachiyo
  Yamashita Kaori Shimizu
Volleyball teams from: Kanagawa Prefectural Hiratsuka
  School for the Deaf Mito School for the Deaf
  Gunma Prefectural School for the Deaf Gifu School
  for the Deaf
Tap dancers: Yuta Hori, Ikken, Takayuki Matsumoto
Juggler: Maro
Members of the theatrical company: Marie Machida
  (Kegawazoku), Namiko Hatori (Kegawazoku),
  Yurako Takano (Kegawazoku), Kiyomi Ensou
  (Kegawazoku), Ikue Takada (Kegawazoku),
  Yoshiki Wakura, Yosuke Morita, Yuji Inanobe

Associate Producer: Corinne Golden Weber
Production Controller: Steev Beeson
Accountant: Allen Wong
Making of Filmmakers: Pedro González Rubio,
  Carlos Armella
Script Translation: Alan Page
Post Production Supervisor: Michael Tinger
First Assistant Editor: Keith Sauter
Assistant Editor: Denise Crise